KNIGHT OF THE TURF

By the same author

BRED FOR THE PURPLE

LORD PARAMOUNT OF THE TURF

STEVE – LIFE AND TIMES OF STEVE DONOGHUE

INTERNATIONAL STALLIONS AND STUDS

HISTORY OF STEEPLECHASING (in association with Mortimer, Willett and Lawrence)

DERBY 200 (in association with Mortimer)

HISTORY OF THE CRESTA RUN

THE LONG HAUL

TWO HUNDRED YEARS OF RICHARD JOHNSON AND NEPHEW

Michael Seth-Smith

KNIGHT OF THE TURF

The Life and Times of Sir Gordon Richards

HODDER AND STOUGHTON

LONDON SYDNEY AUCKLAND TORONTO

British Library Cataloguing in Publication Data

Seth-Smith, Michael
    Knight of the Turf

    1. Richards, Sir Gordon
    2. Jockeys - Great Britain - Biography
    I. Title
    798'. 43'0924   SF336. R5

ISBN 0 340 24657 X

Acknowledgments

I wish to thank all those who generously provided me with information and opinions which assisted my research whilst writing this book. Sir Gordon Richards and his wife showed me much hospitality and kindly answered a barrage of questions. His sisters, Vera Richards, Rhoda Miller and Barbara Dawes, were equally helpful, whilst his son, Jack, and his daughter Marjorie, took the trouble to talk to me about their childhood memories. At Oakengates I was helped by G. C. Murphy, C. R. Nicholls and the Archive Department of *The Shropshire Star* who published a short notice giving details of my commission to write *Knight of the Turf*. Many people contacted me in consequence of this notice and I am grateful to them all, particularly Margaret Parkinson who allowed me to reproduce her poem about newly-knighted Sir Gordon Richards. Others whose assistance proved invaluable included Dudley Williams, Geoffrey Hamlyn, Gerard Fairlie, Herbert Blagrave, Walter Lawrence, Morgan Scannell, Peter Makin, Sir Michael Sobell, Norah Wilmot, Rufus Beasley, Scobie Breasley, Harry Wragg, George Hartigan, Charlie Smirke and Cecil Bromley.

My especial gratitude goes to John Hislop, one of the most outstanding amateur riders in Turf history and a brilliant racing journalist, for reading and criticising my manuscript; to Ann Hoffman of Authors' Research Services; to Betty Lewis for patiently pasting a veritable mountain of newspaper cuttings into scrapbooks; to Morag Robinson of Hodder and Stoughton for the charming and competent manner in which she has helped and advised in the production of this book; and finally to my wife Mary, who devoted so many hours to typing and retyping my original handwritten manuscript, in addition to tolerating my absentmindedness.

SYLVANS, FARNHAM

798
43

Contents

Illustrations

ACKNOWLEDGMENTS

[1] Vera Richards
[2] George Hartigan
[3] Peter Makin
[4] Gordon Richards
[5] Sport and General
[6] The *Illustrated London News*
[7] The *Daily Mail*
[8] The *British Racehorse*
[9] Fox Photos
[10] W. W. Rouch and Co. Ltd.
[11] Popperfoto
[12] Reuter
[13] Dudley Williams
[14] Central Press Photos

Introduction

During the past one hundred years three champion jockeys—Fred Archer, Gordon Richards and Lester Piggott—have dominated their profession on the British Turf. Their achievements have made them immortal in the history of Racing, and although other jockeys of such artistry and skill as Fordham, Maher, Donoghue, Carslake, Smirke and Wragg deserve paeans of praise, it is the outstandingly successful record of 'the great triumvirate' which will remain unchallenged for ever. Genius is the common denominator that they share, but if their childhood and the background to their youthful life are considered and comparisons made, it becomes apparent that there is a more noticeable similarity between the early careers of Archer and Piggott than between either of these careers and that of Richards.

Archer, whose father had ridden a Grand National winner and had spent several years in Russia training and riding the horses of the Czar, was brought up at Prestbury, the village nestling within sight of Cheltenham racecourse and once the home of 'Black Tom' Oliver and Adam Lindsay Gordon. He was taught to ride as soon as he could walk, quickly became totally confident of his ability in the saddle, and was still only twelve years of age when he rode in public at Newmarket. Six months before his twenty-first birthday he triumphed for the first time in the Derby when he won on Lord Falmouth's Silvio.

Lester Piggott is steeped in Racing to an even greater extent than Archer, for the blood of Cannons and Rickabys courses in his veins. In his youth memories of the nineteen Classic victories of Thomas and Mornington Cannon, and the Grand National heroes ridden by his grandfather, Ernest Piggott, who married Thomas Cannon's daughter, were instilled into him. So too were reminiscences concerning his mother's father, Frederick Rickaby, who was first jockey to the Hon. George Lambton and the powerful Stanley House stable from 1893–1901. Piggott, like Archer, began his career at a time when Racing England was flourishing, and received many mounts from his father, who had ridden more than five hundred winners as a steeplechase jockey before taking out a licence to train.

Piggott followed the example of Archer by riding in public at the age of twelve, and six years later became the youngest jockey of the twentieth century to win the 'Blue Riband of the Turf' when he succeeded on Never Say Die in the 1954 Derby.

Gordon Richards, who retired from the saddle within two months of Piggot winning his first Derby, did not enjoy the benefit of a similar background, for no member of his family had ever had the remotest association with horseracing. For this reason alone his achievements as a jockey stand out as being more remarkable than those of Archer or Piggott. In 1933 when he broke Archer's record of riding 246 winners in a season, the Speaker of the House of Commons said in a reference to him, 'It would be a bad thing to eliminate sentiment from English life. It is just that sentiment which springs from the knowledge that men may rise from humble beginnings and humble birth to big places which affords hope for our country — the hope that everyone may have a chance . . .' Gordon Richards' chance commenced when he was apprenticed to a comparatively unfashionable trainer soon after the Armistice.

During his apprenticeship post-war conditions and unrest amongst the coalmining industry brought Racing to a standstill on more than one occasion, whilst the nation was in the throes of economic depression unknown at the outset of the careers of Archer or Piggott.

Eventually Gordon's ability and ambition, allied to honesty, integrity and dignity in all his actions gave him success and recognition. The statistics show that he was Champion Jockey for twenty-six seasons, but such statistics, although highlighting his professional career, cannot be expected to do justice to his great character. To millions of people who never met him he was, and still remains, a hero who has been idolised since their interest in Racing was first awakened. To his credit he has never failed them. In his birthplace, the small Shropshire town of Oakengates, he is beloved as a man, admired as a jockey and honoured as a generous benefactor to the neighbourhood. In the years between the two World Wars when there was no television coverage of sport, Jack Hobbs, Fred Perry and Henry Cotton were acclaimed by a host of supporters as outstanding sportsmen, but none of them aroused such hero-worship as Gordon Richards.

One of his finest attributes has always been his willingness to help others. Throughout the decades when he was Champion Jockey he was the supreme example to apprentices, not only by his own demeanour and behaviour, but also by his consideration in giving them useful advice and cautionary words of warning when they were needed. He was the staunchest of friends to his contemporaries in the saddle; seldom entered into an argument concerning the outcome of a race; invariably attempted to keep the peace when an altercation took place; and would rarely complain if he was the victim of misfortune. In a tribute to him on his fiftieth birthday the Duke of Norfolk spoke for millions when he said, 'The object of a jockey is to win races, and this has never been shown to better advantage than by Gordon Richards . . . If you meet him you are carried away by his ever-enduring enthusiasm and by the example and the leadership that he has set in his profession . . . his will to win and his honesty of purpose are what a grateful public will remember about him with pride and esteem . . .'

He has been one of my heroes since the day that I was taken to Epsom races in the spring of 1935. To a small inexperienced boy, the hustle and bustle on the

Downs, with the excitement of the side-shows, the fortune-tellers and the gypsies, was bewildering. However, my bewilderment did not make me overlook my conviction that the two shillings that I had been given to invest would be multiplied due to the genius of Gordon Richards. A borrowed racecard told me that in the first race he was riding Lone Isle, owned and trained by Mr F. Hartigan. With no thought of possible defeat I gave a shilling to a bookmaker and requested that it was invested on Lone Isle at the offered price of 6–1. Sitting on the bonnet of a car parked alongside the rails is not the ideal way to watch a race—but as the shouts of the crowd heralded the approaching horses, and I heard for the very first time the exultant cry, 'Come on, Gordon', my excitement became intense. I had taken it for granted that I would see the 'white, blue sleeves, black cap' of Gordon in the lead, but in reality Lone Isle was never in the race with a chance and finished unplaced.

Whatever childish emotions I felt as the numbers went into the frame, I know that amazement and surprise were the strongest, for the fact that my hero had been defeated seemed unbelievable. Perhaps from my point of view it was appropriate that in the second race the name of his mount was Merry Conceit—for I wagered my remaining shilling on the horse with no thought for further failure. My faith was totally restored when Merry Conceit won with ease. The rest of the afternoon seemed to go entirely according to plan, with my conviction that Gordon Richards was unbeatable proving correct. In the third race, the City and Suburban, he rode Montrose, owned by Lord Woolavington and trained by Fred Darling, and won by two lengths. Admittedly in the fourth race he only squeezed home by a head from a colt ridden by his brother, Clifford, but in the fifth he triumphed by three lengths on a horse owned by Mrs Martin Hartigan and trained at Ogbourne by her husband to whom Gordon had been apprenticed. My bookmaker scowled with singular displeasure as he paid me my winnings for the fourth consecutive time, and kept muttering that he was thankful that Gordon was not riding in the final race of the afternoon. As the race was an Apprentice Plate the fact that his name did not appear on the number-board was understandable.

The thrill of seeing my hero win four races caused me to follow his mounts with growing interest. I smuggled a wireless into my preparatory school classroom in the hope of listening to his success in the Derby on Pasch and Fox Cub, and like many other schoolboys pasted photographs of him wearing the racing colours of Mr Dewar, the principal patron of Beckhampton, on to the door of my school locker. During the War I was miserable that Big Game did not win the New Derby at Newmarket, whilst Tudor Minstrel's failure at Epsom made me indignant and angry at the apparent unfairness of my hero's fate. Six summers later his achievements on Pinza and the knighthood bestowed upon him seemed to redress the balance.

In the winter of 1978–9 Hodder and Stoughton Limited invited me to write *Knight of the Turf*. They had already published *My Story* in 1954 which took Gordon's autobiography to the moment of his enforced retirement from the saddle, and believed that the time had arrived to up-date his life story in the light of the events of the past twenty-five years. When I explained the proposed project to Gordon Richards he was understandably a little reluctant to agree to co-operate, explaining that he had contemplated writing the story covering his years as a successful trainer and his subsequent appointment as racing manager to Sir Michael Sobell and Lady Beaverbrook. However, for a man who has reached the age of seventy-five such a task is not as attractive as it might at first appear, for the putting of pen to paper takes time and energy, with procrastination the unwanted and constant companion. When his wife casually and diplomatically implied that perhaps the work might become burdensome, added weight was introduced to weaken his resolve to undertake his intended task.

Consequently, he gave his generous consent to my proposals and offered his help. I accepted the commission from Hodder and Stoughton Limited and began my researches. Gordon admitted that in 1957 when he left his large Marlborough home for a smaller house at Ogbourne he deemed it necessary to destroy a vast number of letters and interesting memorabilia concerning his career. There would not have been available space for such impedimenta in his new bungalow, and to make a huge bonfire was the logical solution. Nevertheless, it was a great pity that such a bonfire caused a great deal of significant material, including fan-mail, details of retainers and letters from owners, trainers and jockeys literally to 'go up in smoke'.

I commenced my researches at Oakengates where it immediately became abundantly clear that his career had been followed day by day for more than fifty years by the majority of the local inhabitants. There are several people still living in Oakengates, Donnington Wood and Wrockwardine who remember Gordon when he was a schoolboy, and they kindly gave me reminiscences of those pre-First World War days. Subsequently I visited Ogbourne, the village near Marlborough, where Gordon had commenced his life as an apprentice before I attempted to follow step by step his inexorable advance to the summit of his profession. He has always been reticent about his private life, but as I spoke to his sisters, his children and his closest friends, it became obvious that they were all fully aware of his immense goodness and charity as a husband, father, brother and friend. After being in the limelight for more than fifty years it is natural that he now feels like 'putting up the shutters'. He is inclined to believe that his private life can be of little interest to others – but in doing so he overlooks the curiosity of the vast legion who desire to learn as much as possible about the famous and the distinguished, and have an insatiable appetite for every minor detail in the life of those that they admire. His marriage has been a boundless success story for more than fifty years, and in Margery Richards he has a wife who has loved, stimulated and consoled him, lifted much of the burden of day-to-day routine from his shoulders, and provided a home to which he has longed to return whenever he has been away. Equally, a vital ingredient in the happy story of their marriage has been the love and affection reciprocated by Gordon towards her and all his family.

Fundamentally shy and reserved, although a first-class teller of stories when roused, Gordon has always been incapable of saying an unpleasant word about anyone. On many occasions he has gone out of his way to help others in trouble, and when one of his employees faced a prison sentence he appealed for leniency, explaining to the Judge that there were extenuating circumstances. Jockeys who have fallen upon hard times and who have asked for financial help have seldom been refused, although he has preferred to remain an anonymous contributor to their welfare.

He would have made an immense success of any career that he chose, and it has been the Turf's good fortune that he elected to become a jockey, and subsequently a trainer, for he has brought honour to Racing England for more than half-a-century.

Much of his philosophy of life, and his sense of duty towards his fellow men, was summed up when he admitted in a newspaper article (*Observer Weekend Review* 31 May 1964), 'Public life would have been a wonderful thing. If you like people as I do, and if you can take action about things that you believe in, I think that would be wonderful . . . there is something of Racing in the British character, and when you are in Racing, as I am, you feel very much part of the country and of the community. As far as I am concerned Racing is a form of public life. Once you are in that, you never want to get out of it . . .'

I

Childhood of a Shropshire lad

Britain attained the zenith of her power during the final decade of the nineteenth century when the sun never set upon the far flung outposts of her glorious Empire. The affluence of her aristocracy and the fortunes harvested by her industrialists and her businessmen were the envy of the world, yet a clamour of reproach was being voiced by such champions of the working classes as Keir Hardie and George Bernard Shaw against the unenviable poverty suffered by countless thousands of her families. It was claimed that one-fourth of her population were living in squalor and that no civilisation could be sound or stable which had at its base such a mass of stunted human life. To this claim was added the opinion that the stunted human life reached its nadir in the coal-mining areas where men aged prematurely after years working in cramped, dark and hot underground passages for wages that seldom rose above a few shillings for a fifty-six-hour week.

In many areas the coal owners cared little for the welfare of the miners whilst in other districts the charity and humanity shown by the proprietors entitled them to be considered benevolent. At Oakengates the small Shropshire township in the shadow of the Wrekin where Gordon Richards was born on 5 May 1904, miners were fortunate in that the Lilleshall Company, whose influence dominated their lives, had been led by men of vision for more than a century.

The company had been founded in 1764 by Granville Leveson-Gower, a pioneer of the Industrial Revolution, whose first wife, Lady Louisa Egerton, was a sister of the famous Duke of Bridgewater, known as 'The Canal Duke'. Granville Gower appreciated that East Shropshire was rich in the minerals upon which industrial wealth could be established, and devoted his life to winning coal, limestone and iron ore from beneath the green and pleasant lands of rural England. As a result the peace and solitude of Oakengates which the Romans had used as a Watling Street posting station, where couriers and charioteers recounted the latest news, was replaced by the roar of machinery and the crashing of steam hammers which filled the valley with acrid smoke from the foundries. Chimneys belched forth smoke and grime which blackened the outside of every house, and refuse thrown into the newly-built canal covered the surface of the turgid water with debris.

By the middle of the nineteenth century the Lilleshall Company was playing an influential part in the industrial prosperity of the kingdom, with furnaces and brick works at Donnington Wood, their own canal for transportation, a blast engine manufacturing plant at neighbouring Snedshill, and new pits sunk to replace hundreds of old 'bell' and 'gin' pits which had been worked by lessees of land owned by members of the local aristocracy. During the second half of the century further progress was made, colliery equipment designed, heavy mining machinery built, the reputation of the company enhanced and the fortune of the Gower family increased. By the year 1900 the company owned and controlled collieries, quarries and pits yielding limestone, coal, iron and stone and provided more than a thousand terraced houses for its miners and other employees in the vicinity of Oakengates.

It was in one of these houses, in Ivy Row, Donnington Wood, consisting of a living room and a back kitchen on the ground floor, two bedrooms and a small garden, which included a pigsty and an earthen closet, that Gordon Richards was born.

Gordon's father and mother had been married on 30 April 1894 at the register office in Wellington. Nathan Richards, a twenty-one-year-old coal miner from the Lilleshall Company's Granville Pit, had first become the centre of attraction for twenty-year-old Elizabeth Dean when he was the cornet player in a local brass band. On summer evenings crowds would gather at the street corners to listen to the band whose music was often followed by an address given by a Methodist missionary. Elizabeth would offer to help the bandsmen pack up their instruments once the meeting was over, deliberately giving most assistance to the handsome young cornet player. Their courtship was brief for Nathan became smitten by the beauty and innate goodness of the young dressmaker whose father, William Dean, also worked at the Granville Pit where he was a stoker responsible for the winding engine. Like so many other men in the locality Dean was a devout Methodist whose religious beliefs and convictions dominated his life.

The first Methodist preachers had arrived in the Oakengates area from Staffordshire in 1821 and had been greeted with fervour. They had been given a plot of land at Wrockwardine Wood upon which to erect a chapel, and within a decade had gained a strong religious influence in the neighbourhood. This influence was never lost, and in future decades was to become even stronger amongst those who lived at Oakengates.

Every Sunday William Dean put on his best suit and left his humble home in Chapel Row to deliver the address at the nearby chapel. As a lay-preacher he brought up his children strictly, and eight years before her marriage Elizabeth had received a card-bound certificate signed by the Diocesan Inspector of the Archdeaconry of Salop in Lichfield stating that she had passed a satisfactory examination in the Bible and Prayer Book at the Wrockwardine Wood School. At the bottom of the certificate was printed a text from 2 Timothy 3, 'continue thou in the things that thou has learned'.

William Dean was a close friend of William Latham, who lived at Donnington Wood, and who was to become one of the leaders of the Trade Union Movement and Secretary of the Shropshire Miners' Association throughout their prolonged and bitter struggle against the coal owners. Latham was a man of passionate religious convictions, a magnificent orator who could sway crowds and, like William Dean, a preacher in the Methodist churches every Sunday. The miners from the local collieries of Granville, Grange, Woodhouse, Freehold and Stafford were inspired by him and would pack the churches to listen to his firebrand sermons.

One of those who listened was Enoch Richards, underground manager at the Granville Pit, and father of Nathan. Enoch had no objection to his son's marriage to William Dean's daughter, but opposition came from Elizabeth's father, who fervently believed that it was wrong for a young miner to marry when he earned a mere pittance, which was hardly enough to keep himself, much less a wife and family. He elaborated upon the physical dangers that Nathan faced every time he went down the mine, and attempted to discourage the young lovers. His attempts were to no avail, and after their wedding Nathan and Elizabeth set off for a three-day honeymoon in Blackpool. On their return, their total worldly wealth consisted of seven shillings, some of which Elizabeth Richards squandered upon buying a new hat. Yet this poverty was merely the practical aspect of their new life together, and gave no clue either to their deep love for each other, or to their determination to make a success of their lives. Nathan was ambitious and hard-working, and adored his bride who was the 'apple of his eye'. His father thought highly of Elizabeth, although he made it clear that he would not favour Nathan where work was concerned so that his son could earn an extra shilling in the mine. However, he need not have worried unduly about their future, for Elizabeth had a flair for turning pennies into pounds, and by her skill as a dressmaker and needle-woman was able to add to the meagre weekly earnings of her husband.

Once their short honeymoon was over, Nathan and Elizabeth moved into a Lilleshall-owned terrace house in Ivy Row, which was known as 'Potato Row' due to the potatoes grown in every back-garden to give cheap staple food along with the pig which could provide bacon, ham and pork for almost six months. The rent of each house was two shillings a week, with no rates payable. Within the next twenty years, Elizabeth was to give birth to twelve children, four of whom died in infancy. The eldest of those who survived was Eric, born in 1901, quickly followed by Ewart, Vera, Gordon, Clifford, Colin and years later Rhoda, and Barbara who was born after the end of the First World War.

On the day that Gordon was born the economic plight of the locality was causing the gravest concern, and at an evening meeting of the tradesmen of Oakengates and district held in the Town Hall despairing shopkeepers considered 'whether any means can be adopted to improve the trade of Oakengates and surrounding districts and if so to decide thereupon as may be deemed necessary'. At the meeting it was pointed out that there was no place in the locality at which the daughters of the working classes could be employed, whereas in large towns and cities such as those in Lancashire the daughters of artisans could find work and earn as much as 10/– to £1 a week. Under-housemaids in Liverpool could earn £14 a year, footmen £33 and for those whose enterprises sought new lands it was possible to emigrate to Australia and New Zealand for a very modest sum. In the local newspaper published the next day and which contained a report of the meeting, were advertisements from Dr King recommending his 'Dandelion and Quinine Liver Pills' as the cure for all ailments, and Sunlight Soap proudly announcing that they were entering the fifty-first year of their history—but such advertisements were of little interest to the poverty-stricken miners of Oakengates. Of equally little interest was the news concerning the outside world, which included the war between Russia and Japan reaching its height, the famous composer Dvořák dying in Prague, and King Edward VII, whilst on a State visit to Ireland, seeing his horse Ambush II fail to win a steeplechase at Punchestown.

Gordon's childhood was not unhappy, although he and his brothers and sister received little in the way of luxuries. He and other children of Ivy Row would make their own amusements, often playing a form of childish football with a ball made out of an old woollen sock. At dusk they would throw their caps and hats into the air and, in the gathering darkness, try to catch them before they touched the ground. On summer evenings Gordon and his friends would play rounders in the neighbouring streets and fields, but the exciting highlight of the week was reserved for Saturday afternoons. Many of the miners in Ivy Row had pigeon lofts at the end of their vegetable patch, and the pigeons would be sent as far away as Banff or Bournemouth to begin their race home. There were no time clocks to record the moment that each bird returned to its loft, and in consequence Gordon and his brothers would be sent scampering with all speed to the local Post Office to register the rubber-ring worn on the pigeon's foot. Often a penny bag of sweets was the reward for their help.

As a boy of six Gordon was sent to the Infant School in Donnington Wood where he was taught only the three R's—arithmetic, reading and writing. The school was almost a mile from Ivy Row and he and his school friends would walk four miles every day, for no midday meal was provided at the school, and his mother insisted that he returned home for as nourishing a lunch as she could afford. At the school there were four classrooms for the boys, each with desks for between twenty to twenty-five children, and from his earliest school days Gordon was one of the brightest pupils, with an above-average level of intelligence and intellect. Referred to by the Headmaster of the school as 'General Gordon', a reference to the hero of Khartoum, he was initially taught by Mrs Cooper, whose husband was a foreman in the Lilleshall Wagon shop.

Gordon began his schooldays in 1910. During the year King Edward VII died, 136 men and boys lost their lives in the Whitehaven Colliery disaster, Steve Donoghue rode in the Derby for the first time, and Dr Crippen was arrested aboard the SS *Montrose* as a result of the use of a new medium, wireless telegraphy. It was an era of drastic change, and in the *Westminster Gazette* came the suggestion that:

the better class workman of the new generation is filled with a deep discontent of the conditions amid which his lot is cast. He will not settle down in the surroundings which were good enough for his father. The schools have given him education, he has travelled more, he reads, if it be no more than his daily paper. He is uneasy at the dirt and squalor amid which he finds himself, and yet he scarce knows what is wrong with him. Deep down in his soul is blind revolt against life as he finds it.

Gordon's father, conscientious and ambitious, and not satisfied with 'life as he finds it', was gradually improving his position at work, being made a stall-man responsible for a section of the coal face, and being paid a day rate and a rate upon the tonnage that he and his team produced. Out of these rates he had to pay the wages of his team. However his initiative, urged onward by his wife, did not allow him only to work as a stall-man. Consequently, he negotiated with the Lilleshall Company to purchase some of the pit ponies once their working days in the mines were over, with the intention of using them to increase his earnings. Many of these ponies came from Wales or Dartmoor, with at least sixteen of them working in each pit, pulling the tubs of coal from the coal face to the main shaft exit. The miners were superstitious about the ponies, relying on them to forecast the events of the day. If the pony was listless and sick then the day augured ill, with the possibility of the near-naked miner working with pick and crowbar being injured by falling rock. If the pony was in good health then the day promised to be successful. Once their arduous working lives in the mines were over, the ponies were brought to the surface and the unaccustomed daylight to spend the remainder of their lives grazing in neighbouring fields. A few of the hardiest and strongest of them were still capable of work, and it was these who proved of most benefit to Nathan Richards during the weekends and the hours that he was not working for the Lilleshall Company. There were virtually no motor cars as competition, and he used the ponies in a 'float' to carry out any form of available 'odd job' in the locality. His enthusiasm and his willingness brought him considerable trade; moving furniture, carting coal and meeting people from the railway stations of Wolverhampton, Bridgnorth and Shrewsbury. Nothing was too much trouble, no job too small, provided that it showed a dividend.

Gordon and his brothers found excitement in accompanying their father in the 'float' and longed for the day when they would be allowed to drive it on their own. Meantime there were the ponies to be looked after, and what better opportunity for horsemanship was ever offered to a young boy who wanted the thrill of riding bareback across the fields. Gordon would jump on to the backs of the ponies and happily career up the grass-covered cinder mounds above the disused pits. Often he would arrive at school suffering from a surfeit of fresh air, and wearing a little jockey cap tied under his chin. It has been claimed that Mr Silvester, his father's next-door neighbour in Ivy Row, first put Gordon upon a pony, and that his first ride was to the top of the Barrack House mound on a pony named Bess brought up from the old Freehold Pit. But whether this is correct or not, it is true that the thrill found by Gordon in the saddle stems from these days.

In March 1912 a million resolute miners came out on strike, and the Government declared its intention of using coercive measures against the few intractable coal owners who declined to accept the principle of a minimum wage. The *Daily Mail* cheerfully announced that, 'Whilst chaos and idleness reign in all other trades and distress grows daily keener among the mass of the nation, the holiday-making miners are going to the seaside and playing football . . .' Such a state of affairs could not last, and only days later the same paper commented, 'Unparalleled scenes of privation and distress were witnessed in the great industrial centres of the north. Many a street yesterday possessed not a solitary fire . . .' In Oakengates there was virtually no money for the striking miners and the children were sent to a Baptist chapel to have bread and jam for breakfast, and tea and soup for their evening meal. Such frugal meals did little to assuage their hunger.

However, despite the miners' strikes and the financial plight of the locality, Nathan and Elizabeth Richards slowly began to improve their lot. Gordon's mother was determined to leave Ivy Row, and by dint of immense economy saved up enough money—to which her father generously added a little more—to put down a deposit upon four acres of land at Oakengates. Three houses, numbers One, Two and Three The Limes, Wrockwardine Wood, were built upon this land. The Richards family lived at number One, and the other two houses were rented to friends.

It was not easy for Nathan and Elizabeth to maintain the mortgage payments due upon this ambitious venture, and at times money was scarce or even non-existent as debts mounted. Nevertheless, they erected wooden stables at the end of their garden in which six or seven of the pit ponies were kept, and allowed their sons to harness them to a trap and meet customers at the local station and take them to their destination whenever the opportunity arose. For this service one shilling and sixpence was charged. On one unfortunate occasion when Gordon was returning from the station his pony shied and went through the smoking room window of the Buck Head Hotel. Sadly the pony was so badly injured that he had to be destroyed. Often Gordon would use a pony and trap to take a friend of his father, Charlie Stanworth, to the Grange Pit where he worked as winding engine driver. Charlie usually worked the afternoon shift, so Gordon would return to the pit at night to take him home. As the Sunday shift was only two hours Gordon would wait for him to finish, kicking his heels impatiently until it was time for Charlie to appear.

By 1912 Gordon had become a stocky boy of eight summers. Neither of his parents were tall, and Gordon took after his father's thickset and strong build. Nathan Richards took great pride in all his work, and in addition to being encouraged by his wife, was urged on by the friendly but intense rivalry with his brother Matthew Richards, who had also begun his life as a miner. If either Nathan or Matthew achieved any material success, it became a point of honour for the other to do equally well. Neither man was a scholar, but it did not require scholarship to realise that the dark clouds of war were looming on the horizon. Such events as the sinking of the *Titanic*, the growing strength of the Suffragette Movement and on a happier note the music-hall acts of Harry Lauder and Harry Champion, were of less consequence than the news that Germany was steadily re-arming and was accelerating her policy of naval expansion.

Advertisements for Christmas 1913 offered whisky at 48/- a dozen bottles and a four-course dinner at a Manchester restaurant for the amazing price of 2/-. In Oakengates Nathan Richards had opened a fish and chip shop as yet another new venture, and Gordon would sometimes take delicious portions of golden brown plaice to his appreciative friends. For him, like all other children of his generation, the possibility of a World War did not enter his comprehension and his thoughts ranged no further than riding pit ponies, playing football, saving up money to buy sweets, and above all else to do everything in his power to help the one person he worshipped and loved the most—his mother.

Elizabeth Richards was a woman who possessed every Christian virtue, to whom unselfishness was second nature, and who uncomplainingly devoted every hour and every day to her husband and her children. If any of her children were sick she would stay with them throughout the long hours of darkness. If they cut or bruised an arm or a leg she applied bandages and gave words of comfort. Money was always in short supply, but Elizabeth Richards was a competent housekeeper and saw that her children were as well cared for as was possible. Above all else she gave them love and affection to a high degree, and in return they adored her. A staunch Methodist, she insisted that her children went to chapel three times every Sunday, which meant four visits if Sunday School was included. She had one especial occasion upon which to be grateful to Gordon, who found two hundred sovereigns hidden by Nathan behind a protruding wall in the cellar. Money was particularly short at the time, and the discovery and handing over of the fortune pleased everyone except Nathan.

Throughout the First World War the Lilleshall Company concentrated upon the war effort, with their factories and workshops diverted and channelled to produce shells and armaments, whilst the rolling department received constant orders from the Admiralty. The coal mines continued at capacity production, with the majority of the miners, who had the title 'reserved occupation', not called up for service in the Armed Forces. In consequence Oakengates was a hive of industry throughout the War. At one time it was thought that Gordon would continue schooling after his thirteenth birthday, and he sat an exam, which he failed by one mark, for Newport Grammar School. He may not have been sorry to have failed, for the Newport police had been on the look-out for him. With food in short supply, and only a minimal quantity of such luxuries as butter sold to each customer, Gordon hit upon a plan to increase the family larder. Each week he drove one of his father's ponies and traps to Newport, a distance of some ten miles, taking with him various disguises including a battered trilby hat, a balaclava helmet and a false moustache. Armed with such disguises which gave him a variety of different personalities, allied to initiative and perseverance, he managed on several occasions to hoodwink shopkeepers and thus acquire more than the family's fair share of rations before his activities were discovered and reported to the police.

His mother was adamant that Gordon should not become a miner if a feasible alternative could be found for him, even though his elder brothers, Ewart and Eric, both worked in the mines. Ewart had been awarded a medal by the Royal Humane Society for rescuing a pony trapped in a pit, and Eric had worked with his father before joining the Army. But Elizabeth Richards, like the wives of countless thousands of other miners, lived in terror that a pit disaster might befall one of her sons. The obvious alternative for Gordon was some other employment with the Lilleshall Company. Consequently he began work in 1917 in the Warehouse Department. His tasks included looking after and weighing various items of mining equipment and generally helping Ben Nicholls, who was assistant manager of the Warehouse and Saw Mill Department at St George's. Gordon was not especially enamoured with the work involved, seemed indolent and lazy, and was often found asleep upon bales of rope in the storeroom. One of his jobs was to collect cups of tea for Ben, and more frequently than not the job took him far longer than the allowed time.

Two of the girls in the warehouse with whom Gordon became friendly were Stella Plant and Chrissie Crofts, who was later to marry Ben Nicholls. Anything to relieve boredom and a humdrum existence was acceptable, and on occasions Gordon and the girls would invest a modest number of pennies with the Lilleshall factory bookmaker's runner. Steve Donoghue seemed to be the hero of the factory workers and when he rode Gay Crusader to win the 1917 Derby the local bookmakers were almost ruined. Invincible, who was fourth to Gay Crusader in the Derby, was bred and owned by wealthy sixty-two-year-old Mr Reid Walker who lived at Ruckley Grange at Shifnal, only a few miles from Oakengates. A fine polo player, Reid Walker had begun breeding thoroughbreds in 1902. Before the outbreak of the First World War his horses had won the Kempton Jubilee, the Liverpool Spring Cup, the Chester Cup and the Royal Hunt Cup at Ascot. He was revered in the neighbourhood as the epitome of a sportsman, and when one of his horses won a race the local miners spent evenings drinking his health in the public houses. He had been a dare-devil in his youth, and whilst a schoolboy at Rugby had once walked around the unguarded parapet of a water-tower 150 feet above the ground. On his return to earth he was summoned to the headmaster's study, and once he had admitted to the supposed crime was amazed to hear the headmaster say 'Thank you, Walker, I intend to record your feat in the School annals.'

At eleven o'clock on the morning of 11 November 1918 troops were ordered to stand fast on the positions reached at the hour named. Peace had returned to Europe. When the glad tidings reached Oakengates the Lilleshall factories closed for the remainder of the day, with works buzzers and sirens sounded, flags and bunting produced as if by magic, and workers rushing into the streets to celebrate.

The celebrations were tinged with worry, for a serious epidemic of influenza in the neighbourhood had already caused the death of more than fifty people in Oakengates and St George's, and showed no signs of abating. One of the victims was the assistant master at the Donnington Wood Boys' School and after his death schools and places of entertainment were shut until the epidemic ceased. Volunteers helped the over-worked doctors and nurses and a special service of prayers was held in the Oakengates Primitive Methodist Church, which was in the process of making plans for its Jubilee Anniversary.

'Feed the Guns' week became Thanksgiving Week, and the Oakengates Urban Council arranged a tea for the children and the aged as a celebration for the end of hostilities. The Council was also attempting to build more houses for local in-habitants, but at least one member bitterly complained that 'the hindrance to the better housing of the working classes was the landlords'. Such a feeling against the landlords was responsible for the St George's Branch of the Amalgamated Society of Engineers agreeing to join the Labour Party and forwarding a letter to the Labour candidate for Shrewsbury pledging their active support in his political campaign. However, despite the influenza epidemic and the difficulties in acquiring land to build more houses, the Armistice brought joy to the inhabitants of Oaken-gates, who held a concert in the Congregational School to raise money for the Soldiers and Sailors Fund.

For Nathan and Elizabeth Richards the best news of all was that their son Eric, who had been reported missing for six months, was safe and a prisoner of war. On his return he was given a hero's reception with the neighbours putting out Welcome Home signs to greet him.

Within months of the Armistice, Racing, which had been so adversely affected during the war years, with meetings held almost exclusively at Newmarket, seemed to be on the brink of returning to normal. The War Cabinet's previous admission that horseracing and horse breeding were enterprises of national importance was the vital factor in this return for it enabled the sport to gain momentum once the Armistice was signed and by the spring of 1919 the fixture list included meetings at Lincoln, Gatwick, Windsor, Newbury and Chester. The Derby was held again at its rightful home and huge crowds thronged the Epsom Downs to see Lord Glanely's Grand Parade triumph. The newspapers were able to devote more space to Racing information, and the local meetings at Chester and Wolverhampton caused absenteeism in the coal mines in the vicinity of Oakengates.

Gordon Richards was bored with life at the Lilleshall warehouse long before his fifteenth birthday in May 1919. He had no interest in the work allotted to him, and with the energy and ambition which was in his blood longed for a new life now that the war was over. He had never been to a racemeeting, knew nothing of the ramifications of the Turf, and was unaware of the pitfalls which could ensnare those who chose to make 'The Sport of Kings' their career. Yet Racing offered an alternative existence, and his very nature clamoured for a change. He knew little of the outside world, and war-time conditions had virtually precluded holidays during his teens. He had never been to London, and the few excursions away from Oakengates had become occasions to be savoured and remembered. Secretly, therefore, he decided to attempt to do something about finding a new job. The logical person whom he thought might be able to help him was Mr Reid Walker. Consequently he spent laborious hours composing a letter asking if Mr Walker could give him a job as a stable boy at Ruckley Grange. Gordon possessed more scholastic ability than many of his Oakengate contemporaries, but his handwriting and spelling were not of the highest order. It was not surprising, therefore, that having written to Mr Reid Walker he did not receive a reply. In truth his request, possibly badly worded and illiterate by Mr Walker's standards, cannot have impressed the renowned local owner and breeder in the slightest, and no doubt was discarded without thought.

Nevertheless the uncertainty and the anguish endured by Gordon as he expectantly awaited a reply must have been a harrowing experience for a fifteen-year-old. If Mr Walker had replied immediately, merely stating that he did not require Gordon's services, the misery of the miner's young son would have been lessened, and the period of his dejection shortened. Fate, however, decided to relent in Gordon's favour. Months later Stella Plant and Chrissie Crofts saw an advertisement in the local paper inserted by racehorse trainer, Mr Martin Hartigan, who required stable lads at Foxhill, near Swindon. Knowing that Gordon was still hankering for a new life they suggested that they jointly compose a letter giving details of his brief career and family background and post it to Mr Hartigan, expressing the hope that he would consider Gordon as an applicant.

There is a possible but obscure reason why Martin Hartigan, living and training in Wiltshire, should have put an advertisement in a Shropshire paper. Years earlier Colonel Hall Walker, brother of Mr Reid Walker, had his horses trained at Foxhill. The brothers, when discussing the problem of stable lads, had agreed that, if an advertisement was inserted in Shropshire papers, the unemployment in the Oakengates area might lead to suitable applicants. This resulted in men from the area being given jobs at Foxhill and influenced Mr Hartigan to adopt the same formula in 1919, even though Colonel Hall Walker no longer had horses in the stable.

Within a week of Gordon posting his application a letter arrived at No. One The Limes addressed to 'Mr Gordon Richards'. The letter was delivered whilst Gordon was at the Lilleshall warehouse, and his mother was dumbfounded that her son should receive a letter with a postmark showing that it had been sent from a place of which she had never heard, and written in handwriting that she did not recognise. On Gordon's return the letter was carefully opened, and Mr Hartigan's reply scrutinised by the entire family. To their everlasting credit neither Nathan nor Elizabeth Richards stood in their son's way, and a letter was penned explaining that Gordon would arrive at Foxhill early in the New Year.

2

The new Foxhill apprentice

At the end of 1919 politicians were busily ratifying the Peace Treaty in Paris and promising tranquillity to the world. The great London mansions of Devonshire House, Grosvenor House and Londonderry House were still inhabited by their owners who entertained on a lavish scale, whilst returning ex-Servicemen attempted, with little success, to rehabilitate themselves and earn modest incomes as chicken farmers, window cleaners and carpet beaters. The Atlantic had been crossed by Alcock and Brown, and during the year the first Baby Austin produced. Everyone hoped, even if they did not believe, that the 1920s would herald a better standard of living for all sections of the community, despite the evident post-war problems. On the first day of the decade which was to fulfil the dreams of so many and dash the hopes of others, Gordon arrived at Foxhill, one of the most extravagant training establishments in England. The previous summer forty-two-year-old Jimmy White, financial entrepreneur and theatrical impresario, who had amassed a fortune in the later years of the war, and who was described as 'short, square-shouldered, square-jawed, restlessly alive, very quick of speech and with an unmistakable Lancashire accent', had bought Foxhill in an impulsive moment.

Lunching at a party given by Solly Joel at the Criterion Restaurant in Piccadilly he overheard Frank Curzon, owner of Wyndham's Theatre, telling another of the guests, Harry Preston, that in his capacity as executor for W. T. Robinson he wanted to find a buyer for the Foxhill training establishment, situated on the Wiltshire Downs some seven miles from Swindon. The fame of Foxhill during the three decades that Robinson trained there had been achieved by almost six hundred winners, including five Classic victories with Colonel Hall Walker's Cherry Lass, Witch Elm, Night Hawk and with Vedas—and by enormous gambling coups brought off by Wise Virgin in the Stewards' Cup at Goodwood and Winkfield's Pride in the Cambridgeshire. Robinson had never recovered from the shock of Craganour's disqualification in the 1913 Derby, and by 1918 was suffering from Bright's disease. He spent most of the winter of 1917–18 in a London nursing home before returning to Foxhill where he died on 1st July— only a few hours after having discussed the forthcoming harvest with his workers in the hayfields. Earlier in the century Robinson had sold the red brick Victorian mansion, King Edward's Place, a portion of the Foxhill estate, to Jack Metcalfe, who had resigned his commission in the 13th Hussars, after his regiment returned from India. When Metcalfe was killed in the Battle of the Somme, he bequeathed

King Edward's Place to his secretary, who subsequently sold it to Jimmy White. It seemed logical, therefore, that White should buy the Foxhill training establishment if he wished to embark upon a career on the Turf.

White installed Harry Cottrill as his trainer for the 1919 season on the recommendation of A. L. Ormrod, who was one of his business associates and Cottrill's cousin. During the year White owned eighteen horses who raced in his 'pale blue and khaki hoops, quartered cap'. Best of them were Irish Elegance, Ivanhoe and Gay Lord, a three-year-old bred in Ireland who was considered good enough to run in the Eclipse at Sandown, where he was fourth to Buchan. Yet despite a successful season White and Cottrill did not see 'eye to eye'. There was a clash of personalities, and at the end of the year Cottrill moved to Seven Barrows at Lambourn, whilst White engaged Martin Hartigan as his Foxhill trainer.

Born at Croom near Limerick in May 1889, Martin Hartigan was the son of a doctor and younger brother of Paddy Hartigan, who trained at neighbouring Ogbourne. Brought up with horses, the tall gaunt Irishman rode his first winner at Croom in 1911 and seemed assured of a future as a 'gentleman rider'. Such a glorious existence was soon to be shattered by the Kaiser, and at the outbreak of hostilities he joined the 13th Hussars. For much of the war he served in the Mesopotamia campaign where he won a Military Cross. On demobilisation he had little money but was determined to continue his life with horses, for he detested any form of paper work or office life. It was not easy in the post-war world to find employment either in England or the still strife-torn Ireland, and when Jimmy White, knowing the high reputation of his brother Paddy at Ogbourne, suggested that he trained the horses at Foxhill it seemed that the offer was 'manna from heaven'. It is probable that when White was seeking a new trainer he spoke to Paddy Hartigan's wife, Norah, about the matter. At the time he was beginning negotiations to purchase Daly's Theatre from her, and may have asked her advice about the future of Foxhill in the course of conversation. It was only natural that she should recommend her young brother-in-law.

An added bonus for Martin Hartigan as he reviewed the future prospects at Foxhill was that Lang Ward was the travelling head lad, and Jack Fallon, a brilliant trainer at Druid's Lodge, until he foolishly dissipated a fortune, was to act as his assistant, having been given the job due to the efforts of Steve Donoghue who had persuaded White to employ him. Steve and Jimmy White had much in common and during the racing season Steve was frequently at Foxhill, riding trial gallops and advising White upon the merit of his horses.

Steve Donoghue, at the age of thirty-five, was approaching the zenith of his career. Cast in the mould of Peter Pan – the boy who never grew up – he was improvident, gullible and at times irresponsible. He was also warm-hearted to the nth degree, had limitless charm, was the most lovable of characters and hero-worshipped throughout Britain for his exploits as a jockey. Sadly his domestic life was confused and unstable. In the winter of 1916–17 he had sailed for South Africa to ride for Solly Joel and on the voyage had met Lady Torrington. Within a year

Steve's wife, Brigid, had returned to her native Ireland, Steve had sold his Stock-bridge home and an undefended divorce action was heard in London at which Steve was granted a decree nisi with costs, dissolving his marriage on the grounds of his wife's misconduct with a former jockey and stableman. Subsequently Steve was frequently seen in the company of Lady Torrington, who started to take an interest in his three children, and he began to ride winners in her 'eau de nil' colours. In truth Lady Torrington, born Eleanor Souray, dominated Steve. An actress of limited ability who had played parts in *The Admirable Crichton* and many of George Edwardes' musical comedies, she had married Lord Torrington in 1909. The young newly-weds acquired Homerton House, near Shrewton, on the far side of the Vale of Pewsey from Foxhill, and were soon living 'above their means'. For much of the war Lord Torrington was a prisoner, after seeing military service in Salonika, and by the time of the Armistice it was evident that his marriage was likely to founder, due in part to his wife's association with Steve. She did not care for Jimmy White, but realised that he had a genius and an instinctive flair for making money, and enjoyed the company of the theatrical stars who were invited to King Edward's Place for lavish weekend parties. Martin Hartigan was not enamoured of these extravaganzas, preferring to concentrate on the thoroughbreds at Foxhill and the welfare of the stable lads who looked after them.

All of this was unknown to Gordon Richards, who was met by a chauffeur-driven car at Swindon station after a long uncomfortable journey from Oaken-gates, which had included a two-and-a-half-mile walk with his father to the local railway station, and the necessity of changing trains at Birmingham. For a fifteen-and-a-half-year-old boy dressed in his one and only suit, the transition from the fog and gloom of the Shropshire coal-mining town of Oakengates to the glories of bracing early mornings on the Wiltshire Downs was a stupendous change. That it was successfully accomplished was due in no small measure to Gordon's self-reliance, but also to the help he received from Martin Hartigan, Jack Fallon and the head lad Paddy Gilligan.

From the moment that he alighted at Foxhill after his first ever motor-car ride from Swindon railway station, Gordon was made to feel one of a team—albeit a very junior and unimportant member. There were more than twenty horses at Foxhill, and during the first three months of the New Year the stable grew steadily more and more confident that Sir Berkeley would win the Lincolnshire Handicap. The lives of everyone at Foxhill from Jimmy White to the youngest and most unimportant new apprentice from Oakengates, who was paid five shillings a week pocket money, centred around the proposed coup. Sir Berkeley, who had dead-heated for the Visitors Handicap at Royal Ascot in the summer of 1919, had been bought from the Duke of Portland later in the year and had been the medium of a huge, unsuccessful and typical Jimmy White gamble in the Cambridgeshire. He had subsequently been third under a huge weight at Man-chester on the final day of the season, and hopes were high that he would land the stable coup in the Lincoln. Such was the excitement during the weeks prior to the opening of the Flat season that Gordon had little time to be homesick or to contemplate running away, as Steve Donoghue had done from Kingsclere. Neither had he time to object to the long and arduous hours as a stable lad whose tasks included weary sessions grooming and brushing the coats of his charges until they shone like silk, nor to take exception to the rats which emerged from the floorboards of the apprentices' dormitory. By nightfall, after more than twelve hours of hard work, it would have required more than rats to disturb the innocent slumbers of the youngsters who shared indifferent food, uncomfortable beds and the dream of a fortune to be made upon Sir Berkeley.

Gordon had adapted himself quickly to his new surroundings, and was proud that he was allowed to have the care of the two-year-old filly My Motto without too much supervision from Paddy Gilligan. As February turned to March, Steve came down at frequent intervals to ride Sir Berkeley in preparation for the Lincoln. Pressing his face against the window pane of the tack room, Gordon had his first sight of Steve as the famous man walked into the yard 'with bandy legs and beaming smile'. To his credit Steve was never aloof in his dealings with young apprentices and stable lads. Contentedly, confidently, and without an ounce of conceit, he would shout out on the Downs 'now watch me' before cantering away in his beautiful, perfect and inimitable style. He had little understanding of how or why he was a supreme genius in the saddle, could not put into words his instinctive appreciation of how to ride a headstrong colt with reins which in his hands became no more than silken threads, and thought that the only way of helping embryo-jockeys was to persuade them to watch and copy him. There was no jealousy in his character, no fear that an apprentice would usurp his authority and only a childlike pleasure and enjoyment in being the means of teaching and coaching those less fortunate than himself.

Early in his riding career Steve had met with an accident which caused him to alter his style of riding, since he perpetually suffered a stiffness in his shoulder. Consequently he held his body in a slightly more upright position than normal amongst jockeys. Gordon, to whom Steve became a minor deity, to some extent copied this style and also adopted Steve's technique of riding with an unusual length of rein which was against the established principles of equitation, since it made guidance and control more difficult. There is no doubt that the majority of apprentices had a more gradual introduction to the art of jockeyship during this era than at any period in Racing history, and that the introduction was complete and thorough. If a boy showed no promise he was sent home; if he fell off his mount whilst on the gallops it was considered a disgrace. The logical outcome of this intensive and extensive training was that those who 'made the grade' and had good hands, a secure seat and a sense of balance became jockeys of a very high standard.

Despite the stable confidence Steve could only finish fourth on Sir Berkeley in the Lincoln, for which there were twenty-nine runners, beaten more than four lengths by Furious, owned by Mr Clarence Hatry. The depression and temporary insolvency at Foxhill when the news was brought to the stables stunned the entire staff. Two days earlier Steve had ridden My Motto, the filly looked after by Gordon, in an Auction Stakes, and although she was unplaced Steve told Gordon that he thought that she might win either next time out or at any rate in the not too distant future. Steve's judgment was vindicated at the Epsom Spring meeting, when he rode her to an easy victory in a modest Selling Plate, watched by a proud and jubilant Gordon who was paying his first visit to Epsom. After the race My Motto was sold for six hundred and forty guineas and a lonely Gordon returned to Foxhill without the filly, upon whom he had lavished so much care and attention. Steve generously gave him ten pounds which was unusual since jockeys seldom rewarded stable lads out of their own pockets, but the kind act was typical of the famous jockey.

Throughout the summer Gordon steadily found his feet at Foxhill. With the War over, apprentices in other stables were also beginning to make their reputations, particularly young E. C. Elliott whose father was travelling head lad to Lord George Dundas' Newmarket stable, and the seventeen-year-olds Harry Wragg and Tommy Weston. Wragg, born in Sheffield, was apprenticed to R. W. Colling at Bedford Lodge, Newmarket, whilst Weston, whose father drove a horse and wagon for the Lancashire and Yorkshire Railway at Dewsbury, and who only weighed 4 st 3 lbs when he began his apprenticeship at Middleham, had rapidly come to the forefront as a result of the recommendation he had been given by Steve Donoghue. Newmarket trainers needing a competent lightweight gave him mounts, and he won the 1919 Kempton Jubilee on Arion. Gordon, observant by nature, was improving as a horseman, and was also beginning to appreciate the luxuries that money could buy after seeing the extravagant weekend parties given by Jimmy White at King Edward's Place, where the glamorous guests often included Jose Collins of *Maid of the Mountains* fame, and Ivy Tresmond, with whom White continually bickered in a love-hate relationship. Gerald du Maurier, Gladys Cooper and Marie Lohr were other stars of the London theatre who occasionally came to Foxhill at the time when whisky cost 126/– for a dozen bottles and port, as supplied by Hedges & Butler to the House of Commons, 96/– for a dozen bottles.

It became traditional that on Sunday mornings the house guests at King Edward's Place would stand upon a first floor balcony watching the thoroughbreds being paraded. If the horses, their attendants or the gravel upon which they walked were not immaculate, White would become furious, reprimanding all and sundry for their failure to conform to his ideas of tidiness.

In reality the Foxhill and King Edward's Place establishments were costing White a fortune to maintain, but provided that his financial dealings in the City and his West End theatrical ventures were successful he had no objection to the vast expense involved. He knew little about the complexities of Racing but was not content to leave the stables and the horses in the care of his trainers, and his interference was almost impossible to tolerate at times.

Martin Hartigan, a bachelor, and far more easy-going than Cottrill, was never happy when White was in residence at King Edward's Place, but like so many Irishmen was inclined to be lackadaisical and prepared to overlook the constant demands of his employer, whom he secretly despised. His natural love was for his horses and he was thankful that White was prepared to be totally extravagant where they were concerned. Nothing but the best was good enough in the way of hay, straw and fodder, and so long as the bills were paid Martin Hartigan was content to soldier on. As far as he was concerned the horrors of the First World War were over and amidst the quiet of the Wiltshire Downs he found peace, solitude and happiness. He was not especially ambitious, but to his great credit he took immense interest in his stable lads, about whose welfare he genuinely cared.

Gordon was immensely lucky to have been apprenticed to so kind a master, who was never prepared to treat with excessive harshness those for whom he was responsible, and had the sense to appreciate his good fortune. However, he was bewildered by the weekend house parties and the lavish entertainments provided by White, for they were utterly contrary to his concepts and his experiences at Oakengates, where it was necessary for most people to think twice before spending money on anything other than the necessities of life. His Methodist upbringing had not included even thoughts of such extravagance, and his own idea of how a Sunday should be spent included attending chapel where the singing of favourite hymns was to be enjoyed and savoured. He saw no harm in the donkey races, boxing bouts often presided over by champions 'Bombardier' Wells or Jimmy Wilde, cock fighting, football matches and other entertainments in which stable lads were compelled to participate, but privately he thought it foolish of White to wager hundreds of pounds of his own money upon the outcome of a billiards match — often suggesting that he should receive merely one penny from the loser if the outcome went in his favour. In truth, Gordon did not understand the complicated make-up of White's character. Born penniless in Rochdale, White had the brash courage, initiative and quick wit to make fortunes, but like so many other nouveau riche men he believed that ostentation was an essential ingredient to prove success. He thought that the ordering of champagne by the magnum and lavish tips to all and sundry were expected of him and so he obliged — but underneath the veneer of bonhomie was the solid core of an unbalanced man who craved affection. He genuinely enjoyed football, was an enthusiastic supporter of the Swindon Football Club and insisted that they arrange matches against other local teams, including neighbouring racing stables, especially that of Paddy Hartigan at Ogbourne. White engaged a Swindon professional to coach the Foxhill Stable Lads Football XI and was not averse to employing professional footballers on a day-to-day basis as Foxhill employees when an important match was in the offing. Initially, Gordon considered it wrong to play football on a Sunday, for no such game would have been allowed at Oakengates, where the Sabbath was respected to a greater degree than at Foxhill. However, his scruples were overcome and he happily joined his colleagues in the matches and other Sunday games organised by Jimmy White.

Throughout the long hot summer Gordon steadily improved his prowess in the saddle. The stable was having a successful season, with Sir Berkeley, ridden by Steve, winning three races in quick succession before being retired to the Foxhill Stud where he joined White's other two stallions, Irish Elegance and Polygnotus. The two-year-old filly Pharmacie winning each of her eight races, although she never took on the season's 'cracks', was another achievement which kept the stable 'on the crest of the wave'.

Gordon began riding Sir Berkeley on the gallops and the head lad commented to Martin Hartigan that Richards, whilst giving the big horse his head, showed that he wanted no arguments and would only accept total obedience. He was blessed with legs that were thicker and stronger than average, and he used their tremendous strength and power to the best advantage when riding on the Foxhill gallops. Hartigan appreciated that in Gordon he had a boy of immense promise and his appreciation was endorsed by Vic Smyth, who often rode Foxhill horses. Consequently if horses needed light hands but absolute control Gordon was given the mount when they were exercised. He rode without a hat, with his thick black hair flying in the wind, which caused the other stable lads to nickname him 'Moppy'. Always something of a practical joker, the nearest he got into 'hot water' was one day when he strutted across the stable yard with his inimitable rolling gait. A friend of Jimmy White's thought that Gordon was deliberately mimicking his walk, complained, and proposed that Gordon be sacked. His proposal met with no response.

During the season Racing began to flourish in the aftermath of war. Huge crowds attended the London meetings, even though building restrictions prevented any form of improvement to shabby antiquated grandstands, due to the prohibition of 'luxury' buildings. A third-class single ticket from London to Newmarket cost ten shillings and threepence and, despite grumbles at the excessive cost, such a price was paid by racegoers determined that they would not be denied their sport. The Foxhill stable ended the season with thirty-five winners which was thought to be a highly satisfactory state of affairs, and, more important, Jimmy White professed to having made money from his gambling.

For Gordon the highlight of the year was his first ride in public, on Clock-Work at Lingfield on Saturday 16 October. The two-year-old colt had already had three races, in none of which had he run with distinction. On two of those occasions, at Salisbury and Brighton, he had been ridden by the other Foxhill apprentice, David McGuigan, who had previously been apprenticed to his father at Ayr. At Lingfield Clock-Work ran in the first race of the afternoon, the 5f October Nursery Handicap, for which there were twenty-one runners. Frank Bullock, Brownie Carslake, Vic Smyth and apprentice Harry Wragg also had mounts in the race, but none of them spared more than a glance for the mediocre Clock-Work or her diminutive stocky rider. There was no fairy tale ending to the

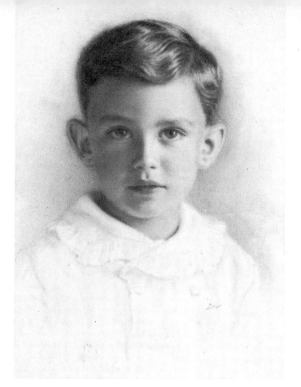

Gordon, Christmas 1908.

Gordon, front row, third from left, as a schoolboy at Wrockwardine Wood
Boys Council School in 1914.

Horses passing Gordon's bungalow at Ogbourne, watched by Mr & Mrs Martin Hartigan, and inset, the home of the Hartigans at Ogbourne.

Mrs Martin Hartigan on her hack, held by Gordon.

race and the unfancied colt finished nearer last than first. However, for Gordon it was a red-letter day. As he cantered to the start with the hubbub of the crowd and the shouts of the bookmakers reverberating in his ears he realised that his career as a jockey had finally started. It was a career which he intended would bring him fame and fortune.

3

Happiness at Ogbourne

During the first three months of 1921 the economic situation of Britain became critical, and politicians began to appreciate the enormity of the problems besetting them. One of the root causes of the crisis resulted from the aftermath of wartime conditions in the mining industry. Government control during the First World War had been so far extended that coal owners had little but day-to-day management responsibility. The miners were satisfied with this state of affairs and were prepared to consider nationalisation in peacetime, a consideration which was diametrically opposed to the views of the indignant coal owners, who thought that the Sankey Commission, set up as a Royal Commission in 1919, was a non-starter.

By 1920 both owners and miners were becoming belligerent and the comment of Lord Birkenhead, 'I should call the miners the stupidest men in England if I had not previously had to deal with the owners', did nothing to alleviate the situation. The owners wanted a return to the pre-war system of bargaining where miners' wages were concerned – and the miners refused to accept a cut in wages, demanding a national negotiating policy. A lock-out began on 1 April 1921, but by the middle of the month, to their bitter disillusionment, the miners found themselves betrayed by the Railway and the Transport Unions and were compelled to give up the unequal struggle. At Oakengates such tribulations totally overshadowed such minor successes as Gordon's first victory, although Nathan Richards gleefully and proudly told his friends of his son's achievement.

Gordon had been given his second ride in public, as a result of scoring a goal. In a match against Paddy Hartigan's lads from Ogbourne the score was level with only five minutes left of play. A penalty was awarded by the referee, and Jimmy White, watching on the touchline, told Gordon that if he scored a goal from the free kick then he could ride a moderate three-year-old, Contractor, at Lincoln. The goal was scored and White's promise kept – but to no avail where success was concerned, for the outsider and unfancied Contractor failed to reach the first four in the humble 11f Kesteven Place, contested by nine virtually useless horses. Nevertheless, the race gave Gordon further experience and his initial victory was not to be long delayed.

A fortnight later he walked the five-year-old Gay Lord the five miles from Foxhill to Shrivenham railway station, travelling with him to Leicester and then walked three more miles to the racecourse stables, saw that he was settled, fed and watered and only then had time to review his prospects as he sat in the Black Dog at Oadby eating jugged hare and redcurrant jelly for his dinner. There were only six runners for the final race of the next afternoon – the Apprentices Plate for three-year-olds and upwards – and Gay Lord, who had been a high-class horse in his younger days, was second favourite. The horse was fit, and strongly fancied by the stable, for he had already had a race at Lincoln, ridden by Vic Smyth, whose brother, George, valeted Gordon at Leicester and was to continue to do so for the next thirty-three years.

The form book showed that at Lincoln Lord Howard de Walden's Sorrel had finished second, with the unplaced Gay Lord giving him a stone. In the Leicester race Sorrel was set to give Gay Lord 6 lbs – a difference of 20 lbs in the Foxhill horse's favour, which augured well for the victory of Gordon's mount. Of the other four runners only the unusually named ZZ seemed to have a chance, so it was with some confidence that Gordon walked the short distance from the weighing room to the paddock together with his fellow apprentices, Forsyth, Mason, Watts, V. Piggott and G. Bowen. Sorrel was favourite at 2–1, with Gay Lord 5–2 and ZZ 3–1. The bookmakers went 10–1 bar three, so it seemed that at least Gordon might be 'in the frame'.

As it transpired he had a bloodless victory, winning by three lengths from Sorrel. Proudly he returned to the winners' enclosure, but having dismounted had to stand on tiptoe while unbuckling the girth to remove the saddle and weight cloth containing over fourteen pounds of lead. After a quick word of congratulation from the travelling head lad, Lang Ward, who was deputising for Martin Hartigan who had a broken leg, the smiling Gordon vanished into the weighing room, whilst spectators were already making their way towards the racecourse exits, oblivious to the fact that they had seen Turf history being made, with the first success of a young jockey whose name and fame were later to become known throughout the entire world. None of his five contemporary apprentices who rode against him at Leicester were to reach the headlines in the future, but for the remainder of their lives were to remember the memorable occasion when they rode against Gordon on the day he achieved his initial victory.

Steve Donoghue was riding at Leicester that afternoon and, having changed from his jockey's silks after being unplaced in the fifth race, wandered into the grandstand to see how the Foxhill apprentice fared in the final race. As Gay Lord and Gordon passed the post no spectator was more delighted at the young boy's moment of victory than the famous jockey, who was confident of winning the Two Thousand Guineas on Humorist in less than a month's time.

However, Racing was temporarily to enter the doldrums due to the coal crisis, and on 16 April, at the request of the Government, the Stewards of the Jockey Club gave notice that no racemeetings under their Rules would be held until further notice. Meetings had been cancelled on a day-to-day basis since 2 April and ultimately the Newbury Spring meeting, the Newmarket Craven meeting, the Epsom Spring meeting and other meetings including those at Sandown,

Chester, Hurst Park, Lingfield and Ripon were abandoned due to the industrial crisis. The reason given was the need to reduce railway traffic to a minimum and thus save coal.

It is salutary to consider that one possible psychological reason for the cancellation of Racing in the spring of 1921 was to deprive the striking miners throughout the kingdom of the enjoyment of backing their selections, and by cancelling Racing, making their enforced idleness a little more drab. In consequence of the strike the Two Thousand Guineas, which Humorist did not win, and the One Thousand Guineas were run on the same afternoon—with the railway companies not able to provide sufficient trains for racegoers. As a result every road to Newmarket was jam-packed with motor vehicles of every description, and it is not too far-fetched to suggest that appreciation of road transport as a means of travelling to racemeetings and the advent of horseboxes were evolved from the 1921 Miners' Strike.

By Whitsun conditions were returning to normal, with racing fixtures resumed. Gordon, worried by letters from home giving details of the serious plight of miners at Oakengates whose financial resources were at their lowest ebb, rode his second winner for Jimmy White at Lewes on 6 June. Gordon had expected to have two rides at Lewes on the Monday afternoon and as he made his way to the weighing room his mind was filled with thoughts of his jockey hero, Steve, who had won the Derby on Humorist the previous week, and who had been fêted at Foxhill when he came to visit Jimmy White on the subsequent Sunday.

On his arrival in the weighing room Gordon was approached by the owner of John Charles, a four-year-old set to carry 6 st 13 lbs in a Selling Handicap, and to his amazement and delight invited to ride the horse, who was having his first race of the season. There was a fixture at Birmingham on the same afternoon, at which the leading jockeys, with the exception of Carslake, were riding, and there seemed little interest in the Lewes meeting. However, the afternoon became a red-letter day for Gordon for he won on John Charles by a neck and still had his arranged two rides later in the afternoon. Although unplaced in the first of them, he was content, for Vic Smyth won on Cyclette, owned by Jimmy White. Half-an-hour later he donned the silks discarded by Smyth before mounting the four-year-old filly, Spiral Spin, who was the even-money favourite for an Apprentice Handicap. Once again Gordon won by a neck, to complete his first double, with both victories being gained by the same margin! He returned to Foxhill on the crest of the wave—little comprehending that his life was soon to change radically, due to the consequences of the tragic death of Paddy Hartigan. This occurred three days after the commencement of the Flat season and resulted in Gordon leaving Foxhill and moving to Ogbourne, a hamlet four miles from Marlborough, which was to play a significant part in his life for the next forty years.

Ogbourne had sprung into Racing prominence in the late 1890s when theatrical impresario, George Edwardes, had bought a one-thousand-acre estate and the manor house. The land stretched across the Wiltshire Downs and from the windswept gallops where he built a large summer bungalow Edwardes could look towards neighbouring Beckhampton and Manton. He loved the large five-bedroomed bungalow where he would frequently spend the night, and thought nothing of marching out of the front door in his pyjamas to see his horses at exercise, before taking a bath and getting dressed.

Known to everyone as 'The Guvnor', Edwardes was generous hearted to a fault, childlike at times, and utterly improvident where money was concerned. At the height of his career he lost a million pounds in two years. Born at Cleethorpes near Grimsby in 1854, he first made his name in the theatre world when he was appointed acting manager at the newly-opened Savoy Theatre in 1881. Five years later he was manager of the Gaiety, which became outstandingly successful under his control. Subsequently he acquired Daly's Theatre where he produced many beloved musical comedies, including *The Merry Widow*, *The Dollar Princess* and *Maid of the Mountains*. Perhaps the most romantic occasion in his life occurred when he was totally 'broke' and owed some sixty pounds to pay his staff at the end of the week. A generous and equally warm-hearted girl friend, Julia Gwynne, who had played at the Savoy Theatre in the D'Oyly Carte first production of *The Pirates of Penzance* and *Iolanthe*, heard of his plight, drew her life savings from the bank and left the money, some fifty pounds, in an envelope on his desk. Her kind action had a happy sequel, for she and George Edwardes were married some months later.

In his heyday Edwardes employed two hundred people excluding artists and chorus at Daly's, with a weekly wages bill of more than three thousand pounds. Yet he reaped fortunes from such musicals as *The Country Girl*, which ran for two years and made him more than one hundred and fifty thousand pounds. Star of the show was Hayden Coffin who refused to change his unusual surname despite 'The Guvnor's' strenuous efforts to make him do so. One evening when Coffin was dining at Edwardes' London home in Park Square West, a nervous maid announced 'Please Mr Cab, your coffin is waiting for you!'

George Edwardes, who loved every sport, found the greatest relaxation from the cares of the theatre on the racecourse, and won his first race in 1897. Four years later, his colt Santoi (named after a successful musical at Daly's Theatre) won the Ascot Gold Cup and the Kempton Jubilee before being retired to the Ballykisteen Stud which Edwardes bought especially to stand his champion.

No sooner had he acquired the Ogbourne estate than he installed his younger brother as his trainer. 'The Major', recently resigned from the 1st Life Guards, was a renowned shot, a fine boxer and a first-class cricketer, who had ridden many winners whilst serving in India, and proved to be most successful as a trainer. Everything at Ogbourne was done on a lavish scale, and George Edwardes loved nothing better than driving down from London for the weekend. On one occasion 'The Major' was ill in bed and so 'The Guvnor' decided to organise some trial gallops on his own initiative. To his delight he discovered one two-year-old who could leave his rivals as though they were standing still. On examining the Entries book he noticed that the horse was entered for a seller the following week. He said not a word to a soul, arranged for the colt to run, went to the racemeeting and backed it to win a small fortune. The colt romped home at a long price and George Edwardes was immensely pleased, until his brother, recovering from his sick bed, heard what had occurred. He was livid, cursed and swore for days, and only begrudgingly admitted that the reason for his fury was that he had been saving the colt for a personal coup.

Eventually in 1909 'The Major', who counted the ambitious 'Whisky King', Mr James Buchanan, amongst his owners, left Ogbourne to manage the Bally-kisteen Stud, and twenty-eight-year-old Paddy Hartigan was appointed to succeed him as 'The Guvnor's' trainer.

He had begun his career as a trainer at Tarbrook, Croom, Co Limerick and proudly led in his first winner as a mere stripling of seventeen summers. Years later he moved to Rathduff House, near Cashel, Co Tipperary, from where he sent out many more winners before coming to England to train the horses of 'The Guvnor'.

One of the horses that he took over was Anchora, a good, second-class stayer, game, sound and with a grand constitution. She was sold in the autumn of 1912 to Walter Alston, manager of the Stanley House Stud, and eventually became the dam of Scapa Flow and the granddam of Pharos and Fairway. Another useful performer was Drinmore with whom Paddy Hartigan won the 1913 City and Suburban at Epsom. In 1914 Hartigan joined the Army and life became less lively at Ogbourne. George Edwardes, visibly ageing, found that the trials and tribulations of the theatre in war-time prevented him from spending as much time as he wished at Ogbourne with his daughter, Norah, who had married Paddy Hartigan.

George Edwardes died in 1915, leaving his freehold estate at Ogbourne to his son, Captain d'Arcy Edwardes, of the 1st Dragoons, with the request that he should carry on the racing so long as it showed a profit. Within a year d'Arcy Edwardes was killed in action in France, and his two sisters, Norah and Dorothy, inherited equal shares of the Ogbourne estate, with Norah, born in October 1894, taking the gallops and training quarters as her share, and her sister the manor house and farm land.

When the war ended the demobilised Paddy Hartigan returned to Ogbourne. In 1920 he won thirty-nine races including the Nassau Stakes at Goodwood, and started the long uphill battle to reorientate himself to peace-time conditions. He had been severely wounded during the war by a shell, which had exploded near him and had lost the sight of one eye, but such a disability did not seem likely to prevent a successful future. His wife, Norah, a fine horsewoman who had the good fortune to possess wealth inherited from her father, proved of inestimable help in his career. However, on the eve of the 1921 Grand National he fell from the bedroom window of his Liverpool hotel and was killed. At the inquest held later in the day, it was stated that he had no financial worries, and although blind in one eye, did not need medical attention. The verdict returned was that he had been killed by falling from the window, but that there was not sufficient evidence to show how it had happened. When he was buried on the Downs above Ogbourne so many people attended his funeral that the procession stretched almost four furlongs, from George Edwardes' bungalow to his grave. On the morning of the funeral his widow received anonymously a short poem, of which she thought so highly that subsequently she had it inscribed upon his tombstone:

> Beneath the clean and spacious sky
> Here let the sleeping horseman lie,
> Nor from his darlings sunder.
> And as the thoroughbreds flash by
> This turf shall quicken suddenly
> To hear the hoofbeats thunder.

Despite the offers of help from many quarters Norah Hartigan, suffering sorrow and personal grief, was at her wits' end as to the future of the stables and the horses. However, a solution was found within months, although it was not to the liking of Jimmy White. Martin Hartigan gave notice that he intended to leave Foxhill, explaining to the Rochdale financier that he was taking over his brother's yard at Ogbourne which he was to manage for his sister-in-law. What he did not know and could not explain was that within a short time he would also marry her. That he did so was largely the responsibility of thirty-two-year-old Norah Wilmot, who had been one of Norah Hartigan's best friends since they were children. The two Norahs had to share a bedroom at the 1921 Newmarket December Sales, since the town was packed to capacity and accommodation difficult to find. In the course of a long gossip Norah Wilmot, whose father was Master of the Berkshire and Buckinghamshire Staghounds, which had been formed in 1901 to replace the Royal Buckhounds, suggested that her widowed friend should marry Martin Hartigan. 'After all he is the next best thing to Paddy in the world for you; he adores you and everyone can see that.' Her advice was taken and Martin and Norah lived in contentment for more than twenty years.

In the normal course of events Gordon and the other apprentice, Herbert Pateman, would have left Foxhill with Martin Hartigan without any undue fuss. However, Jimmy White was under the impression (or pretended to be under the impression) that apprentices signed their indentures with owners and not trainers, and when it was explained to him that this was not correct, he offered a substantial sum, reputedly £3,000, for Gordon's indentures. Thankfully the offer was rejected, for if Gordon had remained at Foxhill with White instead of going to Ogbourne with Martin Hartigan, his future might have been in jeopardy.

Life at Ogbourne was on a more modest scale than at Foxhill, but Gordon found more than ample compensation in his new lifestyle. Although not a prude, he had found it difficult to reconcile the sheer extravagance of Jimmy White's approach to life with the poverty he had seen at Oakengates, and was infinitely happier in the atmosphere of his environment at Ogbourne where the day-to-day routine was on a less exalted level. The stable lads' food was of better quality and in greater quantity than at Foxhill and both Martin Hartigan and his wife took the welfare of the stable lads seriously. In return for this consideration and genuine kindness, the lads gave of their best, and the stable exemplified contentment and happiness. The horses were always well turned out, and although the Hartigans were not able to compete with the huge Newmarket stables, a high percentage of their fancied horses were winners. Fred Darling at Beckhampton, Alec Taylor at Manton and Ivor Anthony at Wroughton were the only other trainers in the vicinity — which provided gallops second to none. Hartigan was patient, methodical and almost parsimonious on his owners' behalf, refusing to enter horses with gay abandon, and as a superlative horseman understood the whims and characteristics of every horse in his yard. He never pretended that his geese were swans, and by careful placing and meticulous attention to detail, never missed an opportunity to win a race.

Behind the scenes he realised, as did many others, that the immediate post-war boom in bloodstock was over. Yearling prices were in the doldrums and owners reluctant to spend money due to the commercial depression both at home and abroad. Only a handful of trainers dared to charge more than four guineas a week per horse, because they believed that if they did so they would have no owners. Few owners beside Lord Glanely and HH Aga Khan, who was beginning to buy expensive yearlings on an extravagant scale in a bid to create a new racing empire, were prepared to expend a fortune on thoroughbreds. Sensibly, Martin Hartigan did not view the future through rose-coloured spectacles, although he was fully aware that in his quest for winners he had one inestimable advantage — the rapidly increasing prowess in the saddle of his apprentice, Gordon Richards.

The next three seasons were comparatively uneventful for Gordon as a jockey, although he was beginning to gain an appreciation of the world at large. Racing was opening his eyes to the enormous opportunities which life with a capital 'L' could offer, and he was determined to take advantage of the fruits of his own ability, however great or small they might be, to better his lot.

In 1921 he rode five winners and received the mention 'he shapes well'; had the identical number of winners in 1922 and the following season, at the age of nineteen, increased this total to forty-three. He was given mounts at Royal Ascot, and at Goodwood won the Draycot Handicap on Lord Woolavington's filly Miss Margaret. In the Cambridgeshire he rode Dumas, trained by Captain Hogg, only losing by a neck and a length to Verdict and Epinard, and thought that he was more unlucky on that occasion than on any other throughout the entire year.

By the end of the 1923 season when he lost his five pound apprentice allowance, he had earned a considerable sum of money, which was kept by Martin Hartigan for him until he was out of his apprenticeship. He asked for two hundred pounds of this money to be advanced, not to be squandered, but to help his parents, who were financially hard pressed due to the plight of those in the coal-mining industry.

Within the next three months the Baldwin Ministry was defeated, and for the first time in the history of Britain the Labour Party were in control. King George V invited Ramsay MacDonald to form a government on the anniversary of the death of Queen Victoria, and in his diary commented that he wondered what 'Grandmama' would have thought of a Labour Government. Before another month had elapsed two world leaders, Lenin and Woodrow Wilson, had died and the new Government in Britain was faced with industrial problems caused by high unemployment and the strikes of engine drivers, dockers and London tramwaymen. However, the new Flat season opened on time at Lincoln and Racing appeared unaffected.

An event which was to affect Racing was the introduction of a new medium — radio broadcasting. At the end of 1922 the British Broadcasting Company, financed by a group of manufacturers, had been given an exclusive licence to send out wireless messages. Under its manager, John Reith, it was to influence every aspect of British life, and by Royal Charter in 1926 was to become the British Broadcasting Corporation. The establishing of the BBC added to the ever increasing circulation battle of daily newspapers such as the *Daily Express*, the *Daily Mail* and the *Daily Herald*, and their quest for more readers resulted in more and more space being devoted each day to 'The Sport of Kings', and caused Racing to gain in popularity with the general public.

During the 1924 season, at the end of which Gordon completed his apprenticeship and received the further accolade in the Press 'this boy has come to stay', he rode sixty-one winners. A highlight was when he had his first ride in the Derby on Mr A. C. Saunder's Skyflight, on whom he had previously won at Kempton. Skyflight, bred by Mr C. M. Prior, author of *The History of the Racing Calendar and the Stud Book*, had been bought by the popular Reading butcher who loved nothing better than a day's hunting, and was the first Derby runner trained by Sir Robert Wilmot. Skyflight was unfancied and finished almost last behind Sansovino, ridden by Tommy Weston, on a day made miserable by torrential rain. Nevertheless it was a proud moment for Gordon as he rode to the start, and the historical importance of the world's greatest race was not lost on him. Later in the afternoon he won the Stewards' Handicap on Helsby to score a Derby Day victory. At Royal Ascot he had two rides on the first day of the meeting, finishing third on both of them. Five weeks later he had the honour of riding Weathervane for King George V in the Stewards' Cup at Goodwood, but failed to be placed behind Compiler. Gordon was thrilled to be wearing the royal racing silks, and thought the occasion more memorable than riding Skyflight in the Derby.

By the end of the 1924 season it was evident that he was the 'star of the future' and Martin Hartigan was inundated with requests for his services. Many of these were refused, but not those coming from Captain Thomas Hogg, who trained at Russley Park, between Ogbourne and Lambourn and who was one of the greatest friends of the Hartigans. Forty-three-year-old Captain Hogg, a man of military bearing and demeanour, who had qualified as a veterinary surgeon at Edinburgh

University before serving in the Boer War, was one of the most shrewd judges of a thoroughbred in the kingdom. In 1908 he had come to England on holiday and had been persuaded by Richard Wootton to settle at Epsom, where he worked as a veterinary surgeon and subsequently as a trainer. At the end of the First World War he moved to Ogbourne where his chief patron was Mr Fred Hardy, a Manchester brewer, for whom he trained Happy Man to win the 1923 Ascot Gold Cup. Hogg was prepared to gamble heavily on his horses if he believed that they had an outstanding chance in an important handicap, and thought that Gordon was the most promising jockey that he had ever seen. Vic Smyth, who had first watched Gordon riding at Foxhill, was his stable jockey, but Hogg put up Gordon on the lightly-weighted horses whenever the opportunity arose.

Hogg's first impression of Gordon's ability never altered, and towards the end of the season he told him that he would like him to ride as his first jockey in 1925. It was a wonderful offer, since Hogg, whose patrons included Lord Glanely, had a powerful stable of top-class horses, and appeared to have considerably more chance than Hartigan of winning important races. Gordon explained the offer to Martin Hartigan, who appeared thoroughly disconcerted when he realised that Gordon intended to accept it. Obviously he had no desire to lose so promising a young jockey, and equally obviously was offended that Hogg had not approached him on the question of Gordon's future rather than make overtures direct to Gordon. He attempted to provide Gordon with alternatives, and suggested that he might consider riding for Harry Cottrill's Seven Barrow stables in addition to being retained by his own Bonita stables. His suggestions were to no avail, for Gordon had made up his mind that he would accept the tempting offer made by Captain Hogg, even though there was no doubt that he was immensely happy at Ogbourne. Well fed by Harry Wheeler, the man employed by the Hartigans to look after the stable lads, Gordon was beginning to save much of his earnings and added to his assets when he was presented with a Douglas motor bike by Norah Hartigan after he had ridden a winner for her. On this bike he would roar through the countryside at breakneck speed, gaining the title of 'the phantom horseman'. Occasionally an opportunity arose to travel back to Oakengates on the new bike to see his family and tell them of his exploits and achievements. It was obvious to them that Gordon was on the high road to success, and although his attitude towards them never changed or varied in its love and affection, it was noticeable that he was beginning to acquire far greater self-confidence and worldliness than he would have done if he had remained at Oakengates.

At racemeetings he was associating with affluent men and women who accepted social graces as a mere part of their normal everyday existence, and with his acutely observant nature he absorbed everything that he saw and heard. He was starting to live in a world far removed from that which he had known at Oakengates, and intended to benefit to the full from it. He bought a dinner jacket, and learned to play chess with George Edwardes' widow, who lived at Ogbourne. On Sundays he was often invited to a pre-lunch drink by the Hartigans, who were entertaining their owners, and asked his opinion about the outcome of future races. To the Hartigans' guests he seemed a strong, slightly gauche young man, who had not an ounce of conceit in him, but who was totally dedicated to becoming the finest jockey in the kingdom.

The Hartigans lived in the large gabled house, with a billiard room and rambling staff quarters, originally built by George Edwardes for his brother 'The Major', and employed a bevy of servants at a time when a head lad's wages were little more than thirty shillings a week. The house, surrounded by a croquet lawn and herbaceous borders, stood at the side of the road leading to the gallops, overlooking the top stable yard. The Hartigans had created an almost self-contained unit amidst the Wiltshire Downs, the hamlet of Ogbourne being comparatively isolated, and had built a tiny chapel for their own use and that of the stable lads who were Roman Catholics. The other lads would usually walk to Wanborough for Sunday evensong. The atmosphere at Ogbourne, the beauty of the scenery of the surrounding countryside, and the kindness of the Hartigans, were treasured by Gordon, but in his heart he knew that he had outgrown them and must move on if he was to achieve his ambitions.

Captain Hogg's principal patron at Russley Park was Lord Glanely, born William James Tatham in the Devonshire village of Appledore in 1868, who had commenced his career as a clerk in the offices of an old-established Cardiff shipping firm. Possessed of energy, initiative and ambition he rapidly extended his business interests until he controlled one of the largest merchant-shipping fleets in the kingdom. He also acquired interests in coal mines, docks, wharves and breweries. One of his first trainers, once he had decided to enter the world of horseracing, was E. de Mestre. On a visit to the stables he bitterly complained of the cobwebs in the boxes occupied by his horses and demanded that they be cleaned away. When de Mestre refused, explaining that the spiders killed the flies which irritated the horses, Lord Glanely removed his horses.

After his colt, Grand Parade, won the 1919 Derby he began expending huge sums on yearlings, but with little immediate success. He had married in 1897 and was devoted to his wife, who shared with him his immense grief that their only son had died at the age of six. In 1918 Lord Glanely had acquired the famous Danebury training establishment near Stockbridge, and two years later purchased the Lagrange Stables at Newmarket from George Blackwell. He also bought an estate at Exning which he gradually increased in size and which he made his home for much of each year.

The 1925 season started auspiciously for Gordon when he rode a winner for Fred Templeman on the first day of the Lincoln meeting, and although he was unplaced on Lord Glanely's Grand Joy in the Lincoln, he had ridden six winners by Easter, including a filly owned by Jimmy White and sired by Sir Berkeley, and a handicapper who belonged to one of Captain Hogg's principal patrons, Mr A. Douglas-Pennant. He did not have a mount in either the Two Thousand Guineas or the One Thousand Guineas, but won the Great Metropolitan at the Epsom

Spring meeting on Brisl and the Durdans Handicap on Grand Joy at the Epsom Derby meeting to show that the Epsom course held no terrors for him. He added to his reputation in the eyes of Lord Glanely by winning the Trial Stakes on Sunderland in his 'black, red, white and blue belt and cap' at Royal Ascot and brought further praise by winning the Ebor Handicap at York on Mr H. O. Madden's Chapeau. Madden, the famous jockey who had won five Classics, including the 1898 Derby on Jeddah, and who trained, owned and bred Chapeau, openly admitted after the Ebor that Gordon was the most promising youngster that he had ever seen in action in the saddle.

Occasionally, and without his knowledge, Gordon was put up on a horse whose connections were having a large gamble. One such occasion was at Salisbury with a two-year-old named Stanhope, owned by Sir Alan Johnstone and trained at Binfield by Sir Robert Wilmot. A secret trial was arranged at Russley with three horses, all three-year-olds with Tommy Hogg. At level weights Stanhope, ridden by Vic Smyth, won decisively and was considered a 'stone-cold certainty' for a Maiden Selling Plate at the Bilbury Club meeting in Salisbury after Hogg had expressed his opinion that the trial showed that Stanhope was good enough to win any Selling Plate in England. As part of the subterfuge neither Sir Robert Wilmot nor the owner of Stanhope attended the racemeeting, but to everyone's horror Stanhope, ridden by Gordon, was beaten a short head with three lengths between second and third. The winner was a filly named Click, trained by W. Lines at Clandon near Guildford. Years later Sir Robert Wilmot was told by Click's owner 'You know, you once gave me the fright of my life when Stanhope nearly beat Click at Salisbury'. To the reply 'If you knew how we had tried Stanhope you would not wonder!' came the instant response 'If you had any idea how we had tried Click you would not wonder.' Later in the season Gordon won a hotly-contested Nursery Handicap at Newmarket on Stanhope to prove how unlucky they had been at Salisbury.

A highlight of the season for Gordon was completing hat-tricks on three occasions, at Worcester, Haydock and Wolverhampton and a four-timer at 'Ally Pally' in October when Vic Smyth and Frank Bullock announced that they had both decided to retire at the end of the season. Despite the fact that he weighed so little, Gordon appeared to have the strength of a man at least a stone heavier, and was hailed as the greatest discovery since Frank Wootton, who had retired from Flat Racing before his twenty-first birthday. Described as being a hard-headed and thrifty youngster who realised that a jockey's career was a lottery and that money could vanish into thin air as quickly as it was accumulated, he was praised for not slavishly following the example of Charlie Smirke and the other Wootton-trained boys who invariably attempted to hug the rails whenever they rode in a race.

At the end of the season Gordon headed the list of winning jockeys with 118 winning mounts from 719 races. Twenty-one-year-old Charlie Elliott, who had won the Championship the previous year, finished second to Gordon with eighty-six victories to his credit—so the year was very much one in which youth was not to be denied. Gordon had over a hundred more rides than any other jockey, such was the demand for his services, particularly as he could go to scale at under seven stone. It had been a hard year for him and, even though he did not intend to ride in Egypt or India during the subsequent months, he did not think that the winter would drag heavily on his hands. He planned to spend Christmas at Oakengates with his family, eating and drinking to his heart's content, and then begin losing the weight that he would inevitably put on. However his plans were altered when in December he was rushed into a Marlborough nursing home. On Saturday afternoon whilst he was watching Swindon playing a football match he complained of severe stomach pains. In the evening he felt worse, was taken to the doctor who diagnosed appendicitis and within hours had been operated upon.

When Gordon had completed his convalescence his weight had increased by nearly a stone and the Flat season was about to commence. Understandably, but misguidedly, he began to waste drastically, with fateful results. It was bitterly cold on the first day at Lincoln where he had five rides, and won the Brocklesbury on Secretary for Mr F. W. Wilmot, who was the Secretary at Lingfield Park. So that he should not put up over-weight he rode on a one pound saddle and wore nothing beneath his racing silks. Such an action was folly, and did not escape the notice of one racegoer who told Captain Hogg that Gordon ought not to be riding, and should be in bed. Gordon stayed with the Walkers, the kind-hearted couple who had been introduced to him by Martin Hartigan's head lad, whenever he was riding at Lincoln. In addition to running a fruit and grocery shop, they owned the yard in which the Ogbourne horses had to be stabled since there were no racecourse stables at Lincoln. Hogg heeded the advice and convinced Gordon that he must not ride when he was so obviously ill. Gordon felt too sick to argue and he did not ride for the rest of the week, either at Lincoln or Liverpool, remaining in the care of the Walkers. On his return to Marlborough his doctor diagnosed pleurisy and ordered him to cancel his rides at the Newmarket Craven meeting. He only began riding again at the Epsom Spring meeting, but even then without any success.

By the time of the Guineas meeting at Newmarket he appeared to be improving in health, won the Bretby Handicap, and in the One Thousand Guineas had the mount on HH Aga Khan's outsider Dary Mahal. It seemed that the worst was over and he looked forward eagerly to riding a host of winners. The following week he had several fancied mounts at Chester but the meeting was put in jeopardy by the General Strike. On 5 May, his birthday and the day of the Chester Cup, the *British Gazette* was published for the first time, with the banner headlines 'FIRST DAY OF GREAT STRIKE—NOT SO COMPLETE AS HOPED BY ITS PROMOTERS' and 'THE BRITISH GAZETTE—ITS OBJECTS—REPLY TO STRIKE MAKERS PLAN TO PARALYSE PUBLIC OPINION.' In retaliation the *British Worker*—'the Official Strike News Bulletin published by the General Council of the Trades Union Congress' was produced, but carried no sports news of any kind. However, the *British Gazette* gave a brief résumé of the Chester meeting, the final day of which was to be abandoned owing to the effect of the industrial crisis. For Gordon, however, a personal crisis was about to arise which would put his entire future at risk. He failed to ride a winner on the first afternoon at Chester and twenty-four hours later had the mount on Vermillion Pencil owned by HH Aga Khan in the Chester Cup. The four-year-old colt, set to carry a mere 7 st 4 lbs was much fancied, for he had run promisingly on his season's debut at Newbury. But Gordon rode an indifferent race and finished second to the outsider Hidennis, beaten two lengths, with eight lengths between second and third.

As he returned to the unsaddling enclosure he felt listless, instinctively knew that he could not continue riding and realised that there was something seriously wrong with his health, although he had little suspicion as to the cause. Martin Hartigan was at the racemeeting and immediately arranged for him to be sent back to his home in Oakengates. The following day he went by train to Cardiff to be X-rayed by Dr John Hartigan, one of the trainer's brothers. These revealed that Gordon had a tubercular patch on his lung which would necessitate six months' enforced idleness in a sanatorium at Mundesley, amidst the bracing air of the Norfolk coast.

In the mid–1920s medical science was still 'groping' where the treatment of tuberculosis was concerned, and unbeknown to Gordon the specialists who examined him held out little hope for his recovery and were convinced that his riding days were over. It would have been tragic if he had been halted at the outset of so brilliant a career, but the doctors, based on their experience with other patients, muttered gloomy prognostications and suggested that he may have first been subject to the disease when a boy at Oakengates. They wondered amongst themselves what the young champion jockey might eventually choose as an alternative career.

However, they had overlooked Gordon's determination which was a vital ingredient in his return to health. Another ingredient was the friendship formed with Bill Rowell who arrived as a patient at the sanatorium a few weeks after his own arrival. Bill, whose home was in the Oxfordshire town of Chipping Norton, was much older than Gordon, far more worldly, and a *bon viveur*. In the long tedious hours at the sanatorium Rowell, whom Gordon called 'Uncle', began teaching him the refinements of life, opening up new horizons for the miner's son. Politics, art, society, history, the appreciation of food and wine all came under the closest scrutiny for the benefit of Gordon, who listened with rapt attention. Amongst the other patients were several with an interest in Racing, and to relieve the boredom surreptitious phone-calls were made to the local bookmaker. The excitement caused by anxiously awaiting the results which were relayed from the local post office frequently caused the patients' temperatures to rise. Once the doctors discovered the reason why the thermometer readings rose to unexpected heights all betting was banned. In mid-summer added excitement (always bad for sanatorium patients) was caused by the unexpected arrival of Agatha Christie, who desired a rest away from the hurly-burly of everyday life.

Outwardly Gordon showed confidence that he would eventually be fit enough to return to the saddle, but inwardly had doubts as to what the future might hold in store for him if his health prevented him from doing so. Happily he made excellent progress, and after being allowed out of bed for short periods, was ordered to go out into the fresh air for walks of ever-increasing duration. Proof that he had recovered almost completely came on an afternoon when he found himself crossing a field in which a bull was grazing. To his horror the bull chased him, and his frantic but successful effort to reach the fence and hastily clamber over it, was a sure sign of the progress that he was making.

He was allowed back to Ogbourne in time for Christmas, and Norah Hartigan kindly and thoughtfully gave him permission to use the bungalow built by her on the gallops as his home, and provided a man-servant to cook and care for him. Gordon slept on the veranda, and by the commencement of the 1927 season felt fighting fit. Nothing should be allowed to detract from the kind action of the Hartigans, but it should not be overlooked that from their viewpoint he was an invaluable and probably irreplaceable asset, for they had a second claim upon his services, with Captain Hogg having the first retainer.

A new face that Gordon found amongst the jockeys that he rode against on his return to the saddle was twenty-year-old Rufus Beasley. Rufus, a member of one of the most renowned racing families in Ireland, had received a more expensive and supposedly better education than any of his contemporary professional Flat race jockeys, in that he had been sent to a famous public school — Ampleforth, where he considered that he was wasting his own time and his father's money. On leaving Ampleforth, set in the North Yorkshire Wolds near Helmsley, he rode for Senator J. J. Parkinson's stable at Maddestown Lodge on the edge of The Curragh.

Early in his career he had an experience that he never forgot after riding a winner at 20-1 for the senator, who had told him as he left the paddock on his way to the start that the stable had wagered heavily on the favourite. As he unsaddled his winner some ten minutes later Rufus was not certain how he would be greeted by the senator who had presumably lost his money as a result of the favourite's defeat. To his astonishment the senator told him, 'I had a very good win on you at 20-1. Never forget that the secret of race-riding is to ride horses as if they are not trying. Hold them together until the finish and then push them as hard as you can without getting them unbalanced. With your little experience, if I had told you to win, you would have got excited and ridden the horse into the ground.'

In mid-summer 1926 Rufus' agreement with Senator Parkinson ended. His elder brother Harry was first jockey to H. S. Persse, who had been a great friend of the Beasley family since his own childhood, and it was proposed that Rufus went for a week's trial to Chattis Hill. He had no desire to leave Ireland, but everyone made it clear to him that he would soon outgrow the Emerald Isle. Admittedly, Ireland in the 1920s was a heavenly land in which to live, with open roads unmolested by heavy motor traffic, the sports of steeplechasing and foxhunting playing a predominant part in most people's lives, and the cost of living very cheap. The political troubles which had tormented the country, the bloodshed of the Easter Rising, and the burning and looting of country mansions seemed but unhappy incidents whose scars were healing. Yet Rufus knew that if his ambitions were to be fulfilled, then he must make his career in England. In Ireland prize money was pitifully small, and few Irish horses except two-year-olds who carried out successful raids early in the season on Lincoln and Liverpool, made their mark on English Racing.

Rufus arrived in England at a time when people were obsessed by the flying exploits of Mr Alan Cobham, thankful that the General Strike was over, and delighted that a daughter had been born to the Duke and Duchess of York. He shared 'digs' with Geoffrey Brooke, who was Mrs Persse's brother, and rode his first winner at Hurst Park six weeks later. Rufus often spent his Sundays by riding work for Martin Hartigan at Ogbourne before attending Mass, lunching with the Hartigans and their guests, playing hectic games of lawn tennis and finally driving to Seven Barrows for games of poker, which lasted until the small hours of Monday morning. He was not considered to be at his best at racemeetings held on Mondays.

In the mid-1920s another personality, William Hill, was emerging at the outset of a successful career which in future years would bring him into close contact with Gordon. Born in 1903, and only a year older than Gordon, Hill was one of eleven children of a foreman coach painter at the Birmingham factory of Daimler Limited. He began making a book soon after his nineteenth birthday, and within two years had left Birmingham and was betting in the cheap ring at Harringay and the White City greyhound tracks. Pony racing was beginning to flourish and he also spent many afternoons betting at Northolt Park, the South Harrow track where Tommy Carey, Pat Donoghue, Monty Smyth and Les Hall made their reputations. Hill also ran an illegal book in the Coventry Club in Denham Street, Soho, at a momentous time in the history of Betting. The Chancellor of the Exchequer, Mr Winston Churchill, had included in his 1926 Budget a proposal: 'that a tax should be imposed in all money legally risked by way of betting'. This proposal caused considerable anxiety and controversy in the world of Racing throughout the year. Curiously, however, little complaint was voiced by the huge army of small-time punters, although a vast number of those who did voice an opinion made it clear that they believed that the death-knell of Racing had been sounded.

Gordon did not ride at either Lincoln or Liverpool in the first week of the 1927 season, but he was at Warwick a week later where racegoers gave him a great reception. His absence from the saddle during 1926 had been Racing's loss and race-goers were anxious to show him their pleasure at his return. However, the next few days were to be the saddest of his life, for during the afternoon he received a telegram informing him that his mother was seriously ill. He travelled directly from the racecourse to Oakengates, but did not reach his home in time to see her before she died – the cause of death being asthma.

Martin Hartigan and Gordon.

Portrait of Gordon by J. Berrie.

Gordon winning on Saint Reynard at Worcester. He was now only two short of breaking Fred Archer's record of 246 winners, 2 November 1933.

The wrecked plane, after the 1933 Doncaster crash in which Gordon escaped unhurt, but the pilot was killed.

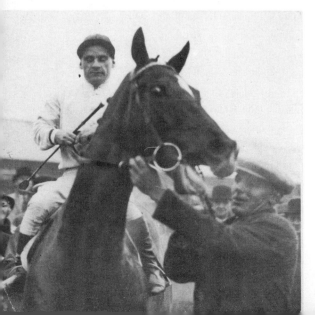

Gordon returning in triumph on Golde King, having beaten Fred Archer record, Liverpool, 8 November 1933.

The Richards family were appalled by the tragedy, and bewildered in their misery. Gordon proved the rock upon whom they all relied, for despite the fact that he was only twenty-three years of age, his judgment and acceptance of responsibility surpassed those of other members of the family. His horizons were broader than theirs, and so was the weight that he was willing to place upon his shoulders. Finance was also a consideration, for his earned income was steadily outstripping that of his father and his brothers. At the time of Elizabeth Richards' death her two youngest daughters, Rhoda and Barbara, were at boarding school. Without fuss or complication Gordon took over the responsibility of their school fees and arranged every detail of collecting his sisters at the end of term and returning them to school once the holidays were over. It was one of the first open displays of his immense qualities, for his actions showed his strength of character, generosity, sincerity, sense of duty and loyalty to his family, and determination to ensure that those he loved wére provided with all that they required. He sought no thanks, demanded no reward for his efforts and sacrifice, and was content in the conviction that he was doing what was right.

1927 was to prove the most successful season and the busiest that Gordon had achieved, with much of his success being due to the fact that he could still ride 6 lbs lighter than any of the other leading jockeys. He had 772 mounts, which exceeded Donoghue's post-war record, and rode 164 winners — more than twice as many as Charlie Elliott, who was again runner-up to him. Charlie, shortly after winning the Derby on Call Boy, gave a celebration dinner to his fellow jockeys. Each of them, when asked to 'say a few words' gave a virtually identical stereotyped speech which implied that they were pleased that Charlie had won, and that he was a great jockey whose Derby triumph was very popular. When it came to Gordon's turn to speak he showed his individuality by saying, 'I am pleased that Charlie did it, he's a great jockey, and I'm glad that he won the Derby because after looking at the papers the next morning I had an idea that Call Boy had won it!'

Less than a month after the Derby Jimmy White committed suicide at Foxhill. Refused credit by his bankers after a disastrous speculation in British Controlled Oil Fields, he was faced with a demand to take up more than a million pounds worth of shares which his brokers could no longer hold on his behalf. Arriving at Foxhill in the early evening he sent the female members of the staff into Swindon to go to the theatre, and after wandering around the house collecting documents, wrote two letters, one to his wife and the other to his estate agent. He then retired to his bedroom where his body was discovered twelve hours later. At the inquest the jury told the coroner that they found that White had died from the effect of chloroform poisoning self-administered during temporary insanity. The coroner told their foreman that he would alter the words 'temporary insanity' to 'while insane'. It was a tragic end to the life of a man who had been a great influence upon Gordon at the outset of his career.

Throughout the season Gordon rode many times for Mr Reid Walker, winning on both Invershin and Delius in his 'sea green' colours. In 1917 Mr Walker, a member of the Jockey Club, had bought the two-year-old Square Measure from his breeder Robert Sherwood. Square Measure proved a wonderful bargain, and won a second Royal Hunt Cup for his owner in addition to a Liverpool Autumn Cup. In 1920 Square Measure was the medium of a stupendous gamble in the Cambridgeshire in which he was to have been ridden by Steve Donoghue. The colt had been doubled up with Bracket in the Cesarewitch, and after Bracket had won the first leg of the 'Autumn Double' the bookmakers' liabilities were colossal. They were saved when the Cambridgeshire was abandoned due to the National Coal Strike. One of those who had doubled up Bracket and Square Measure was Jimmy White. When he heard that the strike would probably cause the cancellation of the Cambridgeshire he offered to settle the strike single-handed and appease the militant miners so that the race could be run. To prove the monstrous bad luck of the gamblers Square Measure proceeded to win the Liverpool Autumn Cup easily—carrying 9 st 2 lbs—once the strike was over.

Mr Reid Walker had tremendous faith in Gordon's future career, and was delighted that an Oakengates boy was beginning to make a name for himself as a jockey. He preferred to forget that Gordon had once applied to him for a job and made it clear that he thought that Martin Hartigan had been a fine master for him. Frequently when Gordon was riding at Wolverhampton he was invited by Mr Walker to stay the night at Ruckley Grange, and after dinner was served a glass of port in a room adjoining the dining room. It would have been unthinkable for a young professional jockey to sit down to dinner with his patron and other guests, and neither Mr Reid Walker nor Gordon would have presumed to allow such an action to occur. On these visits Gordon was shown how to play billiards and snooker by Mr Walker and commenced a life-long enjoyment of the two games.

Although Gordon had a successful season it was not a good year for Racing in general, and racecourse executives were bitter in their criticism at the end of the year.

The Secretary at Hurst Park commented that the betting tax had done much harm and added, 'unless something is done about it there is a dark future before English Racing', whilst Sir Loftus Bates, Clerk of the Course at Carlisle, Catterick, Lanark, Pontefract and Thirsk stated, 'the past season has been most unsatisfactory. In all cases racecourse receipts are considerably down. Owing to the continuance of unemployment there has not been the usual amount of money circulating among the bookmakers, but to what extent the tax has affected attendances it is not easy to say. I have no doubt that if the "Tote" is adopted it will be of considerable assistance in bringing us new revenue.'

An unusually wet summer and high admission charges also adversely affected racecourses, and it was even suggested in some circles that the introduction of greyhound racing was a contributory factor to the parlous state of the Turf. Lord Lonsdale even went so far as to suggest tentatively that horseracing should be held at a later hour, with a view to competing with greyhound racing. When various personalities were canvassed for their views at the St Leger meeting at Doncaster,

Frank Butters, Lord Derby's trainer, turned down the proposal on the grounds that it would be unfair to the horses. His view was endorsed by both Basil Jarvis and Alec Taylor, and proved to be that of Steve Donoghue, who astonished everyone by adding the information that a late start to Racing was customary in Russia. Joe Childs, twice the age of Gordon, was another who disapproved of Lord Lonsdale's suggestion. Off the racecourse Childs lived exceedingly quietly, living in a small house at Reading and spending much of his time digging in his garden. He had not the greatest sense of humour, particularly if he was at the receiving-end of the jibes of others; but he never failed to see the funny side of an incident which had occurred during the First World War when he joined the ranks of a cavalry regiment. On being received initially for training at The Curragh he was despatched with a dozen other recruits to the riding school, where a sergeant asked him if he had ever ridden before. 'Just once or twice,' replied Childs. 'Yes, on a donkey at Brighton, I suppose,' sneered the sergeant. 'You've the worst seat on a horse that I have ever seen in my life.'

In the autumn Gordon was involved for the first time in a race which brought him a rebuke from the Stewards when he rode Saint Reynard in the Cesarewitch. The gelding was trained by Martin Hartigan and most of the Ogbourne villagers backed the four-year-old who was much fancied and started second favourite having won five races earlier in the season. However, one Ogbourne inhabitant who did not support Saint Reynard was Edwin Martin who had ridden Don Juan to win the 1883 Cesarewitch. Martin trained only a few horses at Ogbourne, but thought that one of them, Eagle's Pride, had an outstanding chance of winning the Cesarewitch despite the support for Saint Reynard. He and the owner of Eagle's Pride, Colonel F. T. Halse, backed their horse heavily and on the day of the race Eagle's Pride was third favourite. The two Ogbourne horses had the finish to themselves with Eagle's Pride winning by a head with the third horse two lengths away. The two tiring horses came very close inside the final one hundred yards and afterwards Gordon said:

as you know, Dines and I were riding very close together. He was very keen on winning and so was I. My mount, Saint Reynard, was very tired. He had changed his legs coming down the hill and was fading away fast. The gelding began to hang and lurch, and became very difficult to keep straight and up to his bit. I was looking straight in front of me, and straining every muscle to get my mount first past the post. As I made my big effort I lifted my whip to hit Saint Reynard. It slipped slightly out of my hand. Like a flash I grasped at it, and caught Dines in doing so. It was all done in a fraction of a second, and was purely accidental. I am very sorry it occurred as such incidents only serve, in a lot of cases, to create a wrong impression.

In the *Racing Calendar* it was stated that: 'It was reported to the Stewards after racing on the Thursday that Richards had seriously interfered with Eagle's Pride, and they held an enquiry on the Friday. Having heard the evidence of Dines and other jockeys who rode in the race they were satisfied that, whilst the interference which had taken place was accidental, it was due to Richards' reckless use of his whip. They severely cautioned Richards as to his future riding.' Weeks later, at Liverpool, Gordon received a second warning after the Stewards had enquired into the alleged interference when Steve Donoghue claimed that he had been almost forced over the rails. However, no further action was taken.

Shortly after the end of the season, Bernard Carslake, who was virtually the only jockey from overseas between the wars to attain the high general standard of contemporary English jockeys, and who was so powerful a rider with his hands and his heels that he could get more from his mount without the use of whip than the average rider could achieve by using it, wrote an article for a Sunday newspaper giving his views upon Gordon as a jockey

. . . Having ridden against him often enough, I have had ample opportunity of studying his methods. I attribute his success to one word, *balance*. Richards chose the profession of race-riding. He might have been equally successful as a disciple of Blondin. Do you remember the little figure that you cannot knock over? Every time that you push him over he bobs back again. That is Richards. It is all a question of balance. The two best balanced jockeys today are Donoghue and Richards. Watch them canter to the post and you will see how similar are their styles. Donoghue was the originator of the style, and Richards has not only copied it, but exaggerated it. I have never discussed this with Richards, but you cannot mistake the similarity. Donoghue and Richards are the only two jockeys with perfect balance, and it might be said that they are part and parcel of the horse. Each rides with a long rein, and has only a very light hold of a horse's head. Horses run best that way. Richards, because of his perfect balance, is really carrying less weight than would another jockey of the same weight. At least that is the effect that it would have upon the horse . . . Whatever part of a race may be taken it is the same — balance is the first and last word in the champion's make-up . . . He is a quick beginner because his balance enables the horse to find his stride quickly . . . Richards is more successful on round courses than on straight ones. That is balance again. Richards has one good fault, when he comes to beat you in a finish he is not satisfied to stay with the leader and just win, as many of us do. He goes right through to the end and does not care by how far he wins. That is a good fault because he will never be caught napping as, I suppose, most of us have been at one time or another. While Richards has most of the qualities which go to make a good jockey, he still has something to learn. He is young and he will continue to profit by experience. That he will make progress is certain, for he is as well balanced in mind as he is in the saddle. He is never likely to suffer from a swollen head, for he has not changed in the least since his apprentice days. It is mainly in versatility that he will improve. In that respect I do not regard Richards as the equal of Donoghue. Steve has always been able to vary his style according to circumstances, and I still look upon him as the finest jockey of my time . . .

Gordon was flattered by the continual comparisons with his hero, Steve Donoghue, but insisted that it was Martin Hartigan and not Steve who had modelled his style and taught him all that he knew.

Carslake, born in Australia in 1886, was himself one of the most stylish jockeys ever to grace the saddle. Riding in Austria and Hungary at the outbreak of the First World War he escaped to Rumania and then to Russia, where he was Champion Jockey in 1916. He rode countless winners for Hon. George Lambton and H. S. Persse, but his great reputation never fully recovered from the unhappy 1924 St Leger which he won on Salmon Trout, despite rumours that he would 'stop' the Aga Khan's colt. Carslake, who always had great trouble with his weight, was never a light jockey and therefore did not receive as many mounts as some of his contemporaries. His daily diet was described as 'hot air and hope' and his daily existence a misery. He was obsessed by the importance of 'balance', and claimed that he established such sympathy with his mount that he could lie far out of his ground and still call upon his horse for a final accelerating spurt which would bring victory. He was left-handed, could not swat a fly with his right, and hated using the whip, even in his left hand. On many occasions he voiced his opinion that few top jockeys belaboured their mount unmercifully, even if it seemed that their whips were constantly going up and down.

Before Christmas Gordon, as Champion Jockey, was given a dinner by his fellow jockeys at the New Princes Restaurant, where the chef created a model racecourse in sugar as the table decoration. One of the distinguished guests was Gordon's father, who never failed to attend any dinner given in his son's honour until his death at the end of the Second World War.

4

Champion Jockey

In January 1928 Captain Hogg suggested that Gordon join his family for a holiday in St Moritz. Gordon, who had never been on the Continent, accepted and took his sister Vera and also Jackie Sirett, who had won the Manchester Cup eighteen months earlier on Vermillion Pencil, the horse upon whom Gordon had his final ride before succumbing to tuberculosis. Gordon did not lose his heart immediately to the intense beauty of the Engadine, although in later years he was to become passionately fond of St Moritz. Legend claims that in 1864 four Englishmen were spending an autumn evening in a St Moritz hotel, when the hotelier pointed out his belief that they would enjoy the winter far more in the Engadine than amidst the fog, snow, sleet and drizzle of England. He explained that during the hours of winter daylight the sun was never hidden at St Moritz and that under cloudless skies the warmth of the sun could be so great that there would be no necessity to wear a coat. Carried away by his own enthusiasm, the hotelier, Johannes Badrutt, proposed that if the English returned for the winter and were displeased with the weather he would not charge them for their accommodation.

They returned, Badrutt's claims concerning the weather proved correct, and the future of St Moritz as a winter resort assured, although many of the first visitors were affluent English suffering from tuberculosis.

By the 1920s St Moritz was the Mecca for international society during the winter months and was described as 'lying in a hollow of the mountains like a jewel at the bottom of a crystal cup'. Intrepid sportsmen came from all over the world to ride the famous Cresta Run, whilst others spent their days curling and ski-ing. In the evenings beautiful and glamorous girls were escorted to Gala occasions at the Palace Hotel and the Kulm Hotel by the rich young men who had risked their necks on the Cresta Run earlier in the day. For Gordon it was a completely new world, and he was at first an unwilling spectator of the entire scene.

Captain Hogg, who had been responsible for proposing that Gordon went to St Moritz where the sunshine did him the power of good, had first claim on his services for the 1928 season. Second claim was held by Martin Hartigan and third by Fred Darling at Beckhampton.

Darling had first claim on Joe Childs, but as the season progressed the personalities of the trainer and jockey began to clash, and Darling started offering more and more mounts to Gordon, especially upon the flying filly Tiffin whose victories in the National Breeders Produce Stakes and Cheveley Park Stakes caused her to head the Free Handicap at the end of the year. She was unbeaten in five races and Gordon rode her on each occasion.

As a result of the tuberculosis that Gordon had suffered in 1926 he still continued to live in the large wooden bungalow on the Downs above Ogbourne, faithfully looked after by his man-servant, Towning. Unbeknown to anyone except Towning, from the spring of 1928 he had another companion to look after him—his wife Margery, whose father, Thomas Winckle, was a railway carriage fitter in the GWR workshops at Swindon. Married in secret at Gerrards Cross in Buckinghamshire a few days before the Flat season—the only two others who knew their secret were the clergyman and the registrar! No news was relayed to Oakengates, the reason for keeping the wedding secret being that Gordon was uncertain as to whether or not he would make a come-back as a jockey. Eventually, those who were closest to him shared his secret. The Hartigans unexpectedly arrived at the bungalow one morning, having heard rumours that there was an additional occupant, were told the happy news and introduced to Mrs Gordon Richards.

A week later Gordon's father and his young sisters Rhoda and Barbara, home from school for the holidays, went to stay with him at Easter, and to their astonishment, as their car climbed the hill from Ogbourne to the Downs, found an embarrassed Gordon attempting to block their path, in order to give Margery time to temporarily evacuate the bungalow and Towning time to clear their home of any incriminating evidence that his master was a married man. Gordon's efforts ended in chaos, for at that moment a flock of sheep decided to cross the road and nearly knocked him over. Nathan Richards was introduced to his daughter-in-law and instinctively recognised that in marrying Margery, Gordon had made the best decision of his life.

A wife can be the making of a man, and in Gordon's case Margery proved from the outset to be perfection. Theirs was a true love-match which has blossomed and flourished throughout the years and brought to both of them the happiness which they deserved. It was not until the end of August that the general public knew of the marriage, for Gordon had told Margery that they would not publicly announce their wedding until he had ridden one hundred winners during the season. Ironically, the announcement was eventually made at the wrong moment.

Having ridden ninety-nine winners Gordon went to Haydock Park where, in the Friday Selling Handicap, the Judge announced that his mount, The Countess of Hainault, had triumphed after a very close finish between four horses. Gordon, not doubting the Judge's verdict, rode back to the winners' enclosure in great glee and immediately told gathering reporters that he had been happily married for six months. Moments later the Judge revised his verdict, giving the race to Wypo, ridden by Tommy Weston. However, the exciting news of the wedding could not be withheld a moment longer—and banner headlines in the stop-press of late editions of the evening papers—announced the existence of Mrs Gordon Richards. Gordon did not ride a winner the following day, was second in each of the first three races at the Ebor meeting the next week and had to wait until he won the Convivial Stakes for the Senior Steward of the Jockey Club, Lord Ellesmere, on his flying filly Tiffin on the second day of the meeting, before he notched up his century. Tiffin had a will of her own and had an infallible way of putting the stable lads who rode her at exercise on the ground—much to their disgust—but she and Gordon seemed *simpatico* and were far too good a combination for their rivals.

Three days before the Ebor meeting Gordon and his wife had attended a farewell dinner party in Marlborough for Captain Hogg, who was moving to Newmarket to become private trainer to Lord Glanely, who generously gave Gordon a magnificent radiogram as a belated wedding present when he learned that his jockey was no longer a bachelor. It had been rumoured that Mr J. B. Joel intended to take over the Russley Park Stables, after the departure of Captain Hogg, but the rumour proved to be incorrect.

A month earlier Gordon had won the Stewards' Cup at Goodwood on Navigator, much to the delight of his owner, Lord Glanely. Gordon put up 4 lbs over-weight, but Captain Hogg had tried the colt to be a 'certainty' and the stable had a very substantial gamble. Earlier in the season he had ridden Jurisdiction into second place behind King George V's Scuttle in the One Thousand Guineas, and in the Derby rode Sunny Trace for Lord Dewar. With the impetuosity of youth he began having a mad race with Charlie Elliott on Flamingo as though the Derby was a six-furlong sprint, and by the time that they reached the foot of Tattenham Corner Sunny Trace was a spent force. Lord Dewar was not amused. There was no excuse, but Darling, who trained Sunny Trace, quickly forgave Gordon, even though he told him exactly what he thought of his riding tactics. However, at Goodwood he approached him with the proposal that he accepted a first retainer from the Beckhampton patrons for 1929.

The thought of going to Beckhampton appealed more than anything else in the world to Gordon. However, it was in keeping with his character and his complete integrity that he decided that if Captain Hogg and Lord Glanely would offer him a similar retainer to that suggested by Darling, then he would not desert them. His decision was totally honourable and when made public brought him deserved acclaim. There had been rumours that Stanley Wootton intended to offer him an enormous retainer, but this never materialised.

Hogg, very anxious not to lose Gordon's services, quickly made Lord Glanely accept the fair terms upon which Gordon would remain with them, and did not object when Gordon insisted that he would not live at Newmarket. Darling regretted Gordon's decision, but secretly admired him for making it. However, he was a determined man who did not give up easily, and his future plans still included the services of Gordon. Consequently, he bided his time, retaining Freddie Fox to replace Joe Childs, who was intending to retire.

When Gordon began riding out at Newmarket in the spring of 1929 he immediately realised how very different were the training routines at Headquarters compared to those at Ogbourne, Russley and Beckhampton. There was no privacy as hundreds of horses worked on Warren Hill and the Limekilns, and he began to miss the peace and solitude of the Wiltshire Downs. Hogg had a useful string of horses, including two expensive two-year-olds bought by Lord Glanely at Doncaster — Singapore and Rose of England — but both he and his thoroughbreds took time to acclimatise to their new surroundings. The year was not significant for Gordon and his mounts in the Guineas, Rattlin the Reefer and Grand Idol, and his Derby mount, Grand Prince, were noteworthy only for their mediocrity. Royal Ascot was not an outstanding success, although he won the Churchill Stakes on M. Marcel Boussac's Ramon and the Jersey Stakes on Rattlin the Reefer. The St Leger meeting at Doncaster was little better, but nevertheless the winners kept coming at the minor meetings.

By October 1929 it was evident that the battle between Gordon and Freddie Fox for the Jockeys' Championship would be immensely close, particularly since Gordon had been out of action for a week during July as a result of an accident at Liverpool. As the starter pulled the lever the tapes failed to rise and Gordon and Tommy Weston were both thrown to the ground. Weston only received a bad shaking, but Gordon sustained concussion, had to have two stitches put into a scalp wound and was compelled to miss the Goodwood meeting. This enforced idleness almost cost him the championship.

Early in October Gordon, who had a lead of six, was made 4–5 favourite, with Fox at 6–4; the only other jockeys to receive a quotation being Harry Wragg, Michael Beary and C. Ray, and their odds were more than 20–1. Michael Beary was convinced that Gordon would retain the title, but Harry Wragg, when interviewed, declined to give an opinion, although he added wryly that he would like to back himself at even money for a place! As he was twelve winners ahead of Michael Beary at the time his hope for an even money bet did not find favour with the bookmakers.

The Press latched on to the battle which they labelled 'Youth' against 'The Veteran' — much to the displeasure of Fox who did not enjoy being reminded that he was forty-one years old, and that he had ridden his first winner when Gordon Richards was a boy of three! Curiously he, like Gordon, had been born in Shropshire and like Gordon was unostentatious in his private life, contentedly living at Wantage where his chief recreations were lawn tennis in the summer and fox-hunting throughout the winter. Eventually the 1929 championship became an anti-climax with Gordon taking the title for the third year in succession, his total number of winners being 139 — 19 more than Fox.

On the final day of the season it was announced that Brownie Carslake, who had retired in 1928, was to resume riding, having been given a retainer by Mr J. B. Joel. He had not really enjoyed his year as a trainer, and the fact that he had not put on as much weight as expected since his riding days, influenced his decision to return to the saddle. No one questioned his skill and artistry as a jockey, but his return highlighted the fact that a great jockey does not necessarily possess the qualities needed to make a great trainer.

Once again his fellow jockeys gave Gordon a dinner at the Piccadilly Hotel, with Martin Hartigan presiding. Gordon, modest and unassuming as ever, was eventually induced to make a speech. Smiling at the guests who had come to acclaim him he remarked, 'It is grand to be here again,' and promptly sat down. One of the Turf matters discussed at the dinner was the experiment contemplated in France whereby not only were the rates for a jockey's losing rides to be increased, but also a percentage of the stakes instead of a set fee for winning rides were to be awarded to the jockeys. If the French experiment became standard practice the five guineas paid to a freelance jockey for a winning ride, and the three guineas for a losing ride in England seemed inadequate. Even on this basis, however, it was estimated that Gordon Richards had received approximately three thousand pounds in the course of the season as riding fees, excluding his retainers. In one newspaper article about his career it was estimated that he earned £10,000 for riding magnificent thoroughbreds, driving his six-cylinder Chrysler and wintering in St Moritz, as opposed to working in the dust and dark of a 750-foot deep Oakengates coal mine for less than three pounds a week!

1930 brought Gordon and Captain Hogg their first Classic success when they won the Oaks with Lord Glanely's Rose of England. They may have been a trifle fortunate for the short priced favourite, Fair Isle, owned by Lord Derby and heroine of the One Thousand Guineas, travelled badly from Newmarket to Epsom and on her arrival refused to accept any food. Like her brother, Fairway, who totally dissipated his Derby chance long before the start, Fair Isle had virtually lost the race before the tapes went up. Gordon and Hogg were hopeful rather than confident, but Rose of England, who had been bred by Lady James Douglas, ran on strongly to win convincingly from Wedding Favour and Micmac, racing in the colours of Lord Beaverbrook, who dispersed his stud and sold all his horses in training later in the year since he found that politics took up too much of his time to allow him to find relaxation in Racing.

Lady Glanely had been killed in a car crash a few months previously, and as Lord Glanely led Rose of England into the winners' enclosure he kept on saying to Gordon 'How Her Ladyship would have loved to have been here today'. The weather was almost unbearably hot and on Oaks Day, traditionally 'Ladies Day' at Epsom, the fashions typified the new era of the thirties, with skirts generally reaching halfway to the ankle. Smart two-piece suits of crêpe de chine and skull caps in shiny black straw seemed the order of the day in the members' enclosure, where large hats were conspicuous by their absence.

The year was memorable, not only for Gordon's first Classic winner, but also for 'dope' and 'Tote', with doping cases being severely dealt with by the Jockey Club, and the Tote making steady headway in the popularity stakes.

The word 'dope' was derived from the Dutch 'doop' meaning to dip, which was incorporated into slang to describe the habit of using tobacco adulterated with the seeds of *Datura Stramonium* to stupefy victims prior to robbery. In 1924 as a result of conferences between the Stewards of the Jockey Club and the Home

Secretary, an organisation was created to combat the activities of 'dopers' and other racecourse 'undesirables'. Ring inspectors, many of them retired CID officers, were recruited and although they quickly gained the upper hand in their battle against welshers, gatemen issuing free passes, the sale of bookmakers' pitches and the payment of protection money, their success against dopers was minimal.

A pleasing aspect of the season was the success of Gordon's younger brother Clifford who, after being apprenticed to Gerald Armstrong at Middleham, began riding some of the light-weights in Captain Hogg's stable. He had ridden his first winner at Newmarket in 1925 and four years later won the Cesarewitch on West Wicklow.

Gordon won his second Classic for Lord Glanely, when he triumphed on Singapore in the St Leger, and for good measure also won the Park Hill Stakes on Glorious Devon in the same colours. Lord Glanely had paid twelve thousand five hundred guineas for the fashionably-bred colt by Gainsborough at the Doncaster Yearling Sales, with Mr Cecil Boyd-Rochfort the under-bidder. Singapore had very indifferent legs, did not race as a two-year-old and Hogg at times despaired of ever getting him right. However, by September 1930 Singapore had become a top-class colt and the St Leger result was never in doubt once Gordon struck the front a furlong from the winning post. An enormous crowd was on Town Moor to watch the race, many of them being regaled by the tips of a man who told them that he had been sent down by Mr Ramsay MacDonald to help the unemployed by giving them reliable racing information. Poverty may have haunted many, but at the other end of the social scale Lord Fitzwilliam brought a house party of forty from his enormous house at Wentworth Woodhouse. One of his guests admitted that earlier in the day he had taken half-an-hour to find his way out of the house, and even then had only got into a back-garden used by the servants.

Towards the end of the season Gordon was delighted when his brother Clifford added to his major victories by winning the Cambridgeshire on The Pen owned by Norah Hartigan and trained by her husband. Days earlier Fred Darling had mentioned again the possibility of retaining Gordon, but had added his concern that Lord Woolavington might consider reducing his bloodstock interests due to the death of Hector Macdonald who had managed his stud farm and had died in a London nursing home. Lord Woolavington told the Press:

the death of my godson, Hector Macdonald, will be a shock and a cause of much regret to his large circle of friends. He and his brother, my son-in-law, Captain Macdonald-Buchanan, came under my care as boys when sent to England by their father, the late Sir John Macdonald, of Buenos Aires, an old and esteemed friend of mine. On his retirement from the Army I appointed him manager of my stud and all Racing matters. Up to two years ago he conducted everything in connection with this work with extraordinary ability and thoroughness, and enjoyed in every way my full confidence. The confidence that I had in his ability as manager of my stud and my Racing activities probably accounts for my considerable interest in the sport. I doubt if I should have paid such personal attention to breeding and raising bloodstock had I not had such confidence in his capacity as manager.

Darling thought that Lord Woolavington might now decide to curtail his racing interests, with ensuing detriment to Beckhampton.

Once again the Jockeys' Championship became a battle between Gordon and Freddie Fox. Two days before the end of the season Fox still led Gordon by two — even though he had failed to ride a winner for a week. Owners and trainers with whom Gordon was not usually associated had hastened to offer him mounts, and his brother Clifford willingly had given up a fancied mount at Warwick earlier in the week to enable Gordon to ride another winner. Fox was never happy to accept mounts outside the stables who gave him retainers, but was as equally determined as Gordon, and longed to achieve his life's ambition of heading the Jockeys' List. As the climax to the contest approached, crowds at Castle Irwell on the final day were on tenterhooks. Gordon rode the winner of the first race — appropriately on a filly named Rivalry — to draw level with Fox who felt aggrieved when his well-fancied mount Canfield failed to peg back the favourite in the second race.

Then Gordon rode Lord Glanely's outsider Glorious Devon to a three-length victory in the November Handicap to go one ahead. It seemed to everyone except Fox that the title was Gordon's. However, Fox showed his determination by winning the fourth race by a short head. Level — and still two races to go. Surprisingly, Gordon did not have a ride in either of them, and as Fox cantered down to the start of the Worsley Nursery Handicap on Mr H. F. Clayton's Isthmus he realised that he still had a great chance, for Isthmus was the 6–5 on favourite and on form was a 'certainty'.

Minutes later, Isthmus had won by six lengths to give the delighted and relieved Freddie Fox the championship by one winning mount. It could be argued that seventy-four-year-old Mr Clayton enabled him to become Champion Jockey. The previous afternoon Fox had allowed himself to take another ride outside his retainers, and had won on a filly owned by Mr Clayton, who was almost to bring off a remarkable autumn double and a colossal gamble with Disarmament and Six Wheeler (named after one of the type of cars manufactured by Leyland Motor Company, in which he was a large shareholder) less than a year later.

Days after his triumph Freddie Fox entertained his fellow jockeys at the Champion's Dinner, again held at the Piccadilly Hotel. His speech was even shorter than Gordon's twelve months earlier and consisted of three words, 'I thank you.' After Tommy Weston proposed Gordon's health, the former champion stood on a chair which was supposedly supported by Johnny Dines and said, 'Here I am again. Not quite in the same place, but here I am again.' As he spoke he began his characteristic habit of tapping his finger-tips on his chest, as though playing a tune. It was a mannerism which was an outward and visible sign of his excitement, and he often subconsciously did so as he returned to the winners' enclosure after a particularly exciting race.

Gordon then proceeded to tell his fellow guests that on the previous Saturday at Manchester he went to have a cup of tea after the fourth race. As he heard the huge cheer which greeted Freddie Fox's victory on Isthmus he knew it was all up. He felt in the 'Great Alone', and putting on his cap, which was an old favourite, owned and worn for eight years, he went home. He had always thought that the cap was one of his lucky omens, and had worn it every day throughout the final week, hoping it would bring him good fortune. He added drily that he had since burnt it!

What he did not tell his audience was that he had only reluctantly accepted a retainer from Lord Glanely for 1931. Whenever he had attempted to pin down his patron as to the future, he had been fobbed off with, 'Yes, we must have a chat about it.' Unexpectedly, in the late autumn came the proposal, via an embarrassed Captain Hogg, that Gordon must accept a lower retainer than that received the previous year. It was far too late in the year to make other arrangements and was, therefore, accepted. However, Gordon was understandably and justifiably furious and determined never to allow such a state of affairs to occur again.

A state of affairs which did exist, whether Gordon liked it or not, was that although defeated in the Championship he was the one jockey above all others in whom the general public were interested. In consequence, the Press would not allow his private life to be his own, and scores of articles constantly appeared, detailing his life off the racecourse. It was common knowledge that he was totally straightforward in all his dealings, that he was plucky, dedicated, had a sense of humour, strong convictions and the expressed hope 'ten more years for me, possibly a six-figure sum saved at the end of it all and then retirement'. He bore ill-will against no one, although at times his temper flared — only to subside rapidly. He adored his children, Jack, born in 1927 and Peter in 1930, and treasured the few moments in which he was able to relax with his family. His motto might have been 'anything for a quiet life'. Yet, like all men constantly in the public eye, he had his critics, who claimed that the only reason that he was at the head of the winning jockeys was that he rode at such a light weight that he got far more mounts than any of his rivals. Such criticism seemed unfair, and the only criticism which might have been justifiable was that he did not appear to have the uncanny brilliance of jockeys such as Joe Childs in long-distance races, due to his impetuosity.

He was beginning to love his winter holidays in St Moritz, was never happier than when pulling the leg of his great friend, Johnny Dines, with whom he could have made a fortune on the variety stage as an extemporary knockabout, and had a reputation for honesty and integrity equalled only by Mr Stanley Baldwin. As a hobby he enjoyed racing pigeons, but above all else he loved his home. Whereas

Steve Donoghue and other jockeys including Rufus Beasley would contentedly visit London night-clubs three or four times a week, and would shine and sparkle in the company of débutantes, chorus-girls and society beauties, Gordon wished for nothing more at the end of the day than to drive back to his Marlborough home on the Savernake Forest side of Marlborough. He had bought the house, a modest modern five-bedroomed residence in 1928. Originally named 'Barnfield', he changed the name to 'Singapore' after his St Leger victory. He and Margery loved 'Singapore', and only during January and February would be content to leave on holiday, invariably going to the Palace Hotel in St Moritz. Harry Wragg was another devotee of Switzerland, whilst the Beasleys and Michael Beary preferred to hunt in Co Limerick, and Steve Donoghue would search for winter sunshine in India or the West Indies.

1931 was yet another successful season for Gordon, although he had the chagrin of realising that he would have ridden Cameronian to victory in the Derby if he had accepted the retainer offered by Darling to ride for Beckhampton. At Royal Ascot he was summoned before the Stewards after he had won the Royal Hunt Cup on Lord Glanely's Grand Salute. In the *Racing Calendar* it was reported, 'The Stewards called on the trainer of Grand Salute to explain the running of his horse in the Royal Hunt Cup and the Flying Dutchman Welter Handicap Plate at York. The Stewards, whilst accepting his explanation, considered that he was to blame for running a horse in an unfit condition previous to the publication of weights in a handicap in which he was engaged.' The following afternoon Gordon was beaten a short head in the Gold Cup on Singapore. A furlong from the winning post Joe Childs on Trimdon lost his whip, and was unable to prevent his mount swerving on to Singapore so that Gordon found himself scraping the rail with his boot. Obviously hampered, Singapore ran on resolutely but although many onlookers thought that the finish was a deadheat, the Judge gave his verdict to Trimdon. Gordon wished to object, but Lord Glanely, furious at the Stewards' remarks the previous day about Grand Salute, obstinately refused to allow him to do so. The Stewards took no action on their own behalf, so the lucky Trimdon kept the race.

A week later Freddie Fox gave a dinner to celebrate his Derby victory on Cameronian and deliberately sat Gordon and Joe Childs next to each other. For most of the evening the sparks flew, but eventually Freddie's hoped-for reconciliation was reached between the two jockeys, whose hearts and heads were warmed by fine food and wine.

In mid-summer the economic crisis of the country reached its peak. The Prime Minister, Mr Ramsay MacDonald, resigned and was then entrusted with the task of forming a National Government, which included Baldwin and Neville Chamberlain. The new Government remained in office for three months by which time the crisis was virtually over.

Whilst the crisis was at its height Gordon won the Doncaster Cup for Lord Glanely on Singapore, but was absolutely determined not to allow the procrastination which had occurred twelve months previously to jeopardise his future. Nevertheless, his sense of honour was so great that he would not deviate from his conviction that he could only break with Lord Glanely if there was refusal on his patron's part to match any other retainer that he was offered. Once again Darling tentatively approached Gordon to accept a retainer from Beck-hampton — without the knowledge of Freddie Fox. Gordon went to see Lord Glanely at Exning, where he was given tea, champagne, an harangue on loyalty, the suggestion that money was not everything and the claim that if Hogg ceased training for him and if Gordon stopped riding in his 'black — red, white and blue belt and cap' colours then he would give up ownership. Gordon did not breathe a word about Darling's offer, but when eventually Lord Glanely openly stated that he could not afford to pay the full amount of his original retainer, Gordon felt as though chains of bondage had fallen from his hands and feet. Returning home, he phoned Darling and accepted his offer. Later that evening he made a second phone call to inform Lord Glanely of his decision. Being 'hoist with his own petard' Lord Glanely was furious and made his fury abundantly evident, but no one could accuse Gordon of behaving in anything other than a totally honourable manner. The Beckhampton retainer was reputed to be £4,000 plus 10 per cent of winning stakes and with such influential owners as Lord Woolaving-ton, Lord Ellesmere, Mr J. A. Dewar and Mr H. E. Morriss being patrons of the stable, which was acknowledged as the most powerful in the kingdom, the 'sky was the limit' for Gordon's future.

Without doubt the one innocent party adversely affected by the new retainer was Freddie Fox. Fox had served his apprenticeship with F. Pratt and had ridden his first winner at Warwick in 1907 before riding in Germany and Austria. Short, dapper and always well-groomed, he had first ridden for Darling when still an apprentice, winning the Cesarewitch for him on Lady de Bathe's (Lillie Langtry) Yentoi in 1908. Subsequently, in Germany he had been retained by the Von Weinberg Stable, for whom Darling trained. At the end of 1930, having become Champion Jockey, it was rumoured that he intended to retire. But such rumours were scotched by his remark, 'Why should I retire? Luckily, I enjoy very good health, and I have little or no difficulty in keeping my weight normal.' Business-like, unostentatious, and with a thin high-pitched voice which often trailed into incomprehensibility when he became agitated or excited, Fox did not have Gordon's dominance, and although never spectacular in the saddle, he was a marvellous judge of pace.

In the spring of 1931 Fox had ridden a Beckhampton loser in both Newmarket Classics. In the Two Thousand Guineas he had elected to ride Lemnarchus instead of Cameronian, who became the mount of Joe Childs, and in the One Thousand Guineas he could not make up his mind whether to ride Four Course or Windy-brae. On the suggestion of Lord Ellesmere, the owner of Four Course, Fox and Elliott settled the issue by the spin of a coin. Elliott won the toss and chose to ride Four Course, who won by a head from Mr Martin Benson's Lady Marjorie ridden by Gordon. Lady Marjorie looked assured of success inside the final furlong, but as Gordon touched her with his whip she swerved sharply to her left, losing about two lengths. Gordon immediately straightened her and she ran on strongly, but the winning post came just too soon and she was beaten a head. On returning to the unsaddling enclosure Gordon commented, 'I ought to have won a length. If only I had not hit her.'

Freddie Fox made certain that no such mistake occurred at Epsom in his selection of mount. Winning the Derby on Cameronian was a deserved milestone in his career, and sentimental in that he had ridden as an apprentice for Lt-Colonel E. D. Kennedy, who was a Cameronian, and had stables at Ludlow close to where he had been born. The night of the Derby the Cameron Highlanders printed posters which were distributed as recruiting leaflets throughout Lanarkshire:

> Another Cameronian Victory—
> June 2 1704—Blenheim
> April 29 1931—The Two Thousand Guineas
> June 3 1931—The Derby
> Why not be on a really good thing and join your county
> regiment—The Cameronians (Scottish Rifles).

Also on the night of the Derby Mr Dewar, who had inherited Cameronian on the death of his uncle, Lord Dewar, praised both Fox and Darling in the course of a speech at a celebration dinner and added:

> It is like this, the Government leave only the 'crumbs' to go on with when death duties are paid, and even now Racing with all its joys and big race gains remains for me a problem for the future. They knew the result of the Derby in Australia and far-flung corners of the world a few minutes after Cameronian passed the winning post. I only hope that my uncle has been 'looking down' on the kindest colt that he ever bred and nominated, and knew of our triumph just as quickly.

Three months later, Cameronian finished last in the St Leger behind Sandwich, and put up a lamentable performance for an odds-on favourite. It was later discovered that he had a temperature of 103. Fox told reporters, 'It was obvious when I got Cameronian to the post that there was something wrong with him. He was very upset and kicked Orphen. He then literally went mad, ran himself right out, and was completely done with once the straight was reached.' Darling insisted that the colt was not 'got at' but his comments did not satisfy everyone.

In his heart Darling had considered Fox as nothing other than a very adequate 'stop-gap' until he could retain Gordon, and therefore had no compunction in high-handedly allowing his stable-jockey to discover from the Press that Gordon had superseded him. The truth was that Darling rode rough-shod over Fox and

A famous Tom Webster cartoon.

Above left: Steve Donoghue and Gordon returning to the weighing room.

Above right: Freddie Fox (left) and Joe Childs, two of Gordon's greatest adversaries in the saddle.

Gordon returning from a swim with Jack, Peter and jockey Archie Burns.
Shoreham, 1935.

The christening of Marjorie Richards at Rockley Parish Church, March 1936.
Mrs Margery Richards is on the far left, Gordon's father far right and sons
Peter and Jack in front of Gordon.

was frequently annoyed that Fox allowed him to do so. Initially, he had attempted to get him to agree to ride the Beckhampton horses only when Gordon was not available, but even the mild Fox would not tolerate such a dubious proposal and insisted on becoming first jockey or not accepting a retainer at all.

Darling found it easy to dislike people, and Lord Glanely had fallen foul of him by insisting on his owner's rights and dictating where one of his Beckhampton-trained horses should run, against Darling's advice. The horse won, Darling felt that he had been made to look a fool, and the Glanely horses left Beckhampton in a hurry.

Another owner, with an immense thoroughbred empire and stud, was requested to take his horses away because a personal mannerism irritated Darling. His own foibles may not have pleased everyone with whom he came in contact—and possibly the fact that his German wife insisted on remaining in her own country rather than make her home at Beckhampton added to his apparently abrupt nature which brooked no opposition, his loneliness and his refusal to suffer fools gladly. He disliked the Press, and was never over-enthusiastic about putting pen to paper. If he had troubled to write his memoirs they would have been hailed as one of the most enthralling volumes in Turf literature. He had been accused of being totally cold-blooded, of keeping a revolver in the drawer of his office desk and on one occasion using it to kill a dog who was infuriating him, and of having a temper which at times was ungovernable. However, England has never possessed a greater trainer of thoroughbreds at any period in Turf history, and Gordon's association with him was to bring them immense glory during the next two decades.

5

The breaking of Archer's record

The history of Beckhampton as a racing establishment began soon after the end of the Napoleonic Wars when a red-brick coaching inn and stables on the busy London to Bath road were converted into training quarters. The first Classic winner to be sent out by trainer William Treen was Deception, who won the Oaks in 1839 for the eccentric Mr Fulwar Craven. Two days earlier Treen had ridden the filly in the Derby to be second to Bloomsbury, but Mr Craven thought that he had ridden her injudiciously and replaced his trainer-jockey by John Barham Day in the Oaks. In 1868 the brilliant Beckhampton-trained filly Formosa dead-heated for the Two Thousand Guineas and won the One Thousand Guineas, the Oaks and the St Leger, but it was not until the advent of twenty-eight-year-old Sam Darling in 1880 that Beckhampton began to flourish. Sam had spent much of his childhood at Moreton-in-Marsh with his grandfather who had won the 1833 St Leger on Rockingham.

After a decade training steeplechasers in Worcestershire, newly-married Sam Darling bought Beckhampton in 1880 for five thousand pounds. The local inhabitants gave their unsolicited opinion that he was on the brink of madness to undertake the restoration of land and a training establishment which had been allowed to fall into decay through neglect and mismanagement, but they underestimated his determination and his skill. Within a few years he had bought more adjoining land, improved the gallops and built new stabling so that he could accommodate sixty horses. He created a two-mile gallop and a three-furlong gallop for fast work. Both gallops were perfect for top-class horses, but very severe on those of moderate ability.

In 1897 Darling sent out Triple Crown winner Galtee More, followed in the next fifteen years by such champions as Wildfowler, Cap and Bells, Ard Patrick, Slieve Gallion and Willonyx. Many owners desired to have their horses trained at Beckhampton and Darling was unable to accept all their horses, due to lack of accommodation and stabling. Fate, however, must have been in the best of mood and humour, when Darling agreed to take two horses for Mr James Buchanan, whose fortune stemmed from being sent to London in 1879 to act as the agent for a firm of whisky distillers. In 1912 he trained Tullibardine to win the Goodwood Cup for Mr Buchanan. The year after Tullibardine's victory Darling explained to Mr Buchanan that he intended to retire and asked if he would be willing to leave his horses with his son Fred, who was taking over the licence to train at Beckhampton. Mr Buchanan, who had most of his horses with Robinson at Foxhill, realised that Robinson, utterly offended by the disqualification of Craganour in the 1913 Derby, and seriously ill, was also considering retirement. He therefore not only agreed to Darling's request, he went further and bought Beckhampton.

Fred was the third of Darling's eight children and made his reputation at Beckhampton with Hurry On. The horse was owned by Mr Buchanan, who was knighted in 1920 and eventually became Lord Woolavington, and for whom Darling also trained Derby winners Captain Cuttle and Coronach. The word 'compassion' was not in Darling's vocabulary—but his ability as a trainer made Beckhampton the finest and most successful training establishment in England. Small wonder that Gordon wished to be given the first retainer, for he knew that the unsentimental Darling was dedicated to training Classic winners. A small man, described as having a sharp nose and thin lips, Darling would enjoy driving to London for a party, but however late the party ended, he would be in the stables at first light. As the first lot were paraded in front of him he would know instinctively if anything was amiss. Nothing would escape his notice for his eagle eyes were never bleary from lack of sleep. He was supreme at building up the condition of the thoroughbreds in his care, and he had the inestimable genius of being able to gauge a horse's preparation to bring him to peak condition on the vital day of the race which he had planned the horse should win. All his horses carried an especial bloom and distinctive air, so that as they paraded in the paddock, onlookers immediately recognised them and would exclaim, 'That is a Darling horse.'

He was *el supremo* at training two-year-olds and would never allow them to jump off and gallop helter-skelter. Instead, he taught them to settle down on the heels of other horses and accelerate at a point about a furlong from the end of the gallop. He planned the racing programme for his horses some three weeks in advance, and once a race had been selected for a particular horse the preparation began with no thought or interest as to the possible opposition from other stables. For the most part, his two-year-olds were either Royal Ascot or Goodwood horses and if they fell into neither category, then Darling was disinclined to bother with them.

As Darling had won almost seventy thousand pounds for his patrons during the 1931 season it was not difficult to calculate that Gordon's earnings in 1932 might exceed ten thousand pounds. Such an income seemed a fortune, even by film-star standards of the era, but where business was concerned Gordon had a wise head upon his shoulders. Three years earlier it had been suggested that he wrote his autobiography in return for a large sum of money. He refused the offer on the grounds that he ought to be Champion Jockey for many more years and in consequence when he retired his life story would be worth a far larger sum.

Gordon's business acumen was evident, even at an early age. While still an apprentice, a jubilant owner had offered him a gold watch as a present. Gordon declined and asked for a different gift, giving as his reason the fact that a gold watch could be stolen. Yet even as the news of Gordon's retainer from Fred Darling was released, and also that his brother Clifford had been engaged to ride the Manton light-weights, came word that there was a growing feeling amongst owners that the time had come to call halt to huge retainers, with many owners declaring that they could not afford to continue making the enormous 'cash' presents demanded by the most successful jockeys. Some of these jockeys exchanged their cash presents for stocks and shares which, if wisely bought, yielded huge dividends and capital appreciation. One group, consisting of a famous trainer, jockey and professional backer, was reputed to invest more than one hundred and fifty thousand pounds annually on the Stock Market.

On New Year's Day 1932 the Prime Minister sent a message to the nation: 'The year that we have just rung out has not been one on which we shall gladly dwell in our memories. It has been a year of crisis and hard struggle which has borne heavily on all sections of the community to prevent crisis from developing into catastrophe. I am afraid that in many a home this Christmas the severity of the times has made itself harshly felt . . .'

Certainly in mining areas such as Oakengates such severity resulted in considerable hardship, but Gordon did all that he could to help his father and his family until the crisis abated.

In February Edgar Wallace had died. He had loved Racing, and believed that he was bound to make money if he followed Gordon's mounts through thick and thin. In reality a complete 'mug punter', he had contributed to the sport by instituting the court action which ultimately led to Cameronian being permitted to run in the Derby, and as Chairman of the Press Club founding the annual Derby luncheon.

Gordon began the 1932 season in fine form, with his winners highlighted by victories in the Newbury Spring Cup and the Wood Ditton Stakes at the Newmarket Craven meeting. The Craven meeting also brought him a salutary lesson from Fred Darling when he rode Lord Woolavington's Cockpen in the Column Produce Stakes. The colt, who was a great favourite of Darling's, and had won the 1931 Coventry Stakes, started odds-on despite the fact that he was giving a stone or more to each of his seven rivals. After being beaten into third place Gordon was taken on one side by Darling and criticised for not letting Cockpen run his own race. Darling added, 'Newmarket demands that a horse should run his own race, so do not fight him.'

During the meeting Gordon also received an insight into Darling's views on punctuality. He had arrived five minutes late on the gallops due to the insistent request of Darling's brother, Sam, that he rode a trial for him, despite Gordon's concern that he would not reach Fred Darling at the appointed time. At the end of the morning Gordon apologised to Fred Darling for being late. The curt manner in which Darling remarked, 'My time is seven-thirty', resulted in Gordon never again being unpunctual during the twenty years that he was associated with the Beckhampton trainer, whom he virtually worshipped as a god.

Beckhampton did not have a runner in the Two Thousand Guineas, but Gordon finished third on Lord Woolavington's Safe Return in the One Thousand Guineas, two lengths behind M. E. de St Alary's Kandy. At the meeting he won the first of five races upon Supervisor, a brilliantly fast two-year-old owned and bred by Fred Darling. Supervisor's victories included the Queen Mary Stakes at Royal Ascot, but she was far inferior to another Beckhampton two-year-old — Myrobella — who raced in the colours of Lord Lonsdale, to whom she was leased from the National Stud for her racing career. Darling, who loved nothing better than allowing his horses to make their debut at Salisbury, decided that Myrobella should have her first race the week before the Derby. Salisbury was chosen, and to Darling's and Gordon's complete amazement she was beaten. This lapse was overlooked after Gordon won a maiden race on her at the Bibury Club meeting six weeks later, before she proceeded to win the National Breeders Produce Stakes by five lengths, the Champagne Stakes at Doncaster by six lengths, the Hopeful Stakes at Newmarket by four lengths and finally the Prendergast Stakes a fortnight later by the same margin, to show her enjoyment of the Newmarket course.

Gordon did not have a memorable Derby week in 1932, for Cockpen failed behind April the Fifth in the Derby; Cameronian could only finish third to Salmon Leap in the Coronation Cup; and in the Oaks Will o' the Wisp started favourite but was beaten into second place by Udaipur.

Royal Ascot proved more successful with victories on Manitoba in the Coventry Stakes, on Supervisor in the Queen Mary Stakes, Cockpen in the Fern Hill Stakes, Forab in the Britannia Stakes and Lemnarchus in the King's Stand Stakes. Gordon won the Goodwood Cup on Lord Woolavington's filly Brulette who beat Brown Jack by four lengths, and a month later won the Yorkshire Oaks on Will o' the Wisp to make amends for her Epsom failure. At the Ebor meeting he took another Cup when he stormed home on Foxhunter with Sandwich and Brown Jack trailing in his wake.

An unhappy incident occurred in the Middle Park Stakes when Gordon rode Lord Woolavington's Manitoba in a three-length victory over Felicitation and Scarlet Tiger. Beary lodged an objection to Manitoba on the grounds of crossing three-quarters of a furlong from home. The objection was sustained, and the Stewards made further enquiries, at the request of Lord Derby, into an allegation made by Gordon against Tommy Weston who rode Scarlet Tiger. After hearing evidence they exonerated Weston but told Gordon that they considered that in bringing the matter to the notice of his employer he had acted in good faith and a proper manner.

Throughout his career Gordon was involved in few objections. However, one amusing incident in which he was indirectly involved occurred as a result of the disqualification of a well-known amateur in a point-to-point for 'coming away from the rails'. The Sunday after the disqualification, the amateur was complaining disconsolately about his misfortune to his lunch guests, who included Gordon. The Champion told him that if he had said 'so and so happened and it

69

was not my fault at all', he would have kept the race. Many years later the amateur was acting as a Steward and after Gordon had won a race the jockey of the second objected on the grounds that 'Richards came away from the rails'. At the Enquiry Gordon said 'so and so happened, it was not my fault' and to the Steward's intense amusement his co-Stewards decided that Gordon could keep the race.

Gordon registered his one hundred and eighty-seventh win of the season at Warwick in late November, thus equalling Frank Wootton's record number in 1911 – the highest of the twentieth century. When praising Gordon's feat, certain Press reporters were quick to point out that Fred Archer had achieved the huge number of 246 victories in 1885, whilst Tommy Loates had ridden 222 winners eight years later. In their opinions these enormous totals were unbeatable . . .

Gordon was disappointed not to have achieved 200 winners in the season, and was prepared to point out that if he had always chosen correctly when offered chance mounts he would have easily broken the magical double-century barrier. When he gave his celebration dinner to 150 guests at the Piccadilly Hotel one absentee was Harry Wragg who had broken his leg in a terrible fall at Newcastle a few weeks earlier. The accident occurred on the way to the start of the Astley Nursery handicap when a filly ridden by Tommy Weston lashed out, kicked Wragg's mount and sent jockey and horse crashing to the ground. Wragg's leg was badly smashed. Taken to Newcastle Infirmary, he was operated upon by the famous surgeon Gordon Irwin who instructed that ether was to be poured over the leg many times a day to ensure that it remained clean. Penicillin had not been discovered and without the care and attention received by Wragg from doctors and nurses acting on Irwin's instructions the riding days of the brilliant jockey might have been over. However, Gordon was determined that Wragg should not be forgotten, and on his left was a vacant chair occupied by a caricature of Wragg drawn by Tom Webster. He always regarded 'Sheff' as the best jockey riding against him, and never failed to point out how wrong racegoers were who thought that Wragg could only ride a waiting race. He suggested that they should see him jump a horse out from the start, and added that just because he sometimes pulled back, people thought that 'Sheff' had not got well away.

He then proceeded to tell his audience that once again he intended to go to Switzerland after Christmas, but that until then he would give free rein to his interest in soccer in general and Wolverhampton Wanderers in particular. Whenever possible he would attend 'Wanderers' matches and would also play right-back for the Ogbourne team against the Manton and Beckhampton stables.

The following morning in a Press interview he admitted that he had only witnessed two National Hunt meetings in his life – other than when at the mixed meetings at Liverpool – and that he was unlikely to increase that number to three during the forthcoming winter months. Several renowned National Hunt jockeys stayed in the same 'digs' as he did for the mixed meetings at Aintree and to see their anxious bravado in the evening before an important race over the huge fences including Becher's Brook and the Canal Turn strengthened his decision to ride only under Jockey Club Rules. In philosophical mood he next admitted that he believed the most important thing for a successful man to do when glamorised by fame was to keep his head. Asked a question about his use of his whip when riding a typically forceful finish, he replied that because he swung his whip a lot when he was riding it did not mean that he was using it on the horse. He added that many of the horses that he rode for Beckhampton won in the early part of the season and also at the end of the year. That was positive proof that they got no whip. When his views upon the advice to be given to a young jockey setting out on his career were invited, he commented: 'You really cannot advise them. A boy has a certain head upon his shoulders, and if it is in him then he will emerge from the ruck. When he's at the top, again everything depends upon him as to whether he will stay there. That is life in any profession. A level head, that is the only secret.' He continued, 'If I had my time over again, and the choice of a career, I should still elect to be a jockey. I love every minute of the life.'

He also loved every minute of his trips to St Moritz. The Pullman coaches at Victoria, the cross-channel voyage, the French countryside, and finally the last leg of the journey when they changed trains at Chur for the magical trip up the mountains to St Moritz never failed to exhilarate him.

During his stay in St Moritz the news seeped through that Herr Hitler had reached the summit of his ambition and had been appointed German Chancellor. The Swiss did not seem perturbed and neither were the English visitors at the Palace Hotel.

During this visit Gordon mentioned to a Swiss friend that he was not sleeping well. The Swiss recommended that if a specially prepared wire contraption was placed under the mattress, then a perfect night's sleep was guaranteed. He went further and generously gave one of these wires to Gordon who told Margery that she was to put it under their mattress once they returned home. For the next few weeks Gordon slept marvellously, and remarked, 'That wire has done the trick.' To his mortification, Margery replied, 'Good heavens, I forgot all about it and left the wire in Switzerland.'

Gordon's life on his return from St Moritz in February 1933 necessitated his losing seven to ten pounds in weight. Wisely he appreciated that this weight must not be lost drastically and he settled on a long, slow and arduous campaign. He rode before breakfast, participated in as many as twenty gallops before lunch, played football with stable lads in the afternoon and in the evening trained in a gym. The only consolation to this rigorous and spartan existence was that he ate like any other hungry man and did not need to starve himself, with thin wafer biscuits as a treat. If he had known what the season would hold in store for him he might have trained even harder, for 1933 was to be the most memorable year in his life as a jockey.

He began the season unsuccessfully, failing to be placed in the Two Thousand Guineas on the favourite Manitoba, and only managing to be third in the One

Thousand Guineas on Myrobella, who flagrantly did not stay a mile. However, a week later he won the Chester Cup on Dick Turpin to give Martin Hartigan one of his greatest training successes. The margin was only a head, but the victory gave Gordon almost more pleasure than any triumph he had previously achieved. To commemorate the triumph he was given a silver replica of the cup by Dick Turpin's owner, Mr R. F. Watson. At the Epsom Derby meeting he began by being second on four consecutive mounts, on the first of which he was defeated by his brother Clifford. In the Derby he was again unplaced riding Manitoba behind the brilliant colt Hyperion, and fared no better in the Oaks on Arethusa.

At Royal Ascot he won the Coventry Stakes on Mr Dewar's Medieval Knight; the Queen Mary on Maureen for Lord Woolavington; the Chesham for Lord Ellesmere on Merenda, whose dam was Tiffin; the Fern Hill on Myrobella; and the New Stakes on Lord Glanely's odds-on favourite Colombo.

For Royal Ascot Gordon usually rented a house near Swinley Bottom. He shared the house with Harry and Sam Wragg, Bobby Jones, Phil Lancaster, the New-market bookmaker, and Major Sam Long, a much respected member of the Press. Lancaster and Long were both appalling tennis players but often insisted on playing a set after dinner whilst still dressed in their dinner jackets. The object was to prove which of them was the worst player. Each morning during Royal Ascot Gordon would ride work on the course before returning to his rented house for two hours' sleep.

By 1 July he had ridden his hundredth winner of the season, and the Press began to ask him inane questions about his chances of breaking Fred Archer's record. Tersely, monosyllabically, but politely, Gordon answered their questions. During the next two months he had the misfortune to be stung by a wasp whilst racing at the York Ebor meeting, and to be booed for the farcical pace chosen when he rode Colorado Kid and Michael Beary rode Nitsichin in a two-horse race for the Doncaster Cup. Admittedly, a cab horse could have gone faster than the two opponents for the first mile, but nevertheless the cat-calls were unjustified from a crowd who seemed to have overlooked the fact that Gordon and Michael Beary were riding to the orders of the trainers and that he had already ridden three winners that afternoon.

Two hours after the Doncaster Cup, Gordon, who had been in brilliant form and won five of the six races, was involved in a fatal and tragic air-crash. After racing, he, Fred Darling, Fred Lane, Archie Burns, Herbert Blagrave and Norah Hartigan were due to take off from Armthorpe Aerodrome in a plane piloted by Captain G. A. R. Pennington to return to Beckhampton. The aeroplane, a ten-seater De Havilland Dragon, which had flown up from Heston, failed to clear a six-foot hedge and hit the ground with the front of the plane crumbling, the undercarriage being torn away and the engine totally wrecked. Hundreds of racegoers, including Freddie Fox, waiting to take off in another plane, saw the crash and rushed to the rescue. It was a miracle that all seven occupants of the Dragon were not killed outright. Norah Hartigan and Fred Darling were taken to hospital with cuts and bruises, with Darling also suffering a broken nose. Tragically, the pilot died from his injuries half-an-hour later.

One of the most experienced of fliers, Captain Pennington had flown Gordon to Ostend the previous Sunday in the same aeroplane. Chief pilot of the Skegness and East Lincolnshire Aero Club he had been in the RAF until 1925 and during the First World War had sunk a German submarine in the Mediterranean with a bomb dropped from his plane—a feat which brought him the Order of the Nile from a grateful foreign Government. After the crash Gordon told a reporter 'We had just got comfortably settled in our seats and the machine began to rise when we struck the hedge and overturned. Most of us scrambled out little the worst. I intend to motor back to London and shall ride at Alexandra Park tomorrow.' Not only did he keep his promise but rode a winner and two seconds to prove that he was unharmed by the near-catastrophic crash.

When the inquest on Captain Pennington was heard at the Markham Main Colliery in October a verdict of 'accidental death' was returned after the coroner had said that there was no adequate explanation for the crash. The representative of the Accidents Branch of the Air Ministry told the coroner that he had examined the aeroplane and found all the controls in order. There was an adequate supply of petrol and oil, no defect in the engine and the brakes were working well. The only possible explanation was that the throttles were not fully open and that there was insufficient power to make flying speed.

By the end of September Gordon was under greater pressure than at any other time during his career as a jockey, for it seemed conceivable that he might break Fred Archer's record of 246 winners in a season. Wherever he went he was hounded by the Press, who built up a campaign eulogising him and giving the general public so graphic a day-to-day account of his winning mounts and his private life that he became the most discussed man in the kingdom and for many a national hero. Small punters began backing his mounts in crossed doubles and were winning so much money that bookmakers refused to pay more than 3–1 against any horse that he rode. Only twice before in Turf history had that happened— once with Archer and once with Sloan. This action on the part of bookmakers caused considerable ill-feeling, particularly when Gordon rode a supposedly unfancied horse whose starting price was returned at 10–1 or even longer odds. Punters thought that the champion was infallible, and at Birmingham a badly-bred colt with no form which he rode in a seller was backed to win £20,000. After being beaten the useless horse was sold for eighteen guineas!

The summer was almost over, and the relaxation that Gordon found at Silver Spray, his rented Shoreham seaside home during the Sussex fortnight at Good-wood and Brighton, was but a happy memory. However, his ambition and his strength of character enabled him to withstand the pressures put upon him. One phrenologist, having made a study of the champion jockey's features, wrote that Gordon's face showed large intellectual powers combined with great muscular activity. He added that in temperament and disposition Gordon was sensitive and energetic, tense and sprightly, with his brain and nervous system highly developed. With the forehead of a thinker he would always be a pace-setter who worked harder than his fellows. As a speaker he would never waste words, time or energy in florid, idealistic vapourings, for he would invariably be direct and to the point. His sympathies would invariably be with the underdog. The great height of his head from the opening of the ear to the crown of his head indicated firmness, stability and perseverance. It also showed that he had a sense of humour and that he could be witty and droll on the spur of the moment. The fact that his eyebrows were full and over-hung his deep-set eyes implied that he was able to receive rapid and accurate impressions from surrounding objects—and that he could make quick decisions. The fact that his nostrils were large and elongated denoted histrionic talents of no mean order, whilst his wide broad chin signified fidelity and tenacity in affection to family and friends. Such an analysis may have seemed little more than 'poppycock' to Gordon, but to others it was the truth about him!

By early October Gordon was almost the only man in England not prepared to commit himself on the subject of breaking Archer's record. He claimed that he did not think about it and added that to speculate on whether or not he would ride more than two hundred and forty-six winners was a waste of time and energy. He pointed out that there had been moments in his career when he had ridden more than forty consecutive losers and that his job was to ride winners, not worry about records. His days began at dawn when he would frequently be driven by his faithful chauffeur to Binfield Grove to ride work for Norah Wilmot before returning to Beckhampton for more trials. Home for breakfast, a bath, half-an-hour's relaxation with five-year-old Jack and two-and-a-half-year-old Peter, and it would be time once again to enter his juggernaut-sized Rolls-Royce to be driven to the races. It was typical of him that although his first Rolls had been grey in colour he had changed it to black on hearing a much respected friend saying that black was a more suitable colour.

He was invariably philosophical about his hectic existence, taking the attitude that the work had to be done, so there was no point in making a fuss about it. It was his job, and the state of affairs was as simple as that. He spent a few hours each week with his racing pigeons, which he kept in a loft at the bottom of his garden, and read thrillers and Wild West stories whenever he could find the time. He loved the stories written by his friend Edgar Wallace, but above all else he relished a good night's sleep which he claimed was the best thing in the world for a jockey.

When requested by the Press to state her interest in Racing, Margery Richards claimed, 'I have quite enough interest in looking after Gordon. My racing is to keep his bath water hot, and see that his meals are ready and that there are dry things when he comes home wet through.' She never bet, and seldom went racing, but every afternoon appeared to be on tenterhooks until she learned the racing results. In September she drove with Gordon to Newmarket to watch him ride his two hundredth winner of the season, but that was one of the few occasions throughout the year on which she attended a racemeeting. The children were still too young to go racing, but the belief that Jack, whose favourite toy was a car, wished to become a racing motorist did not prevent his buying his son a pony. Baby Peter, being tubby, was expected to become a successful heavyweight boxer.

Every day newspapers gave details of Gordon's life and on one occasion his supposed death. Telephone wires throughout the country were set buzzing at 2 a.m. when it was thought that he had been involved in a fatal motor-car accident. Shortly before dawn, Gordon's great friend, Bobby Jones, learned the news and rushed to the house in Newmarket where Gordon invariably stayed, to verify the information. To his relief, Gordon was sound asleep in bed and, when awakened, was more annoyed that the rumour was spreading than at anything else; particularly as he had travelled to Newmarket by aeroplane and did not even have his car with him.

Two months earlier, it had been suggested that he was seriously ill with blood poisoning and the latest rumour only added to the thought, shared by the police, that some misguided individual with a warped sense of humour was responsible for the malicious gossip. The police believed that from the same source came the malicious rumours that the Arsenal football team had been involved in a train crash and six of the team killed.

On 4 October Gordon took his total for the year to 212, 34 short of Archer's record established in 1885, by riding all six winners at Chepstow, and regaling the crowd who had gathered to cheer him outside the weighing room after the last race by singing 'Little Man, you've had a busy day'. Gordon possessed a fine voice, had frequently sung in Methodist choirs as a boy, and had the natural talent for singing enjoyed by those of Welsh descent. As he had won the final contest at Nottingham the previous day his Chepstow feat meant that he had ridden seven consecutive winners. Archer had ridden six winners in one afternoon on two occasions, at Lewes in 1882 and Newmarket in 1877, and George Fordham had also achieved this remarkable feat at the Bibury meeting in 1867. Twenty-four hours later, Gordon rode the first five winners at Chepstow before losing the final race, the 'unlucky thirteenth', when riding the 3–1 on chance Eagleray. Eagleray was beaten a head and a neck in a desperately close finish.

The next afternoon at Haydock Park, Gordon, on the St Ina colt, was defeated a head and a short head by Harry Wragg and R. Perryman in the first race before triumphing in the second race on Mr F. Hartigan's Mr Pitman. The total distance of less than one length by which he was beaten on Eagleray and the St Ina colt prevented him from riding fifteen consecutive winners and probably from bankrupting every bookmaker from Land's End to John o'Groats into the bargain.

To commemorate his unique achievement at Chepstow he was presented by the Directors of the Race Company with a silver bowl bearing the names of all eleven winners. It was a generous gift, but one which was shortly to be overshadowed by other gifts as Gordon inexorably drew closer and closer to Archer's record. Another unexpected gift was the dedication of a new slow foxtrot called

'Well done, Gordon' written by Jos Gilbert, at the suggestion of a man who had 'won a packet' on an accumulator nominating all six of Gordon's Chepstow winners.

Gordon took time off to lessen the intense pressure of his existence to attend the annual charity Donkey Derby at West Ham, which followed the football match between jockeys and boxers, and rode with Freddie Fox in a race against Flanagan and Allen for a side stake of £25. As Flanagan appeared in a racoon fur coat and Allen in a dilapidated morning dress coat the two comedians were at a weight disadvantage before the race began. Eventually Gordon and his donkey passed the winning post a stride ahead of Freddie Fox—due to the feverish endeavours of a dozen supporters who manhandled the unwilling donkey forward. Flanagan beat Allen for third place, but only after deliberately taking a short-cut across the football pitch instead of going round it as the more circumspect Allen continued to do!

Such light relief helped to lessen the tension from which Gordon was suffering, tension made worse by his involvement in an unauthorised edition of his life story. At Haydock he vehemently denied having given his permission for such a story to be published by the *Sunday Express* under the title *Gordon Richards—Life Story—edited by Geoffrey Gilbey*, and stated that he had not contributed a single word to what was supposed to be his 'real life story', nor had he been allowed to see one word of what the *Sunday Express* intended to publish. He added that he had not given his permission for his life story to be written—although he might consider doing so at some future date. When Geoffrey Gilbey's first instalment appeared it had a sub-title stating that it was 'from details collected from close friends'.

During the next few weeks, Gordon received an offer to ride in India throughout the winter from the Maharajah of Rajpipla and the offer of a mount in the Centenary Melbourne Cup in Australia; and a Liverpool labourer was sent to prison for a month after admitting that he drew one pound nine shillings dole, gave one shilling and threepence to his wife and put the rest on a mount of Gordon's which lost! And music-hall comedians were saying, 'Gordon Richards is now so famous that his initials are on all the letter boxes!'

By 19 October with twenty-nine racing days remaining, Gordon had ridden 234 winners, and had announced that whatever happened he would go to St Moritz in the New Year and not ride either in India or Australia. He also pointed out that to break Archer's record would not be as easy as it seemed, for in the final month of the season huge fields were the order of the day and winners far harder to find outside one's own stables. On a light note, one of his contemporary jockeys announced that Gordon wanted to beat the record of snooker player Walter Lindrum more than the record of Archer.

Nevertheless, the racing public were convinced that Gordon's moment of triumph could not be long delayed and were delighted to learn that their hero was the star of a film being made by Ace Films Limited, which would be shown at the Plaza Cinema on 24 November and also released to the Paramount Astorias. He was far too busy to go to the film studios, and in consequence the camera crews, with their equipment, followed him from racecourse to racecourse and also went to his Marlborough home to continue filming.

Day after day the national press became chock-a-block with news of Gordon's imminent achievement, and the newspapers announced such banner headlines 'THAT ELUSIVE RECORD', 'RICHARDS ONLY TWO OFF RECORD' and 'GORDON HAS ONLY ONE TO GO'. Every racecourse executive in the land wanted the privilege of having Gordon beat Archer's record on their course, and on 2 November the Mayor of Worcester, the Chief Constable and the Town Clerk formally told Gordon how proud they were that he had ridden at Worcester races that afternoon and how much they regretted that he had only ridden one winner – Saint Reynard, trained by Martin Hartigan – in addition to three seconds. If they had all won, he would have provided the racecourse with its most historic day.

Norah Hartigan was asked for her opinion of Gordon and said:

Gordon was shy as a boy, and will always remain so. He was devoted to horses from the first, even when he had to stand on a stool to groom them. He has a 'way' with horses. Another of his gifts is that of making friends. He got on well with everybody. I wish that my old cook was still alive to see him beat the record. She mothered him. He would go into the kitchen and torment her with his jokes, but he always came out with a piece of cake or had a cup of cocoa. Sometimes when I invited him into the house he would refuse, and go to the kitchen instead. I remember that once an old woman who was over seventy and weighed more than seventeen stone, went off to a fair with this tiny boy. Gordon was taking his friend for an outing. How proud she would have been of him now . . .

When he rode at Thirsk on Friday 3 November the town was packed to capacity with crowds expectantly awaiting his two hundred and forty-sixth winner. Excursion trains and omnibuses from all over the north of England converged on the town, but to everyone's disappointment Gordon did not ride a winner. On Saturday he rode at Hurst Park. He was expected to win the first race on the favourite, Stratfold, owned by Mr G. F. X. Hartigan, a younger brother of Martin Hartigan. It would have been a totally appropriate victory for Gordon to have equalled the record for an owner with such close connections with Ogbourne, but sadly Stratfold finished unplaced. However, later in the afternoon, he rode El Señor for Mr E. Thornton-Smith, to win the Mitre Selling Plate, thus equalling Archer's record. The cheering as he passed the post was tumultuous and police had to restrain the excited crowds who threatened to mob him.

After he weighed in, he was presented with a huge bouquet of red and white carnations by a well-wisher, who had unwisely attempted to give them to Gordon as he unsaddled El Señor. Gordon had brushed the well-wisher aside and moments later an official came out and explained that Gordon could not accept them until he had weighed in. Mr Thornton-Smith promised Gordon that if and when he surpassed Archer's record he would give him the spurs and whip that Archer had used when he achieved his two hundred and forty-sixth winner. It was a remarkable coincidence that Archer had his final mount on a racecourse on exactly the same date, 4 November, when he rode Tommy Tittlemouse at Lewes forty-seven years previously.

Gordon failed to ride another winner during the afternoon, and thus had the frustration of having to wait for four days until the Liverpool Autumn meeting began the following Wednesday before he had another opportunity to gain Racing immortality. After going to the White City on Saturday evening to present the Gordon Richards trophy he spent Sunday at his Marlborough home, relaxing with his family. He went for a ride on the Downs, then joined his children and their nanny, who had been out for their morning constitutional, taking with them the latest addition to the household, a bull-mastiff puppy. In the afternoon he slept, before driving one of his three cars to visit friends at Beckhampton.

His sister Vera, working as a nurse at the Pendlebury Children's Hospital in Manchester, was one member of the family with whom the Press made contact, hoping that she could tell them intimate details of her famous brother. But Vera was on the night staff of the hospital and made it clear that during the hours of daylight the following week she would be catching up on sleep—whatever the chance of her famous brother defeating Archer's record.

No course had ever seen so many cameramen and reporters as swarmed on to Liverpool racecourse on Wednesday 8 November for, instinctively, they knew that history would be made—curiously on the anniversary of the day that Archer committed suicide. There were eight runners for the first race on the programme, the Wavertree Selling Plate, which was named to commemorate the Liverpool brewer, who leased Minoru to King Edward VII and gave his stud at Tully to the nation.

Gordon was riding the 11–4 on favourite Golden King, owned and trained by Frank Hartigan at Weyhill, and as he rode down to the start in Hartigan's 'white, light blue sleeves, black cap' the crowds were strangely silent. The other seven jockeys were Tommy Weston, Harry and Sam Wragg, Eph Smith, Jo Canty, Dick Perryman and Bobby Jones. They were as conscious as Gordon that history seemed likely to be made within moments, for Golden King had already won a very hotly contested seller at the Doncaster St Leger meeting and appeared of a slightly better class than his opponents. The autumnal mist hid the five furlong start down at the far end of the Melling Road from those in the grandstand who, not knowing the exact moment of the start, were still hushed as the bell announced the off. For almost thirty seconds the silence of the huge 15,000 strong crowd was uncanny as they searched to identify the horses approaching the halfway stage of the race. One horse was lengths clear, and when it was realised that the leader was Golden King and that none of the others had the remotest chance of catching him, the silence turned to an uninterrupted roar of pleasure. It was a roar caused by pent-up emotion changing to delight and relief that their hero, their champion, their own beloved Gordon Richards was achieving a record which would never be equalled. As 'Come on, Gordon!' reverberated across the course, the cheering showed the immense popularity of the jockey, and was an outward and visible sign of the crowd's affection for him. Gordon never relaxed for a moment, never looked round for the non-existent danger, and only as he passed the post did he glance back over his shoulder. The Judge would have been the only man on the course to spare a thought for the second and third horse.

In the steadily increasing drizzle, under a grey sky which seemed to be weeping a requiem for Fred Archer, Gordon returned in triumph, escorted by two mounted policemen, as the crowds, including bookmakers, women, old and young, scampered, pushed and shoved their way to the unsaddling enclosure. His face was taut and pale, and he hardly smiled at the cheering crowds. Anti-climax, relief and the realisation that an ambition had been fulfilled affect men in different ways, and it was not in Gordon's nature to be over-exuberant. Dismounting, he gave Golden King perhaps a slightly more deliberate and affectionate pat than was his custom after riding a winner, and disappeared into the weighing room. He weighed in formally and quickly, before being surrounded by officials, jockeys, valets and Stewards. There was little time for celebration for he had to weigh out in the cerise colours of Mr Martin Benson for the second race. Unplaced and still emotionally drained of energy he returned to the weighing room, having failed on Mandritsare, to be met by a young telegraph boy, who handed him the first of the hundreds of telegrams he was to receive. The message stated 'I am commanded to express to you His Majesty's hearty congratulations on winning 247 races, and by this splendid achievement establishing a record in the annals of Racing in this country.' The message was signed by Sir Clive Wigram. There was no prouder man in the world than Gordon as he read the telegram. He sent a telegram to his wife modestly stating, 'Record broken. I have received a wire from the King,' and then asked a friend if it mattered that he had shown the King's telegram to those in the weighing room. He was quickly reassured on this point of etiquette.

The remainder of the afternoon sped by in a jubilant haze. Lord Derby, Lord Lonsdale and Lord Sefton were three of the first to shake Gordon by the hand as owners and trainers queued up to congratulate him. To many of them he admitted that Golden King's victory had taken a great weight off his mind. He added that until he had ridden four winners at Worcester the previous week he had thought he might suffer a spell of bad luck, as so often happened to jockeys. But his luck seemed to be in, and as he rode Golden King to the start he felt very confident. Only later was it realised that the result of the second race of the afternoon had another bearing upon Fred Archer: the winner was owned by Mr F. Pratt, to whom Freddie Fox had been apprenticed, and trained by C. Pratt, the brothers being the nephews of Archer, whose Newmarket grave had not received a wreath or token for more than fifteen years.

Before the afternoon ended, Thomond beat Gregalach easily in the Becher Chase and Gordon ended a memorable day by winning the final contest, the Liverpool St Leger, to take his total to 248. Amongst the praise heaped upon him by his fellow jockeys Steve Donoghue spoke for all of them when he said:

> He has good friends to support and encourage him, and it is to his credit that he has always heeded their counsel. I remember the fine determination that Gordon showed during the critical period of his early career when he was very ill. It was by sheer grit and determination that he pulled through and recovered his health. It is my sincerest hope that he will round off his successes with an early Derby winner.

Freddie Fox added further praise when he explained that he thought that Gordon's performance was a wonderful one and emphasised the admiration that his contemporaries had for him as a man and a jockey. He further explained his extra pride that he and Gordon were fellow Salopians who had been born within fifteen miles of each other. Perhaps, however, the most notable tribute was from Joe Childs who said: 'In my long experience I have never ridden against a straighter jockey than Gordon. Trick or foul riding does not enter his head.'

Another jockey had told a reporter at Worcester the previous week:

> You must not tell this yet, but we who see Gordon every day in the weighing room away from the crowds and when all is quiet, are very frightened. We are very fond of him. No other man would we prefer to do so well at our expense, but the strain is getting him down, and if the record remains intact much longer I think that the strain will be too much for Gordon and we doubt if he will break it.

In the evening Gordon broadcast from the Adelphi Hotel in Liverpool, where he was staying. From 7.30 p.m. until 9.15 p.m. he remained in his room, rehearsing his speech before going to the Manager's office, from where the broadcast was to be made. Nervous in front of the microphone, he told listeners that comparisons had been made between Fred Archer and himself, but generously added that in his opinion Archer would have held his own with the best at any time in Turf history. There was a special Gala ball in his honour arranged in the hotel, but Gordon preferred to stay in his room with Steve Donoghue and a few close friends.

The remaining weeks of the year were taken up with celebrations to mark Gordon's achievement. Endless comparisons were made with Fred Archer, with a constantly recurring theme the probability that Gordon would make even

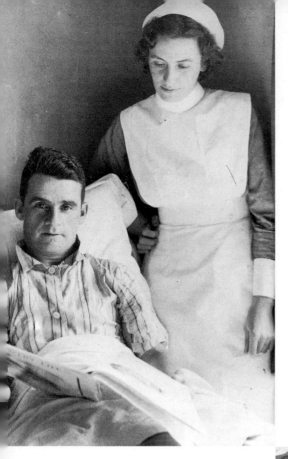

Recovering at Savernake Hospital from injuries received when Tommaok fell in the Newbury Autumn Cup, 1935.

Gordon taking it easy with his son Peter after winning the Jockeys' Championship for the eleventh time.

Gordon with Fred Darling at Epsom on the morning of Derby Day 1937.

greater Turf history in the future. Whilst Gordon stood hardly five foot Archer was five foot ten inches in height, slim, with remarkably small hands and feet, and possessed, according to Hon. George Lambton, 'the shadow of melancholy in his face which indicated a side to his nature never far absent even in his brightest days . . . The one object of his life was the winning of races and from the beginning of the racing season to the end, health, leisure and pleasure were sacrificed . . .' Archer ate practically nothing all day and if he had a good dinner his weight would rise by three or four pounds. Ultimately such privations and the Turkish baths undermined his constitution. Gordon luckily never needed to bother about such enervating and depressing aids to wasting, and his stocky body, which seemed to roll as he walked, was diametrically opposite to that of the slim Archer. Yet Archer was only seventeen when he rode his first Classic winner and went on to ride five Derby winners, four Oaks heroines and six St Leger victors. By the end of 1933 Gordon had ridden only two Classic winners, both for Lord Glanely.

One of the happiest of the celebrations after he had broken the record occurred at Oakengates when Gordon was presented with an address contained in a casket. The presentation took place in the Market Square which was totally inadequate in size to accommodate the thousands who wished to pay tribute to Shropshire's hero. Whilst the Oakengates Town Band played 'Auld Lang Syne' Gordon stepped on to a specially constructed platform to be greeted by the MP for Wrekin Division, the Chairman of the Urban Council, other officials and his old friends Steve Donoghue, Freddie Fox and Jimmy Wilde, the ex-flyweight boxing champion. Nathan Richards was also on the platform to greet proudly his famous son, who was described as Shropshire's greatest hero since Captain Webb, the first man to swim the English Channel. In reply to the speeches before the presentation of the casket, Gordon told the crowds, 'It is the greatest moment of my life to come back here to my old town after fourteen years, and I can tell you that throughout those fourteen years Shropshire has never been out of my mind. I have followed your local football team and other sport with interest, and wherever I am, Shropshire always comes first . . .'

In the evening Gordon attended a banquet given in his honour at the Forest Glen Pavilion at the foot of the Wrekin. Amongst the 250 guests were Gordon's father, his brothers Clifford and Eric, Martin Hartigan, Jimmy Wilde, Steve Donoghue, Freddie Fox and Archie Burns. During the evening Gordon was presented with a silver model of Golden King, and was called upon to tell some of his Racing reminiscences. Mentioning his early days at Foxhill he referred to the fact that he had received £6 as the lad who 'did' My Motto on the two occasions that the horse had won. When he added, 'Like a true Shropshire lad I walked five miles to put that £6 into War Loan. Today it is worth nearly £11,' his comment was greeted with laughter mixed with derisory annoyance at the miserable financial state of War Loan. Typically, Gordon wished to give something in return for the hospitality that he had received, and before he left gave each member present at the banquet a signed photograph. Subsequently, he ordered a large number of pale blue silk scarves with details of his record, and a portrait of Archer, giving them to his family and friends as souvenirs.

Throughout the remaining weeks of the season which Gordon ended on a high note by riding his two hundred and fifty-ninth winner in the final race of the final day at Manchester, the celebrations continued in Gordon's honour. Whenever possible he attempted to see that charity benefited from his achievements. He gave a Liverpool racecard with his autograph alongside Golden King's name to be auctioned for the YWCA Girls' Club, and in conjunction with the *Daily Sketch* selected his ten best rides of the season. This choice was sealed in an envelope and deposited with Lloyds Bank, with £500 being awarded to the first reader who guessed correctly the horses that Gordon had chosen. The entire proceeds of the competition went to hospitals. Gordon also suggested, when asked to name a suitable memorial to commemorate his achievement, that donations should be sent to the Savernake Cottage Hospital at Marlborough. Inevitably, advertisers attempted to cash in upon his feat and Gordon's Gin produced an advertisement with the banner headline 'Gordon's hold the Record'.

When Gordon made a visit to the White City Greyhound Stadium with Steve Donoghue to present prizes he was given a fitted dressing case, ornamented with ivory and silver, and his fellow jockeys commissioned the artist John Berrie to paint his portrait. Afterwards Berrie complained that he had been compelled to chase the jockey halfway around England before the sittings were completed and stated that of the three sittings already given him by Gordon, one had been in Liverpool, one in Manchester and one in Derby. When the portrait was given to Gordon at the Champion Jockey's Dinner one of the guests was Charlie Wood, who journeyed from Eastbourne for the occasion. Wood, a contemporary of Fred Archer, had ridden ten Classic heroes including three Derby winners, Galtee More, St Blaise and St Gatien, between 1882 and 1898.

The Champion Jockey's Dinner had originally been established by Steve Donoghue in the 1920s, and in 1933 a hundred guests had been invited to the dinner, but more than two hundred arrived at the Piccadilly Hotel. They included Harry Wragg and Michael Beary who, despite Harry's damaged hand and Michael's black eye, immediately made up for the fisticuffs fight that they had fought at Manchester the previous Saturday. For the most part the evening was both happy and hilarious, with Gordon intently watching the Shetland ponies who performed circus tricks in the ring created in the centre of the enormous dining room. Later, two pantomime comics appeared dressed as the front and rear of a horse. Gordon was persuaded to mount them and was promptly bucked off, to the glee of Donoghue, Wragg, Beary, Dines and Fox, who acted as master of ceremonies for the evening. Gordon's speech was brief, and ended with a serious request for a minute's silence in memory of South African jockey, Cyril Buckham, recently killed in a car crash. The Racing Press gave Gordon a clock, and his valet, George Smyth, presented him with a gold mounted whip with the wish that he would use it regularly—particularly when he rode his first Derby winner.

Days later he received a silver cigarette case from King George V and a pair of pigeons from the Sandringham lofts.

Gordon was also entertained to dinner at the Eccentric Club, where he was presented with a pair of spurs which had once belonged to Fred Archer. After the dinner he was also given a large bottle of liqueur brandy. Both the spurs and the brandy were wrapped up in identical brown paper when Gordon and cartoonist Tom Webster left to tour the night-clubs. Long before dawn the paper parcel containing the spurs had been unwrapped on several occasions before the eyes of admirers who wished to inspect the historic gift—but eventually the inevitable occurred, and the parcel containing the spurs was mislaid. On the next occasion when a parcel was unwrapped the 'historic gift' turned out to be the bottle of brandy! Luckily the mislaid parcel containing the spurs was discovered intact the next morning by a penitent Webster, who felt that he was responsible for the loss!

Other gifts included a large silver salver bearing the engraved signatures of Fred Darling and the patrons of Beckhampton, and from Martin Hartigan a silver frame containing three photographs of Gordon: as an apprentice at Foxhill; of his first winner Gay Lord; and of his dismounting from Golden King in the winner's enclosure at Aintree; and also the tail of Tommy Tittlemouse, the horse upon which Archer had his final ride. This gift was presented at the House of Commons at a dinner organised by Colonel Baldwin-Webb MP for the Wrekin Division of Shropshire. Prior to the dinner, Gordon was given a conducted tour, which ended with him being installed in the Speaker's Chair—the House having risen a few minutes earlier. Ordering Steve Donoghue and Freddie Fox to sit on either side of him, he remarked, 'I promote you both to be Under Secretaries.' In welcoming Gordon, the Speaker voiced the views of all Members of Parliament when he said, 'It would be a bad thing to eliminate sentiment from English life. It is just that sentiment which springs from the knowledge that men may rise from humble beginnings and humble birth to big places that affords hope for our country—the hope that everybody may have a chance.'

At a civic dinner in Marlborough he was presented with a silver salver and an illuminated address emblazoned with the history of Marlborough and a picture of a thoroughbred with Gordon up, wearing the colours of Martin Hartigan. Gordon, with typical thought and kindness, arranged a party for 600 Marlborough school children which was held at the Town Hall in January. Peter and Jack Richards were two of the guests, and it is not too far-fetched to claim that Gordon enjoyed the evening as much as the children.

Before leaving for St Moritz for his annual holiday Gordon announced that his first retainer for 1934 would be for Fred Darling, his second for Martin Hartigan, his third for Norah Wilmot, who had taken over the Binfield stables after the death of her father, and his fourth for Sam Darling. Fred Darling had sixty horses in training, whilst the other three trainers had a total of more than one hundred, so Gordon had less chance of outside rides than ever before.

In early March, on his return from Switzerland, he had one final 'bust-up' lunch consisting of asparagus, a dozen oysters and champagne, before going into serious training for the season. He had put on a stone during the winter and had to lose most of it within a few weeks. He delayed his weight-reducing campaign for a fortnight due to a painful septic gum, and his physical training expert was compelled patiently to wait for his recovery. He had not ridden a horse since he had dismounted after the final race of 1933, and eagerly awaited the new season even if he did not expect to ride as many winners as the previous year.

6

The mid 1930s

In May 1934 the weather prophets forecast a glorious summer. Imperial Airways proudly announced that their flights to Cape Town now took only nine days and Miss Jean Batten broke the woman's flight to Australia record when she flew from Lympne to Port Darwin in less than fifteen days. At Glyndebourne, the lovely Sussex village nestling at the foot of the Downs, a season of opera was instituted, and in Westminster Abbey a bust was unveiled to Adam Lindsay Gordon in Poets' Corner.

At Chester races Gordon was lucky to escape serious injury when his mount, Roi de Paris, was brought down in the Chester Cup. Three horses were in the pile-up, and one of them had to be shot, but happily Gordon and the other two jockeys, T. Bartlam and T. Barber were not seriously hurt. In the evening Gordon motored to Oakengates to see his father, whilst Steve Donoghue went to Warrington to visit his seventy-four-year-old mother, who had been knocked over at Chester races that afternoon.

A week after his accident at Chester Gordon achieved a victory which gave him tremendous pleasure when he won his first pigeon race, the Newbury and District Homing Society's race from Weymouth and a month later secured second club prize in the San Sebastian race. On another occasion he suffered the misery of seeing one of his favourite pigeons fly into her loft only to die moments later having been shot whilst flying home over Savernake Forest.

He was optimistic about his mount in the Derby, for although Lord Glanely's Colombo was a red-hot favourite, he thought that Lord Woolavington's recent purchase, Easton, who had finished second to Colombo in the Two Thousand Guineas, when he had raced in the colours of Mr R. B. Strassburger, had a reasonable chance. Easton, named after a town in Pennsylvania, had been the subject of several offers, with Sir Hugo Cunliffe-Owen tentatively offering £10,000 and Mr Martin Benson £12,000, before Lord Woolavington's £15,000 was accepted. Once Gordon had elected to ride Easton, Fred Darling offered the mount on the other Beckhampton runner, Medieval Knight, to Steve Donoghue.

The Derby was to prove one of the most dramatic in modern Turf history with Windsor Lad defeating Easton by a length with the ill-fated Colombo a neck away third. The first three were all exceptional colts, and in many years Gordon's mount would have been a comfortable winner. Horses such as April the Fifth and Felstead would not have been able to match strides with him and it was Easton's and Colombo's misfortune to be born in the same year as Windsor Lad.

During the next six weeks Gordon won the Gold Cup at Royal Ascot on HH Aga Khan's Felicitation, who trounced Hyperion; finished third on Easton in the Grand Prix de Paris—Europe's richest race—to Admiral Drake who was a last-moment mount for Steve Donoghue; and read in the newspapers that it was expected that he would have the mount on Colombo in the St Leger, since Rae Johnstone had returned to France after severing his connection with Captain Hogg's stable. Prior to the St Leger, Gordon and Easton took their revenge on Steve Donoghue and Admiral Drake when they won the Grande Internationale at Ostend, but at Doncaster Gordon rode the Beckhampton-trained Lo Zingaro in the St Leger with Colombo a non-runner.

The week after the St Leger an incident showed up another creditable and typical aspect of Gordon's character, and his desire to do the best possible for the owners who gave him mounts. In an unimportant race at Worcester he finished second and immediately lodged an objection to the winner on the grounds of crossing. The jockey on the winner whom he accused of this action was his brother Clifford.

Early in October Gordon flew to Paris to ride Felicitation in the Prix de l'Arc de Triomphe. He had a terribly rough crossing and felt unwell, but even at his brilliant best it is unlikely if he and the Aga Khan's colt could have lowered the colours of the winner, Brantôme. Weeks later he was unplaced on Loosestrife, trained by Norah Wilmot, in the Cesarewitch in which the total age of four of the jockeys exceeded one hundred and ninety-five years. The day of the race was Steve Donoghue's fiftieth birthday, B. Carslake was forty-eight years old, Joe Childs was in his fifty-first year and Freddie Fox had seen forty-eight summers.

At the end of the season Gordon was champion jockey with 212 winners, 80 more than the runner-up Freddie Fox, and once more entertained his fellow jockeys and countless others to dinner at the Piccadilly Hotel. Tommy Weston voiced the opinion of many when he claimed that Gordon would keep the championship for another twenty years and wryly added, 'Nobody can afford to take it from him and take this on.' Despite this reference to poverty, it had been a vintage Racing season with Miss Dorothy Paget paying nine thousand one hundred guineas for a yearling at Doncaster—the highest price since 1929; the Tote breaking all turnover records and the great sire Blandford achieving immortality through the Classic triumphs of his progeny, Windsor Lad, Campanula, Brantôme, Primero, Umidwar and the unbeaten two-year-old Bahram.

The main topic of conversation towards the end of the season was the supposedly huge offer made to Gordon by HH Aga Khan, who wanted to give him a three-year contract. There was little doubt that the offer, reputed to be in the region of £7,000 a year plus 10 per cent of winning prize money was more than his Beckhampton retainer—but once again Gordon highlighted his conviction that loyalty came before money.

Almost as soon as the offer was made, Darling asked Gordon point-blank what he intended to do about it, and when told by Gordon that he hoped that Beckhampton patrons would match the offer, promptly agreed. Thus Gordon deprived himself of riding Bahram to win the 1935 Triple Crown. Another owner who hoped that Gordon might ride for him in 1935 was King George V, and in a letter to his racing manager suggested that Darling be approached on the subject. The King thought that a retainer of £1,000 might be acceptable, and added his conviction that the greatest factor in Gordon's favour was that he was absolutely straight and always tried to win.

Nothing illustrated Gordon's loyalty more than the fact that he gave Martin Hartigan a second claim for the 1935 season when there was every likelihood that he could have received considerably more money from other stables with more fashionably-bred horses and more chance of success than would be achieved by the Ogbourne trainer.

In the summer of 1935, with the Silver Jubilee celebrations of King George V at their height, and Bahram, whom Gordon would have ridden instead of Freddie Fox if he had accepted the Aga Khan's offer, was carrying all before him. Gordon was again the only jockey to ride 100 winners before the end of July. These victories included the Queen Anne Stakes at Royal Ascot on Fair Trial whom Darling had been unable to train as a two-year-old. Since his first victory in 1921 he had ridden 1,725 winners, only 25 less than the total recorded by Steve Donoghue who had begun riding in 1909. Yet his life was nearly forfeited a second time – in an air-crash *en route* for Worcester races. The monoplane, piloted by the thirty-eight-year-old Earl of Amherst, who was known to the Olley Air Services, for whom he worked, as Mr John Amherst, had taken off from Shoreham. Forced to crash-land at Powick two miles outside Worcester, the plane came to rest in a ditch with its nose in a bank, and its propeller, wing, under-carriage and tail badly damaged. Neither Gordon nor the pilot suffered more than a few bruises, and later in the day Gordon showed that he was in fine form by riding two winners.

His annual 'Shoreham fortnight' were two of the happiest weeks of the year for him. The visit coincided with his wife's birthday and also that of his youngest son Peter, and a family party was held to celebrate the two events. Years earlier, his sister Vera had been staying in the Richards' seaside bungalow when Peter Richards was born prematurely and had acted with the greatest competence as mid-wife. Most years she and Nathan Richards and Gordon's two youngest sisters enjoyed his hospitality at the sea, when early morning and evening swims after racing were the order of the day.

After the death of Gordon's mother, his father continued to live at Bonita, the Oakengates villa where he was efficiently cared for by a housekeeper, Miss Jones, who was beloved and respected by the entire family. Nathan, who was seldom seen other than in riding breeches, a hacking jacket and a bowler, took immense interest in Gordon's career. He relished the thought of having so famous a son and was never happier than when discussing Gordon's achievements over a glass of beer with his friends. Gordon never forgot a birthday or a family anniversary, and brought musical boxes and other presents for his sisters and his children when he returned each year from St Moritz.

In August 1935, only a week after Lord Woolavington died, Gordon flew from Shoreham to Redcar and on arrival was greeted with a telegram telling him that Margery had given birth to twins, a boy and a girl, in a Marlborough nursing home. Coincidently, his mount in the first race was named Fairbairn, who won easily. Gordon and many others thought that this was a happy omen for his twins. It was intended that his son should be christened Gordon and his daughter Marjorie, but sadly his new-born son died within hours. Understandably, Gordon and his wife were heart-broken and for the next few days he shunned the race crowds who knew of his bereavement, and did not leave the weighing room of the racecourses at which he was riding, except when walking to the paddock.

By the end of the month it seemed that he might break his own 1933 record for the number of winners he rode in a season, for during August he rode 38 winners to bring his mid-season total to 159. He had trebles on consecutive days of the York Ebor meeting, and was so far ahead of his rivals in the Jockeys' Championship that Johnny Dines sent him a telegram: WHY NOT HAND IN YOUR LICENCE AND RIDE AT NORTHOLT. However, hopes of the possible achievement of a further record were dashed when he was seriously injured at Newbury.

Riding Tommaok, the favourite for the Autumn Cup, he was thrown to the ground three furlongs from home, and was sent sprawling under the hooves of the oncoming horses. To spectators, the accident looked disastrous, but to their relief, Gordon, although concussed, had no bones broken. His wife, making one of her rare visits to the racecourse, Norah Hartigan, whose husband trained Tommaok, and Norah Wilmot were three of those who rushed to the racecourse hospital to discover how serious were Gordon's injuries, and were thankful to be told that although he could not remember what had happened, he appeared reasonably unharmed, although his neck was badly bruised. However, as a precautionary measure, he was taken to the Savernake Hospital for observation and remained there for several days. From his hospital bed, Gordon insisted that no blame could be attached to any other jockey for the accident and added that as he fell the picture that flashed through his mind was of Freddie Fox falling in front of so many flying hooves when he was seriously hurt at Doncaster on the afternoon prior to the St Leger—thus losing the ride on Triple Crown winner Bahram. Fox had made the mistake of not remaining still until the entire field had raced over his prostrate body, and in the split-second it took for Gordon to fall, he determined to stay motionless for as long as possible. Gordon was out of action for a fortnight and did not resume riding until Brighton, where, although he claimed, 'I'm still a bit of an invalid', he thrilled the crowds by riding in all six races and winning four of them. It seemed that there was still an outside chance that he would ride a prodigious number of winners during the remainder of the season, but suddenly luck deserted him, he rode seventeen consecutive losers, and did not ride his two hundredth winner until early November, when he won the Quorndon Plate at Leicester on Galvani who started at 20–1 on.

A gesture which typified Gordon's care for others, was his generosity in allowing the boots that he had worn for three seasons, and in which he had beaten Archer's record when winning on Golden King, to be sent to America. Inside the boots metal canisters had been placed to act as 'collecting boxes' for Liverpool children's hospitals, and a world tour in aid of the hospitals was to begin in New York.

Gordon ended the season with 210 winners before going to the West Country for a three-week holiday, Christmas at Marlborough, and then his annual St Moritz fortnight. Captain Hogg and Willie Griggs joined him as members of the Junior St Moritz curling team on the Grand Hotel rink—but without success. A week later they nearly achieved victory, being beaten by the Pontresina team by one stone in the final of the Black and White Cup.

On his return to England it seemed that Gordon was all set for another successful year, with retainers from Beckhampton, Martin Hartigan, Mrs Corlette Glorney, Norah Wilmot and Sam Darling. Yet the one unanswered question was 'When would Gordon win the Derby?' Since his first ride in the 'Blue Riband of the Turf' in 1924 he had been unplaced on Solitary, Chichester Cross, Sunny Trace, Grand Prince, Grand Salute and Coldstream—none of whom had the remotest chance of success—before joining Beckhampton for the 1932 season. In 1932 he rode Lord Woolavington's Cockpen who started second favourite and was unplaced to April the Fifth; in 1933 he rode Manitoba in the same 'white, black hoop, scarlet cap, gold tassel', who was also second favourite and never showed with a chance behind Hyperion; and the next year he had the mount on Easton who was beaten a length by Windsor Lad, possibly the best Derby winner of the decade; and in 1935 rode HH Aga Khan's second string Hairan.

On the first day of the 1936 season at Lincoln Gordon scored on Mrs Martin Hartigan's Even So. Two days later, he rode in a terrifying Lincolnshire Handicap, in which three horses fell and his great friend Johnny Dines was badly injured. The accident occurred when jockeys drawn on the outside of the thirty-four runners crowded over towards the rails. At first it was thought that thirty-nine-year-old Dines had broken his neck and suffered severe internal injuries, but mercifully his injuries proved to be less serious than at first thought. Bobby Jones broke his collar bone. Gordon, on Hidalgo, was lucky not to be embroiled, for his mount was on the heels of the fallers at the time, but he managed to extricate himself from the mêlée.

A month later he rode HH Aga Khan's Taj Akbar to win the Chester Vase in a common canter, with the favourite Thankerton, ridden by a fully recovered Johnny Dines, in second place. Frank Butters, who trained Taj Akbar, was impressed by the capable performance, but with Mahmoud, Bala Hissar and Noble King in his stable, all of whom were preferred to Taj Akbar in the Derby call-over, he was not unduly optimistic as to the future of his Chester Vase hero. However, when it was announced that Gordon would have the mount on Taj Akbar at Epsom, the public promoted the colt to second favourite and Gordon made no secret of the fact that he believed that at long last he had a great chance of fulfilling his ambition of riding a Derby winner. Four days before the Epsom meeting began, he showed that he was in near-invincible form by riding eight consecutive winners at Bath and Salisbury, and his hopes for Epsom grew stronger.

Yet the Derby again proved a bitter disappointment for him, and the best that he and Taj Akbar could do was to finish second to HH Aga Khan's Mahmoud, ridden by Charlie Smirke. The ground was hard-baked, and the supposed non-stayer, Mahmoud, revelled in the going which discomfited many of his rivals. Taj Akbar may have been a little unlucky in running and suffered interference, but Mahmoud who won in record time was undoubtedly a brilliant colt. Once again Gordon with true sportsmanship stated there was no excuse for his failure, and that on the day the best colt won.

Taj Akbar had failed to give Gordon a 'first', but a 'first' of a different nature was gained when he began to find relaxation in golf. He quickly became better than a mere 'rabbit' and before Christmas had played at Romford for a team of jockeys, who included Bobby Jones, Harry Wragg and Fred Lane, against a team of international women golfers. Gordon beat Miss Audrey Holmes, who was giving him fourteen strokes, by two and one. Once more, he headed the Jockeys' List at the end of the season, but for the first time in four years he failed to notch up a double century of winners.

The winter found him again in St Moritz where he competed unsuccessfully in the Jackson Cup, the curling championship of Switzerland. Whilst he was on holiday his valet, George Thomas Smyth, came before Kingston-on-Thames Magistrates. He told the court that in 1936 he had earned a total of £1,005; £372 from Gordon, £202 from Cliff Richards; £304 from J. Sirett and £127 from T. Barber and R. Dick. By the end of the Flat season he had only £100 to keep him going until the 1937 season began four months later. Gordon was perturbed at this state of affairs, and may have unobtrusively come to Smyth's assistance. He also expended money prior to the new season when he bought four racing pigeons from the famous Bolton breeder, J. C. Cort, paying the highest recorded price, £4 10s. for a 1934 mealy cock.

In 1937 once again fortune refused to smile upon him in the Derby and he was unplaced on Mr H. E. Morriss' Pascal behind Mid-day Sun. The following afternoon he dead-heated for the Coronation Cup on Mr J. V. Rank's His Grace, with Tommy Weston on Sir Abe Bailey's Cecil. As the two winning owners stood outside the weighing room, Lord Rosebery tossed a half-a-crown into the air to decide the ownership of the Cup. Mr Rank correctly called 'heads', was given the Cup and paid Sir Abe Bailey £100, half the value of the Cup. Gordon and Tommy Weston had no need to toss, for both were awarded gold-mounted whips.

In June Gordon, together with twenty leading jockeys, rode donkeys in the twelfth Pinner Derby organised by Father John Caulfield, known as 'The Jockeys' Priest'. The jockeys had rushed from afternoon racing at Alexandra Park to the fête to take part in the derby, sign autographs and help swell the funds. The Donkey Derby, with donkeys brought from Blackpool, Southend and Brighton,

had originated in 1925, when Steve Donoghue had established the race to commemorate his Derby victory on Manna, and had been a leading light in the annual
event ever since.

At the 1937 fête the boots that Steve had worn when winning the Oaks on
Exhibitionnist (the name of the filly was incorrectly spelt when originally
registered with Weatherbys) and those used by Michael Beary when riding
Mid-day Sun to win the Derby, were auctioned by cartoonist Tom Webster, who
described the donkey race as the 'straightest contest ever run on the most crooked
course'! In the final Gordon and his donkey defeated Steve Donoghue, to provide
him with one derby victory—even if it was not the one that he coveted most
of all!

Earlier in the season Rufus Beasley and Michael Beary had a contretemps after
a trial gallop at Newmarket. Captain Boyd-Rochfort knew that in Spray and
Black Lashes he had two exceptionally useful three-year-old fillies. He gave them
a serious trial on the Limekilns, with Beary on Spray and Beasley on Black Lashes
in addition to three other horses in the gallop. Black Lashes finished far ahead of
Spray, so Beasley thought that she should be his One Thousand Guineas mount,
especially as Michael Beary endorsed his opinion by shouting breathlessly as he
pulled up, 'Rufus, your filly galloped in great style', and was all smiles when
Beasley announced that he was very pleased with her. Later that morning Rufus
was told the truth—that Beary had deliberately not tried a yard on Spray, whom he
was convinced was the better filly by far. Rufus therefore changed his mind, and
rode Spray in the One Thousand Guineas to finish second to Exhibitionnist, with
a furious and fuming Michael Beary way down the course on Black Lashes.

The sequel came at Royal Ascot six weeks later when Beary rode his Derby
winner, Mid-day Sun, in the Hardwicke Stakes. Gordon had the mount on
Plaster Cast for Lord Astor and Rufus Beasley rode Flares for Mr William Woodward. Mid-day Sun won by one and a half lengths from Plaster Cast, who beat
Flares by a head. The race was full of incident and an indignant Beasley returned with
a torn boot, feeling livid at the treatment he had received from Beary, whom he
thought had deliberately and dangerously cut him off every time he tried to find
an opening on the rails before the straight was reached. Eventually he had to come
very wide, and in doing so cannoned into William of Valence, putting paid to
any chance that he might have had. Once in the weighing room Beasley objected
to Mid-day Sun and Beary on the grounds of boring and foul riding. At the same
time the Stewards objected to Beasley for bumping and boring. Beasley's objection was overruled, but the Stewards sustained their own, much to the disgust
of Beasley and the unconcealed delight of Beary. Historically, it was the first time
that there had been an objection at Royal Ascot for more than a decade.

During the summer Baldwin resigned as Prime Minister, Lord Glanely bought
a new Phantom III Rolls-Royce, and the Royal Hotel in Deauville offered demi-
pension accommodation to English racegoers for £1 10s. a day. The Spanish
Civil War raged unabated, Sir James Barrie died and a smart man about town

could buy a suit for £6. Also during the summer Gordon was at Lingfield when he was involved in a sad and macabre incident. As the elderly and much respected starter's assistant, Jim Green, was adjusting the girths before the third race, Gordon jokingly called out, 'Hurry up, Jim, you're getting old.' Jim replied, 'I am, and I'm wondering what you will say about me when I am gone.' Gordon shouted back, 'We'll all say you weren't such a bad old fellow really.' Half-an-hour later sixty-three-year-old Jim Green collapsed and died whilst the horses were at the post for the fourth race.

In September Gordon won his third Classic when he rode Lord Glanely's Chumleigh to win the St Leger. It was a chance mount for him, as no jockey had been engaged to ride the colt until the eve of the race. Gordon was expected to ride Lord Astor's Cash Book, but his eleventh-hour withdrawal left him free to accept the offer of Captain Hogg to ride Chumleigh. Gordon found immense sentimental satisfaction in his St Leger victory, for Chumleigh was sired by Singapore, on whom he had won the 1930 St Leger, and Chumleigh's dam was Rose of England on whom he had triumphed in the 1930 Oaks. There were fifteen runners for the 1937 St Leger and it was remarkable that nine of them were sired by horses who had themselves won the Doncaster Classic.

Gordon headed the Champion Jockey's List for the eleventh time in thirteen years, and was honoured again at the annual end-of-season Jockey's Dinner. Yet it was Steve Donoghue who was the centre of attraction, for at long last he had decided to retire from the saddle. At the dinner there was hardly a dry eye as part of Steve's farewell speech was broadcast to the stable of Brown Jack, who instantly recognised the voice of the great jockey whom he had carried with such glorious distinction to six consecutive Queen Alexandra Stakes' victories. 'Hello, old boy,' said Steve, 'I can see you now, you beauty. I hope that your ears are burning, because I am thinking of you all the time. We are jolly old pals.' It was known that Steve intended to commence training, and in consequence no one was surprised when he told the huge audience who had come to pay homage to him, 'The proudest moment of my life will be when, in my new calling, I produce at Epsom the horse upon which Gordon Richards will win his first Derby. That great race will remain incomplete until the name of Gordon Richards is notched upon its records.'

Sadly Steve's finances were leaving him in a parlous state, and early in the New Year he was sued by a Cambridge car-hire firm for debts incurred by his wife. In an effort to help Steve, Gordon was one of those who organised a dinner at the Dorchester Hotel, ostensibly to raise money to enable Steve to buy saddles, rugs, whips and bridles for his Blewbury stables. At the dinner Gordon summed up the sentiments of the 400 guests when he said, 'No jockey and few men in our time have enjoyed the popularity of Steve, but believe me, however popular he may have been with the public, he was still more popular amongst us in the weighing room.'

7

Derby disappointments

After Pasch, owned by Mr H. E. Morriss and ridden by Gordon, had won the 1938 Two Thousand Guineas, to give him his first Classic success at Newmarket, it seemed that at long last the cry, 'Come on, Gordon', would reverberate across the Epsom Downs as he stormed home to win the Derby, for Pasch appeared immeasurably the best three-year-old in Britain. Gordon made it clear that Pasch had shown no sign of tiring inside the final furlong in the Two Thousand Guineas and that he thought that there was no reason why the colt, by Blandford out of a Manna mare, should not stay the Derby distance. He added that he was confident that Pasch would win the 'Blue Riband of the Turf'. However, fate decided to intervene in the shape of a French-bred colt, Bois Roussel.

Peter Beatty, son of the famous Admiral, was in Paris in mid-April with Fred Darling, looking for a three-year-old who would win races for him in England. Having seen Bois Roussel win the Prix Juigne—a modest race at Longchamp for colts who had not previously run—Beatty determined to purchase the colt from his owner breeder M. Volterra. With Prince Aly Khan acting as an intermediary he offered £4,000, but was eventually compelled to pay twice that sum, far more than he had planned. Bois Roussel arrived at Beckhampton a week later and immediately received approbation from Morgan Scannell, one of Darling's leading stable lads. Scannell was one of the finest judges of a horse in the country, and from the moment he first set eyes upon Bois Roussel he instinctively knew that the colt had the indefinable quality—class. One morning he was delegated to take Mr Peter Beatty on to the Beckhampton gallops to watch Bois Roussel in a trial gallop. He told the delighted owner that in his opinion Bois Roussel had a positive chance of finishing in front of Pasch at Epsom. He had ridden both colts, and Bois Roussel gave him a better 'feel' even though Pasch did nothing wrong. For Gordon there could be no question as to which colt he rode in the Derby. He had ridden Pasch to win the Two Thousand Guineas and Mr H. E. Morriss was a long-standing patron of Fred Darling. To desert Pasch would be unthinkable under any circumstances.

A fortnight before the Derby trouble was brewing in an unexpected quarter, and although Beckhampton was not affected, the training programme of several Derby hopes at Lambourn were seriously interrupted by a strike of 300 stable lads. Freddie Fox came out of retirement to help Fred Templeman; many of the horses were taken to the Downs in police-guarded horseboxes, and girls from

Lady Wright's riding school at Savernake were subject to a torrent of abuse when they arrived at various Lambourn stables to help trainers by riding work. The strikers were demanding an extra five shillings a week which some trainers thought exorbitant.

Derby Day was memorable in that the BBC televised the race for the first time in broadcasting history, and it was stated by a BBC controller: 'Television will provide a new medium for the entertainment and education of the masses — cheaper and more convenient than any yet imagined.' King George V had a runner in the Derby for the first time in thirteen years, and huge crowds flocked to the Downs fully expecting to see the hot favourite Pasch redress Gordon's years of misfortune.

Gordon had broken a toe when he was thrown on the way to the start at Birmingham the previous week, but the X-ray showed that the injury would not preclude him riding at Epsom. Sensibly, he cancelled all engagements until Epsom and spent several days in a London nursing home, with a notice on the door of his room bearing the name 'Mr Gordon Smith'. A special boot was made for his injured left foot, but he proved that he was in good shape by walking in Regent's Park, which was near the nursing home.

Once again the hopes of the crowd were unfulfilled, with Pasch being beaten into third place by Bois Roussel and Scottish Union. Pasch was never out of the first four, but once the final two furlongs were reached he could not sustain his effort, and could not catch the leader Scottish Union, on whom Carslake had ridden an impeccable race. From the grandstand it appeared certain that Scottish Union would provide Mr James V. Rank with a Derby triumph, until Bois Roussel came bursting through to win in a common canter. It was an incredible performance, for Peter Beatty's colt was nearer last than first at the foot of Tattenham Corner. Carslake was heart-broken, for he had never won the Derby, and the result was equally frustrating for Gordon, who philosophically commented, 'It is all in the luck of the game.' Other than Morgan Scannell the one man not totally surprised by the result was Fred Darling, who had been greatly pleased by the improvement made by Bois Roussel in recent weeks. Prior to the race, he disclosed his pleasure to no one, but astutely invested an equal amount, reputedly £1,000, upon Bois Roussel as he wagered upon Pasch.

A month after the disappointment of Pasch's Derby defeat Gordon rode Bois Roussel in the Grand Prix de Paris in which he finished third to the brilliant Italian colt Nearco. Gordon flew from Northolt with a party which included Quintin Gilbey on the eve of the race, and dined at Maxim's, after booking in at the Chatham Hotel. Paris was jam-packed for the Grand Prix and Maxim's fully booked, but the renown of Gordon caused the maître d'hôtel to give him a table for twelve at the very last moment.

Pasch redeemed his reputation by a decisive victory in the Eclipse Stakes at Sandown, but proved that he did not stay beyond ten furlongs when a distant third to Scottish Union in the St Leger, before being beaten by the filly Rockfel in the Champion Stakes. Gordon had few significant winners in the autumn, yet there was no doubt as to his 'star attraction', and he was inundated with offers for his services during the winter. Before November he had declined an invitation from the Victoria Amateur Turf Club to ride in Australia during Christmas week, refused an offer from America and had announced that in 1939 he would no longer have a third retainer from Martin Hartigan. Rumours that he was contemplating retiring were quickly scotched and he made it clear that he intended to continue as Champion Jockey for many more years.

The one change in his life was the purchase of a new Marlborough home, Clements Meadow, to the north of the town. The sizeable creeper-covered house, which cost £5,000, was set amidst grounds amounting to nearly seven acres, and included a gardener's cottage. At the suggestion of Tom Reece a billiard room was built above the garage. When it was completed, Tom Reece, Bobby Jones and other celebrities came to the 'opening night' to which the Mayor of Marlborough was also invited. Bobby Jones, a very experienced amateur billiard player, was requested to play the first frame against Reece who was set to give him two blacks. After a few moments it was evident that Jones was in great form and had an unassailable lead. Reece hated losing, and to the consternation of Gordon, threw down his cue and marched from the billiard room in furious indignation. Clements Meadow had been built by a former master at Marlborough College and over the dressing-room fireplace he had carved a French motto, which translated as 'Who loves you well, aids you doubly'.

Gordon adored his few precious moments each day with his children on whom he loved playing practical jokes, often telling them that it was raining as he poured the contents of a watering can from an upstairs window. One of his many presents to his son Peter was an expensive scale model of a racing stable, complete with its racehorses and jockeys in the colours of renowned owners. Playing with the racing stable gave the family hours of enjoyment until Peter sold it for five shillings to a school friend in order to raise money to go to the local fair in Marlborough.

Gordon bought a caravan, and on Sundays, he, Margery and the children would drive to the most isolated parts of the Downs where they would enjoy their lunch in peace and solitude unmolested by crowds of well-wishers. Another treat for the children was to accompany Gordon to Salisbury racecourse where he would release his racing pigeons, who would make their way back to their lofts at Clements Meadow. Gordon took the training of his racing pigeons very seriously, and was assisted by a great friend, Mr Ellis, in looking after the hundreds of pigeons that he owned and bred. In addition to Mr Ellis, the staff at Clements Meadow consisted of Mrs Robins, the cook, a maid, a daily, a gardener and the ever-faithful chauffeur, Stan Russ, who was immensely strict with Jack, Peter and Marjorie where the Rolls-Royce was concerned. Proud of the invariably clean state of the car, he reprimanded the children severely if they thoughtlessly put finger marks over the highly-polished bonnet. One of the happiest of times for the children was going to the Ramsbury airstrip in the summer evenings with Russ to await Gordon's return from racemeetings. They adored their father and the pride that they felt in his triumphs was evident at all times.

Gordon loved entertaining at the weekends, with Flanagan and Allen frequent visitors. On one occasion they completely fooled a friend of Gordon's, a Marlborough tailor, by pretending that they had recently arrived from the West Coast of America, were distant relations, and as by sheer chance they too were tailors, were prepared to make him a suit of clothes! They criticised the suit he was wearing and steadily tore it to shreds—but their promise to provide a new suit as a replacement was kept.

Another friend was the bulky xylophone player, Teddy Browne, who reduced the children to convulsive laughter when he unintentionally crushed a huge potato under his heel one Sunday lunch. Gordon was lucky in that he did not have to waste or diet, and although he never ate fried foods, he often ate suet puddings which were one of his favourite dishes. Knowledgeable concerning vintage port, he kept a fine cellar and never failed on the score of being an excellent host.

Almost a decade before moving to Clements Meadow Gordon had met Walter Lawrence, who was to become one of his closest friends, his confidante and his personal secretary. Walter's father kept the Roebuck Inn at Marlborough and his sister used to visit Gordon when he was in a local nursing home recovering from his operation for appendicitis in 1925. One evening it was suggested that Walter accompanied his sister to see the patient, now fully on the road to recovery. Walter, who was employed at Marlborough College as the racquets coach, was ten years older than Gordon, but the two men found, as the years went by, that they had much in common.

Gordon seldom carried cash with him, and if he dined in a London restaurant he would sign an IOU, and Walter would promptly send a cheque for the necessary amount. Another of Walter's chores was to answer the enormous weekly fan-mail. If the request was for information about the horses that Gordon was to ride, then the letter was thrown into the nearest wastepaper basket unanswered.

Inevitably Gordon was asked for 'tips' in the course of conversation, but he had the effortless knack of being able to ward off the direct question with a laugh and a smile, a shrug of the shoulders and immediately changed the topic of conversation so that the questioner neither received the wished-for tip nor felt that he had been rebuffed. In some respects Gordon was shy by nature, but this knack stood him in good stead throughout his riding career.

He was supremely happy at Clements Meadow, which was organised with efficiency and precision by Margery. Like so many other wives who stand stalwartly behind their famous husbands, she had a flair for unobtrusive administration, and Gordon probably never appreciated to the full the 'behind the scenes' thought which was needed to ensure that everything 'went like clockwork'.

During the Flat season he spent lengthy periods away from home, particularly if he was riding at Newmarket, York, Doncaster, Liverpool and Ayr, and Margery

Big Game, the Two Thousand Guineas'
hero, 1942.

Pasch, the winner of the 1938 Two
Thousand Guineas.

Sun Chariot, after winning the 1942 Oaks at Newmarket.

seldom went with him on these occasions. When riding locally he loved nothing better than to wander around the Clements Meadow garden before supper and then retire to his bedroom with a book — often a Western written by Max Brand. Walter Lawrence would frequently find that the hour after supper was the only time to discuss business affairs with him and would go upstairs to the bedroom for a session which would only end when Gordon was too tired to consider business matters any further.

One of the outstanding factors in Gordon's life at this time was the almost uncanny appreciation by those who worked for him as to his requirements. It was as though an affinity, based on respect and admiration, resulted in his employees understanding his every need. For example his chauffeur, Russ, knew exactly where to stop the car *en route* for Salisbury races so that Gordon could have a brief nap to recover from the morning's exertions, and equally exactly how long should elapse before he continued the journey. To maintain the staff at Clements Meadow required a considerable annual outlay, but by the standards of the era Gordon earned a very large income. He invariably claimed that the figure of £20,000 a year constantly mentioned in the Press was far too high, but it was certainly over £10,000, at a time when £1,000 was thought to be a very adequate sum. In 1938 a Rolls-Royce Phantom III cost £2,675, a bottle of whisky 13/– and in the Marlborough area a newly-built three bedroom bungalow could be bought for £700 and good farming land rented for 15/– per acre.

Gordon was never extravagant in his personal expenditure, and his staff were employed of necessity, for, given the demands of his working life, he required a chauffeur, a secretary and a masseur. Yet as he so often admitted he loved his work, and equally he loved the countryside around Marlborough and enjoyed walking in the Savernake Forest where, in the tiny hamlet of Cadley, he and his family would often attend church on Sundays. His knowledge of local ancient history, particularly that concerning Avebury, the Druids of Stonehenge and the Romans, was profound and, as he rode upon the windswept gallops of Beck-hampton, he could see the Stones of Avebury in the far distance. He adored the time spent with his racing pigeons, and claimed that when one saw a pigeon drop out of the clouds on to its own perch exactly on time, after a flight of two or three hundred miles, the excitement was unbeatable.

Gordon ended the 1938 season by winning the Manchester November Handicap on Pappageno II, trained by Martin Hartigan. For the twelfth time and the eighth year in succession he was Champion Jockey, but his pleasure in this achievement took second place to his delight that his wife was making an excellent recovery from her operation for appendicitis, and to his sorrow that his seven-year-old nephew, Anthony, son of Clifford, had died of pneumonia.

Although Gordon's prowess in the saddle was far superior to that of his brothers, they maintained a steady flow of winners and when all three, Gordon, Clifford and Colin, rode in an important race it caused mild ribaldry from their contemporary jockeys. In the 1939 City and Suburban at Epsom Gordon rode

Taran for M. Boussac, Clifford had the mount on Pigskin, on whom he had won the race the previous year, and Colin was aboard Hot Bun II. Harry Wragg won by five lengths on Bistolfi, having made most of the running, with the brothers trailing in his wake! Colin never had the same chances on the Flat as his older brother, due to weight problems, but was Champion Jockey in Norway in 1938, the season in which Clifford won both the City and Suburban and the Royal Hunt Cup at Ascot.

Harry Wragg enjoyed nothing better than defeating his long-standing friend, Gordon, and early in the 1939 season at Leicester laughed all the way to the winning post at his own effrontery which had enabled him to outwit Gordon. The fact which allowed him to do so was that the starter, a retired naval officer, was performing his official duties for the first time, and was 'somewhat of a greenhorn'. With more than twenty inexperienced two-year-olds coming under orders he let it be known that as Gordon was riding the favourite he was determined that the champion and his mount should be perfectly poised for the 'off' when the tapes went up. In reality Gordon's mount was somewhat fractious and wheeling round when the starter unwisely asked, 'Are you ready, Gordon?' Quick as a flash Harry Wragg shouted, 'Yes sir, I'm ready', the tapes went up and Harry had poached a clear lead which he never lost. Only in the weighing room after the race did he admit his impersonation to Gordon and his powers of mimicry to the abashed starter, who determined in future to make himself more familiar with the features of the best known jockeys!

Wragg was a great tactician, and always prepared to be flexible in the manner in which he rode a race. He loved to 'come from behind' — but for a reason not always appreciated. In the era when the Judge had no photo-finish to aid his verdict, Wragg became convinced that, if the finish was desperately close, the Judge tended to give his decision in favour of the horse making up most ground in the final strides.

1939, with the war clouds gathering across Europe, proved a less successful season than usual for Gordon where the important races were concerned. He was unplaced on Mr Edward Esmonds' Fox Cub in the Two Thousand Guineas, and did no better on Lord Astor's Light Velocity in the One Thousand Guineas. By Derby Day, when the nation was mourning the submariners who died when the *Thetis* sank in the Irish Sea, Fox Cub had become a high-class colt. But although he finished second, Gordon was compelled to watch the champion Blue Peter sailing past him to win with effortless ease by four lengths. At Royal Ascot he triumphed twice, winning the New Stakes on Mr Peter Beatty's Tant Mieux, and the Queen Mary Stakes on Snowberry, a daughter of Myrobella.

However, Royal Ascot contained one fiasco. In the Cork and Orrery Stakes he rode Miss Dorothy Paget's Colonel Payne, whom Darling thought to be a 'racing certainty'. 'D.P.' backed her colt as though settling day did not exist, but to her horror the wretched colt ran abysmally, failing to reach the first three. As he unsaddled, Gordon was asked by Miss Paget, 'Where's Darling?' His reply: 'On the top of the grandstand cutting his throat,' caused the dejected owner to roar with laughter. From that moment onwards, Gordon was one of the few men whom she admired. Darling never relished Dorothy Paget as an owner, and resented the fact that when she visited Beckhampton she was accompanied by a secretary, who made notes of everything he said.

One of the highlights of the season was the epic battle between Panorama, trained by Captain Boyd-Rochfort, and Portobello, trained by R. J. Colling. Panorama was owned by Mrs James Corrigan, an exceedingly rich and eccentric American. Shortly after the Armistice she had come to London, rented a house in Grosvenor Square, and she began giving lavish parties, to which she invited the whole of London Society. Presents from Cartier and Asprey were showered upon her guests, and she was equally generous to her jockeys after they had ridden a winner in her 'dark blue, red sash and cap'.

At the Newmarket Craven meeting Rufus Beasley on Panorama beat Gordon on Portobello by a head. Gordon and Rufus had the reputation of being faster from the gate than any of their contemporaries in the saddle, and they thrilled the crowd. It was a marvellous race, for Gordon had Portobello into his stride in a flash, and for the first three furlongs Panorama could not match his blistering speed. It was the first time in his racing career that Panorama had been headed, but when Beasley hit him with his whip he surged forward to force his head in front, literally on the line. Gordon and Portobello took their revenge at the Hurst Park Whitsuntide meeting, when they beat Panorama and Beasley by a short head, with Gold Vista, ridden by Carslake three lengths away third.

Panorama started at 9–4 on at Royal Ascot for the Fern Hill Stakes and was surprisingly beaten by Gold Vista, whilst the following day Portobello started at 7–4 on and whipped round at the start of the Granville Stakes giving his disconsolate and dejected jockey, Beasley, no chance. Possibly remembering his two hard races at Newmarket and Hurst Park, he dug in his toes, refused to line-up and as the tapes went up shied away from them. Whether or not he was 'got at' will be a mystery for ever. The following afternoon Gordon rode the miscreant Portobello, who finished third to Mickey the Greek in the King's Stand Stakes. Once again Jack Colling was dissatisfied, ordered an investigation and was informed by the veterinary surgeon that belladonna had been administered to Portobello's eyes, so that he could not see properly.

The colt redeemed his tarnished reputation by a head victory in the July Cup, and ended the season on a high note by a narrow victory in the Nunthorpe Stakes at York, ridden by Gordon who won the Gimcrack Stakes on Tant Mieux for Prince Aly Khan forty-eight hours later.

Goodwood at the end of July was frustrating, for Gordon rode seventeen fancied horses, and only managed one victory—in the Chesterfield Cup. However, there were important and unpalatable events occurring on the Continent, which no one relished, and at Brighton races the unprecedented step was taken of broadcasting a recorded appeal by Gordon for enrolment for National Service. The broadcast, made at the request of the Brighton Race Committee, had the support of the Jockey Club, who gave their permission for Gordon to make the appeal. His speech lasted nearly three minutes and was listened to in almost complete silence as the race crowds appreciated the seriousness and importance of his words. At the end, the broadcast was greeted with patriotic cheers.

8

War-time Racing

Inevitably the outbreak of the Second World War virtually brought Racing to a standstill. There were rumours that Gordon would ride in Ireland, but like other jockeys he considered that it was his duty to remain in England. He applied for a job with the Royal Air Force and, whilst awaiting the necessary papers, he took on ARP work in a village near Marlborough and helped Margery look after four children from London, who had been evacuated to Clements Meadow. His famous racing pigeons, including two given to him by King George V when he beat Archer's record in 1933, were registered with the National Pigeon Service. Many of these birds, from the most famous pedigree strains in the kingdom, had already competed in races across the English Channel and it was thought that their services might prove very useful during the war.

Whilst Gordon was doing his ARP work, Eph and Doug Smith were working on their brother's Berkshire farm, and Newmarket trainers Geoffrey Barling, George Colling, Hugh Sidebottom and Bernard van Cutsem joined the Royal Artillery. Early in December Gordon was returning from Newmarket, having dined with Bobby Jones, with whom he had arranged to play a snooker match in London the following Sunday in aid of the Red Cross, when his car ran into a lamp-post in the black-out. He was concussed and his doctor advised him to stay in bed for a few days. He was not sufficiently fit to play in the snooker match at Thurston's, and his place was taken by the boxer, Eric Boon.

Due to the War there was no possibility of his annual St Moritz holiday, and he spent the winter months rearing chickens and 'digging for victory'. Harry Wragg also worked hard in his vegetable garden, and it was claimed that he was training his cabbages and Brussels sprouts to come with a late run.

Before the spring, when it was evident that Racing would be permitted to continue on a restricted scale, Gordon had fixed up his retainers. Fred Darling at Beckhampton had the first claim, Lord Astor the second, Lord Portal the third and F. Templeman the fourth. It was also announced that for the 1940 season he had been elected President of the Marlborough Bowling Club. More than one of the club members, although delighted that Gordon had accepted the presidency, was worried that he might forget himself and run along in front of his 'wood' sweeping away at the sacred turf with a broom.

At Lincoln he won his first Lincolnshire Handicap, after attempting to do so without success since 1928, when he rode Quartier Maître, owned by the wife of the Chairman of Ladbrokes, Mrs Arthur Bendir. This success left the Derby, the One Thousand Guineas, the Goodwood Stakes, the Cambridgeshire and the Cesarewitch as the only major races that he had not won.

It was obvious, however, that the curtailment of Racing would prevent him riding a number of winners remotely approaching the totals of previous years, particularly since Fred Darling (who had slipped on ice during January and badly injured his shoulder) had a far smaller string of horses than usual at Beckhampton due to labour problems. He had told his owners that he refused to accept horses unless he could ensure that he had adequate stable lads and staff to do them full justice and was not prepared to skimp under any circumstances.

In the Two Thousand Guineas he rode Tant Mieux into third place behind M. Boussac's Djebel and Stardust, and ten days later won the Derby Trial Plate at Hurst Park on the Maharajah of Kolhapur's tough resolute colt, who had headed the two-year-old Free Handicap the previous autumn and had originally run in the colours of Peter Beatty. There was no doubt, however, that Gordon had a problem when deciding his Derby mount, for Fred Darling trained three top-class colts: Tant Mieux, Paques, owned by Mr H. E. Morriss, and his own horse Pont l'Eveque. The decision concerning Paques was determined for Gordon when Darling contacted Mrs Morriss and suggested that her husband's colt should complete his Derby preparation at Newmarket under Hon. George Lambton. Mrs Morriss agreed and Paques departed from Beckhampton. Pont l'Eveque proved a more difficult horse to assess. Darling had always regarded the colt very highly and when, shortly after the outbreak of War, Mr Morriss had decided to reduce the number of his horses in training, and had specified that Pont l'Eveque was one of those to be sold, Darling had promptly bought him. However, as Mr Morriss had bred and originally owned the colt as a yearling, Darling thought it correct, in the spring of 1940, to cable to Shanghai offering Mr Morriss a half share for £2,500, conditional upon Pont l'Eveque, who had wintered so well, winning the Newmarket Stakes. The cable duly arrived, but as Pont l'Eveque was beaten at Newmarket the offer became null and void. Darling believed that Gordon's first loyalties must be towards the Beckhampton patrons and as one of them, the Maharajah of Kolhapur, owned Tant Mieux, who was a certain contender for the war-time Derby, so there was no question of Gordon having a choice between Tant Mieux or Pont l'Eveque. In consequence S. Wragg was engaged for Darling's own Derby candidate.

Thus it came about that it was announced at Windsor races, four days before the Derby, that Gordon would ride Tant Mieux. Possibly, due to the lack of space permitted to Racing in the national Press, the full reasons for this announcement were not clearly stated, and the general public were under the false impression that Gordon had chosen to ride Tant Mieux, who was criticised in some quarters as being too small and too pretty to be a potential Derby winner. In private, Gordon believed that Tant Mieux would not stay more than ten furlongs and regretted that he could not ride Pont l'Eveque.

His belief proved correct and he and Tant Mieux could only finish fourth, beaten some four lengths by Pont l'Eveque, Stardust and Lighthouse II. Disappointed at Tant Mieux's failure, Gordon could only exclaim, 'Just my luck', as he unsaddled. The irony was that Darling had believed that Pont l'Eveque would win the Newmarket Stakes. Had he done so, instead of being thrashed by Lighthouse II, Mr Morriss would undoubtedly have accepted Darling's offer and bought back the offered half share. In which case Gordon and not S. Wragg would have ridden the Derby winner, for Mr Morriss had been a Beckhampton patron for almost twenty years.

The War continued unabated, and Gordon, together with 'Midge' Richardson and his wife and Fred Herbert, had a lucky escape from death when their car was dive-bombed by a German aircraft in the late autumn. Quickly jumping out of the car, they threw themselves into a ditch as bullets thundered into the road. Gordon used to recount this story with exaggerated embellishments.

At the outbreak of the War pony racing at Northolt Park terminated. The previous year William Hill had owned a useful pony in Win Over, who had finished second in the Northolt Derby to Miss Dorothy Paget's Scottish Rifle, a son of 1931 Derby winner Cameronian. Rumours were rife that Dorothy Paget was financing Hill, but such rumours were false. What was not false was the admission of the immense debt that National Hunt Racing between 1930–9 owed to her. She had suddenly changed her allegiance from motor-racing to horse-racing, and devoted her money, her enthusiasm and her energy to supporting Racing during the winter months. Her hero, Golden Miller, captured the imagination of the racing public, and did much to keep alive an interest in Racing once the Flat season ended. That interest, as no one knew to a greater extent than William Hill, spelt *betting*. Hill had opened a small office in Jermyn Street in 1934, and four years later realised that he must find larger and more suitable premises. He found exactly those which he required in Park Lane, at the former residence of Lord Inchcape, and took the plunge to become a national bookmaker. The day that War was declared he assumed that he would be ruined, for his weekly commitments were huge. His assumption proved incorrect, and by 1942 he was acknowledged to be one of the most influential bookmakers in the kingdom. Due to acute gastric trouble he was placed in the lowest grade medically for National Service and was never called up. He was always amazed by the stoicism of the British people in adversity, and frequently stated that when bombs fell on Clapham Junction many people were far more concerned as to whether the train to Salisbury or Windsor races, where Gordon Richards had fancied mounts, would be cancelled or delayed, than in showing a compassionate interest in the casualties inflicted by the bombs.

In the autumn Gordon won a substitute St Leger at Thirsk on HH Aga Khan's Turkhan, and ended the 1940 season as Champion Jockey for the fourteenth time in fifteen years, but due to war-time conditions with the much smaller total of sixty-eight winners. There was a possibility that he would be called up for militay service prior to the commencement of the 1941 Flat season, but as nothing was definite he arranged retainers for the forthcoming season, firstly to ride for Fred Darling's patrons, secondly to ride Lord Astor's horses and thirdly for Lord Glanely, who had become a patron of Joe Lawson at Manton.

Early in January 1941 he registered at Marlborough with his age group, the thirty-six-year-olds, and was given a medical. He had already volunteered for the RAF, but had twice been rejected as unfit, due to the chest trouble that he had suffered in 1926, and now, to his consternation, found that after further medical examinations he was placed in Grade III. In consequence, he was available to ride throughout 1941, together with Michael Beary, P. Maher, Tommy Weston and Tommy Lowrey whenever they were able to gain some leave. The scarcity of senior jockeys gave splendid opportunities to young apprentices too young for military service, and with about one hundred and forty of them, including D. V. Dick, D. Marks and D. Greening, available to replace the ranks of those who had been called up, there was no dearth of riders for the thousand horses who remained in training after owners had drastically reduced their commitments.

Gordon won the first race on the opening day of the new season at Lincoln, but was stopped by the police for exceeding the speed limit on his way to the racecourse and was subsequently fined one pound and had his licence endorsed. A month later he was again fined, two pounds and two shillings costs, and again had his licence endorsed for exceeding the speed limit in Leicestershire. Throughout his life his attitude to motor cars was to get into the driver's seat, put the accelerator to the floorboards and go like Jehu!

Racing was taking place at Stockton, Salisbury and Newmarket, where the substitute Classics were to be run, and Gordon thought that his chance of adding to his total of Classic victories was second to none, for Fred Darling was delighted with both Owen Tudor and Morogoro. In the Two Thousand Guineas Gordon finished fifth on Owen Tudor to Lambert Simnel, with Morogoro, ridden by Harry Wragg, second. However, he was convinced that Owen Tudor would be a far better horse by the time of the New Derby, and fully expected to win. Once again he was defeated by his Derby hoodoo, due to an unanticipated incident at Salisbury on 8 May.

In the Maiden Plate he was riding a filly belonging to Lord Astor, and had been asked by the Duchess of Norfolk to look after a young apprentice, who was having his first ride on an Arundel-trained filly. He agreed to do so, and whilst awaiting the start was giving some helpful advice when the boy's filly lashed out and kicked him. Gordon fell to the ground in agony, and with horror realised that he had probably broken his left leg. Taken to Salisbury Infirmary for an X-ray examination his worst fears were confirmed. Doctors had the unpalatable task of telling him that he was unlikely to ride again for six months, which was tantamount to being *hors de combat* for the entire season. After a few days in hospital in Salisbury, he was moved to the Orthopaedic Hospital at Byfleet, controlled by

Mr Rowley Bristow, which at the time was a military hospital, but in which Gordon was provided with a small room.

Walter Rowley Bristow was respected and loved by all who knew him. Honoured in England and on the Continent for his brilliant work as an orthopaedic surgeon, he was Surgeon to the Army and a Hunterian Professor of the Royal College of Surgeons. Charming both as a host and a guest, he enjoyed an occasional day's racing as much as anyone, although he preferred sports in which he could participate to those in which he was compelled to be a spectator. He had the highest regard for Gordon as a man and as a jockey, and the regard was reciprocated with interest.

Darling saddled four horses for the Derby: Morogoro, Owen Tudor, Thoroughfare and Chateau Larose. Owen Tudor, whom Gordon had implied would have been his choice of mounts, started at 25–1, the longest price of the four, and won by one and a half lengths from Morogoro. As Thoroughfare was Mrs Macdonald-Buchanan's first string it is possible, however, that Darling would have insisted that Gordon took the mount and allowed another jockey to partner Owen Tudor. Gordon listened to the radio commentary from his hospital bed and his sense of frustration when Owen Tudor was shouted home was only equalled two days later when he again listened to the wireless and heard commentator Raymond Glendenning calling home the Beckhampton-trained Commotion, which he would also have ridden, in the New Oakes.

During Gordon's enforced idleness he devoted much of his time to an intensive study of the *Racing Calendar*. His knowledge of the form book was second to none, and he would mark those horses not trained by those for whom he had retainers with 'dots'. One dot for the horse that he thought had the best chance, followed by the next two who were awarded two dots and three dots. However it was to his credit that he never touted for rides.

In July, by which time Harry Wragg had been called up and had been posted to an anti-aircraft battery, Gordon, using crutches, paid his first visit to a racecourse since his accident when he went to Salisbury. His car was drawn up at the entrance to the straight and many of the jockeys stopped for a quick chat on their way to the start. He told well-wishers that he hoped to be able to ride in the St Leger early in September, but had to add that his hope was not a certainty and that until the plaster was removed from his leg the doctors would not commit themselves as to the date of his return to the saddle. He also discussed with some of them the news of the death of Brownie Carslake at Whitsbury. He had been ill for some months and the previous April had collapsed in the weighing room at Alexandra Park. By permission of the Stewards his ashes were scattered over the Rowley Mile at Newmarket, which had always been his favourite course.

At Salisbury Gordon saw King George VI's brilliant filly Sun Chariot win her second race. When Sun Chariot had made her debut some weeks earlier the famous billiard player Tom Reece called to see Gordon on the morning of the race, Gordon told him that he thought Sun Chariot would win. Soon after Reece left, Gordon had two more visitors, Flanagan and Allen, who informed him that they had a certainty that afternoon. To his consternation Gordon saw that the certainty was running in the same race as Sun Chariot. After some difficulty he was able to get a message through to the course telling Tom Reece not to back Sun Chariot. When he received the evening paper and saw the result—Sun Chariot first and the Flanagan and Allen's certainty second—he was covered with confusion, which became worse when he was upbraided by a furious Reece for taking any notice of the information given to him by two 'bum actors'!

Once he felt fit enough to do so, Gordon holidayed in Devonshire and made arrangements to make a tour with Tom Reece, Joe Davis and Steve Donoghue giving billiard exhibitions in aid of the Red Cross. He also became chairman of the entertainments committee of 'Warship Week' in Marlborough.

His absence from the saddle left the way clear for thirty-nine-year-old Harry Wragg to become Champion Jockey. Since his call-up in July Wragg had managed to ride at twenty-one of the thirty-one fixtures, and ended the season by winning on a 20–1 outsider at Manchester early in November. He had no special privileges from his military duties, but received a twenty-four-hour leave at frequent intervals. Sometimes he went direct to a racemeeting, having been at his post all night. Admittedly, he had had the advantage of being based near Newmarket, but even so, did not find it easy to meet all his racing commitments, particularly in the light of the remarks of a pompous Army official that: 'In no circumstances is special leave granted for taking part in professional sports, including Racing. Leave out of turn is only granted to men forming a team or a side for sports approved by the Army Control Board.'

By the spring of 1942 Gordon had fully recovered from his leg injury, and as the new season approached he made clear his ambition to beat another of Fred Archer's records—for he needed only an extra seventy-three winners to surpass Archer's aggregate number of winners. At the first few fixtures he had little success, and whilst Michael Beary celebrated the birth of his son and heir by riding four winners in one afternoon at Newmarket, all of them trained by Hon. George Lambton, Gordon virtually drew a blank.

His frustration was deepened when he rode Sun Chariot at Salisbury in mid-April, for the filly was on her worst behaviour, careered towards the rails on her way to the start, with her tail swishing like a windmill, and although starting at 3–1 on, she refused to exert herself and could only finish third to Ujiji.

However, a fortnight later, Gordon deservedly enjoyed one of the highlights of his career when he won the Two Thousand Guineas on Big Game, and the One Thousand Guineas on Sun Chariot for King George VI. Both the colt and the filly won convincingly by four lengths to the delight of the huge crowd who were equally pleased that their hero, Gordon Richards, rode three winners on the final day of the meeting, to bring his tally to twelve victories in the previous four days racing. It seemed that the Derby and the Oaks were a foregone conclusion, for Big Game and Sun Chariot, and that finally Gordon would ride a Derby winner—albeit a war-time Derby. For the umpteenth time the Fates intervened and although Sun Chariot won the Oaks by a length, having almost dissipated her chances by swerving at the start, the stamina limitations of Big Game were brought to light when he could only finish sixth to Watling Street and Hyperides, despite starting the shortest priced favourite since the end of the First World War.

Oaks Day and Derby Day, both held at Newmarket, were the first war-time visits of the King to a racemeeting, and except for an earlier visit to Beckhampton, he had never seen either Big Game or Sun Chariot. Obviously delighted by Sun Chariot's victory, he was equally disappointed by Big Game's failure.

Gordon had some compensation when he rode Owen Tudor to a comfortable victory in the Gold Cup three weeks later. He won by three lengths from After-thought, who had been second in the Oaks to Sun Chariot, thus giving Lord Rosebery the misfortune of being runner-up in the 1942 Derby, Oaks and Gold Cup. Big Game made amends for his Derby flop by easily turning the tables on Ujiji who had finished third to Watling Street in the New Derby when he won the Champion Stakes, held at Newmarket at the end of August. Fred Darling was immensely pleased by this victory but still remained emphatic that it would be Sun Chariot and not Big Game who would be his St Leger candidate. Gordon made it abundantly clear that he thought that Sun Chariot would defeat the colts, and his conviction was proved correct when she trounced Watling Street, Hyperides and Shahpoor in mid-September.

Harry Wragg, riding Watling Street, was convinced that Gordon's instructions would be to hold up Sun Chariot for as long as possible. As the race progressed Wragg remained amongst the back-markers, but to his chagrin Gordon was still behind him. Eventually he had no option but to make a forward move on Watling Street, but even as he did so he could see no sign of Gordon and Sun Chariot. Suddenly Gordon made his challenge, and his brilliant filly stormed clear of her rivals. After the race Harry Wragg stated that Gordon's performance in the New St Leger was one of the finest 'waiting races' ever ridden by a jockey.

As Gordon dismounted in the winners' enclosure he happily and enthusiastically told reporters that she was the best filly that he had ever ridden, even though he found her more headstrong than any horse that he had ever known. Racing is full of 'ifs'; but if an export certificate had not been delayed shortly after the leased Sun Chariot had arrived at Beckhampton she would have been returned to the National Stud at Tully without ever having seen a racecourse, for in her early trials she gave Darling the impression that she was quite useless. One of Sun Chariot's forbears was Cherry Lass, who won the One Thousand Guineas and the Oaks and was trained at Foxhill, where Gordon had begun his career.

In the summer and early autumn three men died who had greatly influenced Gordon's career. Lord Glanely was killed in a West Country air-raid at the end of June. Days before his death he had called in to see Gordon and Margery at Clements Meadow. Gordon apologised for not having any whisky to offer him.

No comment was made by the guest. However, the following afternoon a case of whisky arrived with Lord Glanely's compliments.

A week before the St Leger Martin Hartigan died at the age of fifty-three, following an operation. At the outbreak of the War he had more than forty horses in training at Ogbourne, but within a year he had dispersed the horses, announced that he had given up training for the duration of hostilities, and had become attached to the RAC Tactical School. For his widow, Norah, the sadness of his death came as a second calamity within a short space of time, for her only son, whose father was Pat Hartigan, had been killed on active service at Sidi Barani in December 1940.

Norah Hartigan erected memorial stone crosses to her son and to her second husband alongside those of Paddy Hartigan, and expressed the wish that in due course she was to be buried next to them on the windswept Downs. On the memorial to her son she had the words inscribed:

> Horses he loved and laughter, and the sun.
> Good sport, the open air, and spaces wide.
> God called him early with his life so short.
> He fought for England's glory, and found his glory there.

The death of Martin Hartigan was hard for Gordon to bear, for the trainer had given him his first chance as a jockey in 1921. Hartigan's kindness, patience and advice were vital ingredients in the success of his early career, and he was the first to admit the inestimable debt that he owed to the Ogbourne trainer.

Three weeks before Martin Hartigan's funeral Gordon had sadly learned of the death of sixty-three-year-old Captain Hogg in a Cambridge nursing home. Soon after the death of his wife in 1937 Hogg had told Lord Glanely that he wished to retire from training at Lagrange Stables, but he was persuaded to stay on for a further twelve months whereupon he was succeeded by Basil Jarvis. At the beginning of the War the urge to train once more became too strong to resist and he started up with a few horses at Heath House. When Martin Hartigan dispersed his Ogbourne establishment Mr Martin Benson sent some of his horses to Hogg. One of them was the brilliant two-year-old filly Lady Sybil.

By the spring of 1943 it was evident that Gordon would soon break Archer's record of 2,749 winners. At the end of the previous season when it seemed possible that he might achieve his ambition in the final day's racing there had been considerable controversy as to whether Archer had ridden 2,746, 2,747, 2,748 or 2,749 winners. *Ruff's Guide*, the recognised authority, stated that the correct number was 2,746, but the *Sporting Life* claimed that it should be 2,749 and this became Gordon's target. Before he reached it Lord Russell of Killowen sent a letter from the House of Lords to the Editor of *The Times*:

Sir — What is all this talk in the Press of Gordon Richards beating Fred

Archer's record of winning mounts? He will, no doubt, ride a larger number of winners, but can he approach Archer's record? Archer rode his first winner in 1870 and died in 1886 aged twenty-nine. Richards rode his first winner in 1921 and is now aged thirty-nine. Archer was a tall, long-legged fellow who had to waste in order to ride at weights which are well within the reach of Richards. Archer, with fewer mounts, rode his number of winners in sixteen years which Richards, with more mounts, will have taken over twenty-one years to equal.

Gordon beat Archer's record at Windsor on 26 April when he won on Scotch Mist. The following day Percy Swaffer, a well-known racing journalist, answered Lord Russell's letter when he wrote to the Editor of *The Times*:

Sir—Lord Russell of Killowen has very rightly observed that Archer rode his big aggregate of winners in considerably less time than Richards has taken and it might be added, with many less mounts. In most other respects the two great jockeys are dissimilar—height, natural weight, shape, style and temperament. Archer stood 5 ft 10 in, and weighed over 10 st in winter-time, although he usually turned up at Lincoln when the Flat opened able to go to scale a few pounds under 9 st. Such fasting had inevitable consequences. Archer's length enabled him to get a good grip of the saddle; Richards rides by balance.

In enthusiasm alone are they alike. It is well known that a leading trainer, when asked by a woman why Archer looked so sad, replied, 'because, madam, he cannot ride two horses in one race'. But whereas Archer sought out the best mounts, Richards will ride a bad horse rather than none.

The peaceful career of the present champion is likely to extend until he approaches fifty or even longer. Archer rode when the Turf was a hotbed of conspiracies, plots, and disputes, and when his brilliant career so tragically ended he was only twenty-nine.

One further letter merits emphasis, for it mentions a unique portrait of Archer:

Sir—Ever since Fred Archer died fifty-six years ago, at the early age of twenty-nine there have been conflicting statements as to the aggregate of his winning mounts.

However, there still exists an informing portrait of Archer wearing Lord Falmouth's racing colours; it is enclosed in an ornamental frame, measuring 14½ by 13½ inches, the contemporary tablet on which records that 'this frame was made to the memory of the late Fred Archer and contains on its face a piece of wood for every winner he rode during his career as a jockey, viz, 2,747'. It adds that the various pieces of coloured woods—of which a list is given—represent the colours corresponding to those of his four principal patrons, Lord Falmouth, the Duke of Portland, Lord Hastings, and the Duke of Westminster . . . The portrait was bought by its present owner at the sale of the effects of Captain Machell, who died 11 May 1902.

In the 1943 Classics Gordon met with no success, although if fortune had been a little kinder he might have won or at least been placed in all five races. Nasrullah, owned by HH Aga Khan, was a far better colt than any of his contemporaries, but stubbornly refused to exert himself. In the Two Thousand Guineas Gordon finished fourth on him to Kingsway, beaten less than a length. Despite self-willed and exasperating performances on Newmarket Heath by Nasrullah in the ensuing weeks, Gordon elected to ride him in the New Derby in preference to the stable companion Umidadd, who was ridden by Charlie Elliott. Once again Nasrullah behaved abominably and finished third, again beaten less than a length. The colt would not go through with his effort and left Gordon with the impression that had he done so, he would have triumphed. The winner was Miss Dorothy Paget's Straight Deal, who beat Charlie Elliott and Umidadd by a head. Without Straight Deal it would have been banner headlines that Gordon had yet again chosen the wrong Derby mount.

In the One Thousand Guineas he rode a backward filly of Mr J. V. Rank's, Why Hurry, into fifth place behind Herringbone, and when Why Hurry won the New Oaks he was claimed for Beckhampton's Tropical Sun, who started favourite and could only finish third, beaten a length. The three-year-old fillies were evidently a very high-class vintage, and Herringbone and Ribbon finished first and second in the St Leger, with Gordon fifth on Tropical Sun, who showed up her stamina limitations. Nasrullah, however, if he had put his mind to it, could have trounced all of them — and only in subsequent years when standing as a stallion in America did he prove his true merit.

By mid-season it seemed a possibility that Walter Nightingall's jockey, Tommy Carey, who had won the New Derby on Straight Deal, might beat Gordon in the Jockeys' Championship, for he was only three winning rides behind him. However, Carey admitted that he did not think that he would do so as he could not go to scale at less than 8 st 4 lbs — 9 lbs heavier than Gordon. This disadvantage meant that he did not have so wide a range as Gordon who was able to accept a greater number of rides.

In August the King, in the uniform of a Field Marshal, attended Ascot races where he presented both Fred Darling and Gordon with paintings of Sun Chariot by Alfred Munnings. In the royal box the King told them of the great pleasure which her victories had brought to his family, and indicated that his eldest daughter was beginning to take a considerable interest in the racing careers of the Royal horses. Munnings had spent four days at Beckhampton making notes for his commission but after the first twenty-four hours he and Fred Darling were virtually at loggerheads.

By the end of the season, in which there were only sixty-seven days' racing, a drop from eighty in 1942, on six racecourses (Ascot, Newmarket, Pontefract,

Salisbury, Stockton and Windsor), Gordon, once again Champion Jockey, was announcing 'no change' in his 1944 retainers. Beckhampton was to have first claim upon his services and Frank Butters second claim, and as he looked to the future he felt confident that during the subsequent season his ambition to ride the Derby winner would be fulfilled. It had been frustrating that Nasrullah, who could have made his dream come true, had refused to do so, but despite this further set back he believed that amongst the potential treasure trove of the Butters-trained colts sired by Bahram, Fairway, Hyperion, Mahmoud and Bois Roussel there must be one champion.

At Beckhampton there was less confidence, although Fred Darling, who had reluctantly agreed to again train some of Miss Dorothy Paget's horses, had high hopes of the Blue Peter colt, Blue Moon, whose dam was a full sister to Derby winner Trigo. Blue Moon, who had cost four thousand eight hundred guineas, proved moderate in the extreme, and Mustang, whom Fred Darling sold to Mrs Philip Hill for ten thousand guineas, became the most successful three-year-old at Beckhampton.

In the early part of the season some confusion was caused when a certain Gordon Richards, aged thirteen and apprenticed to Mr J. C. Waugh, made his appearance in the saddle. Scaling 5 st 10 lbs he came from a family living in Somerset besotted with Racing, and had two young brothers, Steve named after Donoghue and Archer after Fred Archer. Eight years earlier, his mother had dressed him up as a jockey, borrowed a white pony from her husband's fire wood cart and allowed him to take part in a carnival procession through the streets of Bath. Young Gordon Richards rode in public for the first time at Salisbury where he saw the Champion Jockey win two races, and was encouraged with a word of advice from his illustrious namesake.

Within days of celebrating his fortieth birthday, Gordon rode a hat-trick of winners at Windsor. He was lucky not to have been involved in a serious accident during the afternoon, for in the fifth race he and J. Marshall were sent crashing to the ground when their mounts collided. The Stewards found that the accident was the fault of no one, but Gordon returned home with a knee the size of a football.

Gordon had no Classic successes until he won the St Leger on HH Aga Khan's Tehran, beating Borealis and Ocean Swell. On St Leger Day there was almost open war between taxi drivers and 'pirate' lorry drivers along the roads near Newmarket. Car hire restrictions made it impossible for racegoers from the Cambridge and Bury St Edmunds districts to take a taxi for the entire journey. Consequently, relays and a change-over point were organised, and although this action saved no petrol, profiteering taxi drivers hoped to reap a golden harvest by charging two pounds a head for a seven-mile journey. This harvest was prevented by enterprising lorry drivers who offered to drive twenty to thirty spectators to the racecourse for ten shillings a head.

Tehran's victory benefited the Indian Army Comforts Fund, for HH Aga Khan had decided at the beginning of the War to give all his winning stake money gained in England to this charity. Living in Switzerland throughout the War, Tehran's owner did not listen to the radio commentary given by Raymond Glendenning on the race, and only learned the St Leger result at his Geneva home the following day.

During the summer and early autumn, when the news that the Allies had landed in France and that the invasion of the Continent was successfully achieved was uppermost in everyone's minds, Gordon consolidated a friendship with Dudley Williams—a friendship which was to strengthen throughout the next three decades. Dudley came from a much respected Carmarthenshire family, who had served the community as councillors for generations. He had been a brilliant amateur steeplechase jockey in the 1920s before being compelled to turn professional by Sir William Bass. No jockey has ever ridden Aintree with greater skill and verve, and his victories on the Liverpool course included the Topham Trophy, the Grand Sefton and the Grand National on Kellesboro Jack, owned by his friend F. Ambrose Clarke, the rich American who made Melton Mowbray his base throughout the winter months.

Within a year of his Grand National triumph Dudley Williams, who was assistant trainer to Ivor Anthony at Wroughton, had a crashing fall at Hurst Park which ended his riding career on doctor's orders. Refusing to accept this desperate stroke of misfortune and all its implications he went to America in the early 1930s and studied phrenology and neurology at Lincoln College, Indianapolis. The fees were high and so were the living expenses, but Dudley felt the cost worthwhile for his new profession would equip him to help and cure others whose ailments were preventing them from leading fully active lives.

In 1944, at the request of Mr Mark Ostrer, he began training at Bishop's Canning, near Beckhampton, and sent out a steady stream of winners, many of them ridden by Gordon. Advocate was the star of the stable, and it was upon this colt that Gordon won two races at Ascot.

Dudley, wise, cultured and a loyal friend to those whose company he enjoyed, had a great sense of humour and found that he had much in common with Gordon, whom he always insisted was a Welshman and not a Salopian. Many a winter's evening was spent by the two men in entertaining banter as one tried to out-do the other in repartee, and often the evening ended with a sing-song around the piano with 'cockles and mussels, alive-alive-o' a favourite song which they rendered with relish and gusto. Dudley loved to remark that 'Egotism is the anaesthetic supplied by nature to deaden the pain of feeling a fool,' and his remark deserved consideration for the truth it revealed.

One inestimable good turn done by Dudley was the improvement which he achieved in the eyesight of young Marjorie Richards. Ever since her childhood she had suffered from a defect in her eye which specialists had been unable to cure, despite Gordon's willingness to call in the most respected eye surgeons. Dudley set about a remedy, and under his skilled and loving care a cure was effected over a period of two years.

Gordon admiring a trophy presented to the Marlborough Flying Club and
won by one of his own racing pigeons.

Tudor Minstrel, the most brilliant miler ever ridden by Gordon.

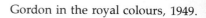

Impassive after scoring an easy victory on
Dramatic in the 1950 Lincoln.

During this time Dudley and Gordon occasionally went to Torquay with 'the gang'—Archie Burns, Ted Gardner, who had been Lord Derby's jockey in the 1920s, Quintin Gilbey and Tom Reece. Golf would be played—with little serious thought being given to the score at each hole—against such worthy opponents as Humphrey Cottrill and boxer George Garrard, who was Gordon's masseur. The evenings were spent in playing poker and drinking port. The emphasis was invariably upon relaxation from the stress and strain of Racing, and in Dudley Williams Gordon found a perfect companion. Gordon was a wonderful host on these occasions, invariably over-tipped his caddie on the golf course, paid for all the drinks and the green fees, but did not accept side-bets on the outcome of the match, which he was always anxious to have the 'honour and glory' of winning.

When he announced his retainers for 1945, Beckhampton, where there were only twenty-six horses in training, of which Mustang was the sole four-year-old, was again at the head of the list, followed by Fred Templeman and Captain Laye, who had recently moved his horses from Marlborough to the stables at Ogbourne used by Martin Hartigan until his death.

In March, Racing was saddened by the death of Steve Donoghue and mourned the Irishman who had enriched the Turf for more than thirty years by his brilliance as a jockey and his endearing character as a man. Utterly improvident, unpunctual, a *bon viveur* who loved nothing more than a night on the town in the company of a bevy of attractive women, he was blessed with more charm in his little finger than many men possessed in their entire body. Lovable and a super-optimist who had enjoyed every moment of his life, he lived completely and totally for the moment and the hour. For him the future could take care of itself, without thought or preoccupation with what the Fates had in store. He died virtually penniless in his London flat, and with his death an era in jockeyship seemed to end. In his Will he left his painting of The Tetrarch to Gordon.

Many years earlier the racecourse cry 'Come on Steve' had been changed to, 'Come on, Gordon', but Gordon never forgot the encouragement and kindness shown to him by Steve when he first left Oakengates for Foxhill, and never ceased to regard Donoghue as one of his heroes. Inevitably, comparisons were made between Steve, haphazard and careless in his business affairs, fanatically fond of horses and seldom out of financial troubles, and Gordon who managed his business affairs with great acumen, was utterly generous to his family and his friends, and was renowned throughout the kingdom for his integrity. His straightness was a household word, and he would take as much trouble with an indifferent colt as he would with a potential Classic winner.

This was one source of his success, for owners and trainers knew that he would always give of his best, whether the race was of immense significance or little importance, and during his racing career in the saddle he did more for the prestige of jockeys than any other jockey before or since. Horses ran for him, and although his style may have been unorthodox his determination and will to win compelled horses to give their utmost.

He earned more than three times the salary of a cabinet minister and deserved every penny of it—and although one owner who gave Gordon a small present after he had won a Maiden Plate at Bath claimed that he felt as though he was giving a cultured pearl to the Nizam of Hyderabad, Gordon never became swollen-headed as a result of his success or his wealth.

Another quality was his humbleness, typified by his insistence on lodging with Mrs Susan Seamans at her Stamford Street home in Newmarket every time that he was riding at Headquarters. He had been recommended to Mrs Seamans when he was a small apprentice. Wearing a bowler hat, which almost came down over his eyes, he could hardly reach the door-knocker when he arrived for the first time, but his quiet determination to succeed, his reticence and his innate goodness appealed to Mrs Seamans. As the years went by and his fame increased he still found time to go into the kitchen and talk to her whilst she prepared and cooked his evening meal. In the mid-1930s she changed the name of her house to Myrobella and a decade later a grandchild was christened Gordon Richard Seamans.

By the early spring of 1945 Gordon was feeling totally exhausted with the strain of race-riding, travelling amidst the inevitable discomfort of war-time conditions, and constantly attempting to 'do his bit' in the Home Guard and on the farm which he had bought near Lambourn. Told by his London specialist that he had an ulcer, he could not eat or sleep. He felt sullen, a bundle of nerves and hated both his own company and that of his family and friends. A trip to Lymington arranged by Margery proved a disappointing failure, and the 1945 season was looming on the horizon. Dejected and despondent he soldiered on valiantly, but fatigue was his constant companion.

Yet he won three races at Salisbury to celebrate his forty-first birthday. Three days later the free world had far more to celebrate. At the end of April Mussolini had been shot by Italian partisans, Hitler had committed suicide, and the German armies in Italy, Holland and Denmark surrendered. At one minute past midnight on Tuesday 8 May the end of the Second World War was officially declared. At Newmarket that afternoon jubilant crowds watched Harry Wragg win the One Thousand Guineas on Sun Stream with Gordon unplaced on Fractious. However, he had the honour and distinction of riding the first winner in post-war England when he triumphed on HH Aga Khan's Rivaz in the opening race.

Although unsuccessful in the first two Classics, no one was more pleased than Gordon at the victory of his younger brother Clifford in riding Lord Astor's Court Martial to win the Two Thousand Guineas. The short-priced favourite Dante may have been unlucky in the first Classic, but took his revenge in the New Derby. Ten days before the race a flint stone flew up as he was being galloped at Middleham and struck him in the eye. It was thought that the injury would blind him permanently, but his owner Sir Eric Ohlson had the perspicacity to call in Mr Williamson Noble, the renowned Harley Street oculist. Mr Noble travelled to Middleham, successfully operated upon the eye of a thoroughbred for the first time in his life, and told the delighted owner that there would be no fee unless

Dante won the Derby. In the event Sir Eric Ohlson generously made certain that Mr Williamson Noble received a very substantial reward for his trouble. As Mr Noble was responsible for looking after the eyesight of Mr Winston Churchill and on the eve of the Derby informed the Prime Minister that Dante would triumph, his reputation in Downing Street was greatly enhanced.

As the St Leger drew nearer the scratching of Dante gave the final Classic, which was to be held at York, a far more open appearance. Gordon, who was to ride the filly Naishapur for the Aga Khan, drove to the meeting in his Rolls-Bentley where he was greeted by Tom Reece, who had been sent ahead to organise the house which Gordon and his friends had rented for the week. Eight months previously Gordon had been put on a strict milk diet by his doctor, and had been advised studiously to avoid alcohol. In consequence his Rolls-Bentley became known to his companions as 'the milk float' on account of the crates of milk that it carried.

Naishapur failed abysmally behind Chamoissaire and Rising Light, much to Gordon's chagrin, for the filly was beaten after three furlongs. The race appeared to be full of scrimmages and Gordon thought that the jockeys ahead of him were making the St Leger more like a football match than a race.

He had high hopes of winning the Gimcrack the next afternoon on the flying filly Rivaz, rated the fastest and best of her sex for a decade, but she was scuttled by Harry Wragg on Lord Derby's Gulf Stream when her stamina gave out inside the sixth and final furlong. It was a hectic week for Gordon, for the day after the St Leger it was planned that he, Harry Wragg, Eph Smith and Michael Beary were to fly with Lord Fitzwilliam to Stockholm. The object of the goodwill mission was to impress upon Swedish owners and breeders the fact that they should 'buy British' — in return for much needed Swedish currency. Unfortunately, the proposed trip did not take place as the Swedish authorities could not guarantee return transport.

Gordon, despite his continued milk diet and his meat-free regime which resulted in his having no need for the meat coupons in his ration book, retained his pre-eminence as a jockey. Constantly asked how long he intended to continue in the saddle he invariably replied that he would not give up until he believed he could no longer ride winners. He had no hesitation in adding that riding was his life, that he was superbly fit and that Steve Donoghue had ridden until he was fifty-five years old.

Due to the War there had been a dearth of apprentices and the young and most promising jockeys of 1939 had all been swallowed up by military service — leaving Gordon, Harry Wragg, Michael Beary, Eph Smith and W. Nevett as the veterans who dominated the Jockeys' Table throughout the years of the Second World War. There was no chance of either of Gordon's sons following in his footsteps, for Jack, who was at school at Haileybury, where he was proving to be a better than average cricketer, had no particular interest in horses, and was thinking of making the Army his career; and Peter, who was at Blundell's School, already appeared too heavy to become a jockey, although Gordon planned that he should work in a racing stable before becoming established as a trainer. Jack was to be called up in 1946 and was to spend three years with the Royal Engineers in Berlin at a time of the Blockade and Air Lift before his demobilisation and his acceptance of a job in the motor industry, working for the garage which had the Jaguar agency in Cheltenham.

Gordon, who won both the Coventry Stakes and the Middle Park Stakes upon Khaled for HH Aga Khan, reached another milestone in his career when he won his three thousandth race on 31 October 1945, a feat no other English jockey had ever achieved. Many of these victories had been gained by narrow margins and Gordon was occasionally told that he had won or lost a close finish due to an error on the part of the Judge. Such errors were to be eliminated in the future, for the Stewards of the Jockey Club announced that the photo-finish camera was to be installed at Newmarket during the next season in an effort to make decisions absolutely fool-proof.

In mid-November Gordon's father died at the age of seventy-two at his home, Bonita, in Wrockwardine Wood. Throughout the final years of his life he had been a keen supporter of the Wrockwardine Wood Bowling Club, and only a fortnight before he died he had been photographed with the victorious team after they had won the Mid-Shropshire Amateur Bowling League. When his funeral took place at Holy Trinity Church, Gordon and Margery were joined as mourners by Ewart, Clifford, Colin, Vera, Rhoda and Barbara. Nathan Richards' only surviving sister was too ill to attend. Amongst the large number of wreaths and flowers were tributes from Tom Reece and Freddie Fox.

Within a month Gordon was appalled to learn that fifty-seven-year-old Freddie Fox, affectionately known as the 'unofficial Mayor of Wantage', had been killed in a car crash when he was involved in a head-on collision with a lorry near Frilford. At the inquest the driver of the RASC lorry claimed that he had been waved on by the driver of another lorry. When the collision occurred, Fox was thrown on to the steering wheel and died instantly. His wife, who was a passenger in his car, was injured.

9

The failure of Tudor Minstrel

In the winter of 1945–6 Gordon was able to holiday for a month in St Moritz, for the first time for seven years. It was the tonic that he needed to restore him to his former self, and racegoers at Lincoln, when the Flat season opened, commented on how fit he looked. During the early spring it was announced that the Derby would return to its rightful home after a lapse of six years, and Gordon was confident that the principal Beckhampton hope, Edward Tudor, would go very close to winning.

The Two Thousand Guineas had not been far enough for Mrs Macdonald-Buchanan's colt, but the bright chestnut had pleased both Darling and Gordon in the weeks prior to the Epsom Summer meeting by the power and zest that he had shown in trial gallops. At the Press Club luncheon, being held for the first time since 1939, the customary toast 'the pious memory of the founder of the Derby Stakes' was proposed and when it came to the owners and jockeys to express their opinions as to the outcome of the race, Gordon told his audience that he was very hopeful of victory, although he feared Gulf Stream who had finished fourth to Happy Knight in the Two Thousand Guineas at Newmarket. None of the pundits was correct, and the race proved a bookmakers' benefit with 50–1 outsider Airborne, the only grey amongst the seventeen runners, out-staying Gulf Stream. Edward Tudor appeared to have a great chance as the straight was reached, but failed to stay, thus maintaining Gordon's twenty-three-year-old Derby hoodoo.

Ten days later at Royal Ascot Gordon won the Coventry Stakes on Mr J. A. Dewar's Tudor Minstrel, the fastest two-year-old seen by many racegoers in their lifetime. A brown colt of perfect size and proportion sired by Owen Tudor out of Sansonnet, the best two-year-old of 1935, who had already produced the brilliantly fast Neola and Neolight, Tudor Minstrel had made a winning debut at Bath and had then toyed with his opponents at Salisbury to win by eight lengths. At Royal Ascot he massacred his rivals and subsequently won the National Breeders Produce Stakes at Sandown by four lengths, before being retired for the season. At Beckhampton he was considered to be one of the greatest racehorses ever to have been trained there and the possibility of his defeat as a three-year-old seemed as impossible as the leaning tower of Pisa collapsing. By mid-summer the bookmakers were quoting him at 10–1 for the 1947 Derby and his jubilant owner was teasingly asking the Press how they intended to compare the already retired

Tudor Minstrel with the colts who later in the year would win such prestige races as the Middle Park Stakes.

In August Gordon, heading for a season's total of 200 winners, brought back memories of former glory when he won at Lewes on Coup de Diable, the only flat horse trained by Ivor Anthony at Wroughton. During the War the famous stables were closed down and Coup de Diable was the first winner under Jockey Club Rules sent out from the 'Brown Jack stables' since Gordon had won the 1940 Lincoln on Quartier Maître. Mrs Aubrey Hastings, presiding genius of the Wroughton stables, and her son Peter Hastings, who was learning the art of training, were both witnesses to Coup de Diable's triumph. A week earlier Gordon had been stung by a wasp whilst riding at Brighton on an afternoon made memorable by amateur John Hislop scoring his sixth successive victory and his seventh in the eight races in which he had ridden during the season. Gordon, more angered than hurt by his wasp sting, was one of the first to congratulate Hislop upon his feat.

Days later Gordon was again 'in the wars' when he thought that he had broken his big toe after being kicked at the starting gate. An SOS was sent out for the racecourse doctor who, on arrival, took one glance at the toe, gave it a sharp wrench and was congratulated by a well-satisfied Gordon as the dislocated joint promptly went back to its correct position. He was less satisfied at Doncaster on the eve of the St Leger when Charlie Smirke insisted that he had been engaged to ride Anwar for HH Aga Khan and intended to do so, despite Frank Butters' statement that Gordon would have the mount.

When Edward Tudor, suffering from a chill, was withdrawn from the final Classic, Butters had made it clear that Gordon must ride Anwar as the Aga Khan had a second retainer on his services. Admittedly, Smirke had been engaged for Anwar when it was assumed that Gordon would ride the Beckhampton colt, but it was also assumed that Gordon's second retainer would override Smirke's engagement. Smirke, smarting with indignation, threatened to take the matter before the Stewards, but the dispute was settled when Prince Aly Khan arrived, and decided that Gordon should have the mount, but that in the event of victory Smirke should be given a present equivalent to that given to Gordon. Anwar finished unplaced behind Airborne.

Whenever he was at Beckhampton Gordon found that Fred Darling was spending more and more time preparing Tudor Minstrel for the 1947 Derby. Already he had won the 'Blue Riband' seven times, but although he would never admit the fact, he was as anxious as anyone to provide Gordon with his first Derby triumph. It has been claimed that whereas Gordon loved horses, Darling treated them with complete strictness and although he admired them as individuals regarded them merely as the means whereby victories could be achieved. Certainly he had no use or time for those that did not conform to his high and exacting standards, and had no sentiment towards any of them. If a horse had no ability, Darling was not prepared to waste his time upon training the miscreant.

If, however, he believed that a horse potentially had great ability he would be willing to show the patience of Job.

Tudor Minstrel had performed in the spring and summer of 1946 with such scintillating brilliance that Darling began dreaming of another Derby success. However there were two worries at Beckhampton. Darling's health was deteriorating and he had to face the fact that before Christmas he would have to spend some time in hospital. The other nagging worry was Tudor Minstrel's stamina, and so for month after month in the late summer and early autumn Darling, who wanted to give his exceptionally speedy champion every chance to develop the temperament of a stayer, arranged the training of Tudor Minstrel in such a way that he refrained from taking hold of his bit, teaching him to settle down and come from behind to win his trial gallops.

On doctor's orders Darling spent three months in a sanatorium at Midhurst and the remainder of the winter of 1946-7 abroad, whilst his brother Sam took charge of Beckhampton. Before leaving for his enforced winter vacation and convalescence Fred Darling told his brother that Tudor Minstrel was 'an unusual horse — sensitive, intelligent, highly imaginative. A lark would rise up in front of him on the Downs and he'll follow it with his eyes and think about it — or perhaps in the night one of those big lorries will rush down the road. Tudor Minstrel will pull himself up and stand and listen until the noise dies.'

The possibility that Tudor Minstrel would enable Gordon to win the Derby was one of the chief topics of conversation at the Albany Club in November when Gordon organised a farewell dinner in honour of Harry Wragg, Bobby Jones and Tommy Carey who were retiring. Lord Rosebery received the guests of honour at the beginning of the evening. Gordon, an accomplished but never patronising or facetious after-dinner speaker, told the guests in the course of his speech, wishing future success and happiness to the three jockeys, that Harry Wragg had given him 'a crick in the neck whenever he had pulled in behind me, and I had always been anxious until the winning post had been reached'.

Gordon had a short holiday in December in Penzance with Dudley Williams and Tom Reece, spent Christmas at Clements Meadow, and on Boxing Day left with his family for his St Moritz vacation. He had never been bitten by the bug of riding in India or Egypt during the winter months, and whilst Smirke, Richardson and Weston travelled East to accept mounts on horses owned by influential potentates, Gordon was content to relax either at home or in Switzerland. He enjoyed his golf, although he was none too happy if his partner or opponents mentioned any of the errors that he was making. If they suggested how he could cure a hook, or improve his putting he would cry out, 'Don't tell me, don't tell me!'

Fred Darling returned to Beckhampton in the early spring of 1947 to find that Tudor Minstrel had wintered well under the competent care of his brother, to whom he gave neither thanks nor praise. At Newmarket he cantered away with the Two Thousand Guineas to give Gordon his eleventh Classic victory. At the winning post the brilliant colt was still on the bit, with Gordon looking around for non-existent danger. Unfortunately, the race was marred by an accident to Petition, the only colt who might have tested Tudor Minstrel. At the start Petition crashed into the tapes and fell back on his haunches, throwing his jockey. When eventually the starter released the tapes Petition ran a listless race, obviously suffering from the effects of his fall. Nevertheless, Tudor Minstrel's victory was so awe-inspiring that punters wagered colossal sums at 6–4 against his Derby chance, and it was obvious that he would start one of the shortest priced favourites for the Derby in living memory.

As Saturday 7 June grew closer, there seemed no point in looking beyond him for the Derby winner, for his authority, power and speed were far superior to that of any of his Epsom rivals. Mr Dewar was supremely confident, and so was Gordon, who had stated after the Guineas that he would never know the distance by which Tudor Minstrel would have won if he had been ridden out. He admitted that the Guineas had been the easiest victory of his career, and was not in the least surprised that every jockey to whom he spoke thought that his Derby victory was a foregone conclusion.

The only possible 'fly in the ointment' seemed to be another colt trained at Beckhampton, Blue Train, owned by King George VI. Blue Train's sire was Blue Peter, his dam the incomparable Sun Chariot, and when so superbly bred a colt won at Sandown in April and then, in the presence of Princess Elizabeth, proceeded to slam his rivals in the valuable Newmarket Stakes, he proved that he was a force with which to be reckoned. Bookmakers made him second favourite for the Derby, and the Press began to question whether or not Gordon might make the mistake of choosing the wrong mount at Epsom.

Michael Beary was engaged by Fred Darling for whichever colt Gordon elected not to ride, and the dilemma was heightened when it became apparent that Blue Train was improving every day. His Beckhampton trials were brilliant, but so were those of the headstrong Tudor Minstrel. In the midst of this dilemma Gordon announced that he had sold his Lambourn farm because 'a man cannot do two jobs properly' and the post-war demands on his services as a jockey precluded any other career. The fixture list had regained its pre-war look, with racing on forty-seven courses from Alexandra Park to York, and Gordon was far too busy to concentrate upon his farming. Yet he had enjoyed it, and so had his children. Jack and Peter had vied to drive the tractor and both agreed that their father was second to none at delegating the farm work and supervising the efforts of others as they struggled with hay bales.

As Derby Day approached, Darling announced that if the going at Epsom was firm he would not run Blue Train, for he was a heavy horse who needed some give in the ground. He also announced that a final decision as to Gordon's mount might not be made until the eve of the race. At the annual Press Club luncheon, where the President, Colonel Astor, referred to the Derby being run on a Saturday 'presumably so that we may work our five-day week without feeling that it is really our duty to take Wednesday off', it was obvious that everyone longed for Gordon to win the Derby. A final Derby gallop at Beckhampton at 5.30 a.m. two mornings later made Gordon decide upon Tudor Minstrel, for Mr Dewar's colt won the trial in the most convincing fashion. Tipsters and touts complained that they were not allowed to watch the trial, since the Beckhampton gallops were privately owned, and wished that both Derby horses were trained on the wide expanse of Newmarket Heath where their every movement and every trial could have been reported upon.

Once it was announced that Tudor Minstrel was definitely to be Gordon's Derby mount, his price shortened still further. Charlie Smirke in a newspaper article, gave his views upon riding in the race, explained that he thought that Tudor Minstrel was so brilliant a horse that even if he found himself in any sort of trouble he had the speed and the ability to extricate himself, and added, 'To me the Derby is much the same as any other race. The only difference is that the jockeys like to wear their best breeches and boots and turn out as smartly as they can. This is not too easy these days. Weatherbys allow jockeys coupons for only two pairs of breeches a year.'

At an eve of the Derby Charity Dinner a generous Michael Beary bought a pair of boots worn by Steve Donoghue when successful at Epsom for sixty guineas and presented them to Gordon. As he did so, he reminded Gordon that Eph Smith had borrowed his brother Doug's lucky boots when he won the Derby on Blue Peter and wished him success. It was a gracious gesture, typical of Michael Beary and much appreciated by Gordon. In fact he did not wear these boots, because Beary had forgotten to ascertain whether Gordon took the same size as Steve! He did not, so the boots were useless for the purpose for which they had been bought.

It was an austerity Derby Day, with King George VI and the Stewards of the Jockey Club wearing lounge suits and bowler hats instead of morning dress and top hats. In the days before the race Dr Malcolm Sargent and Laurence Olivier had been created Knights Bachelor in the Birthday Honours List; Earl Mountbatten, as Viceroy, had outlined plans for Independence to Indian leaders; and Trooping the Colour was held for the first time in seven years, but was a battle-dress parade which replaced the usual colourful pageantry of scarlet and gold uniformed soldiers. A noticeable feature of the parade was that seventeen-year-old Princess Elizabeth made her first appearance at the ceremony on horseback.

Members of the Royal family walked to the paddock at Epsom on Derby Day and joined the thousands who crammed the side of the rails hoping for a glimpse of Tudor Minstrel. A smaller horse than either Sayajirao or Pearl Diver, but with a massive girth, he carried his head high as Gordon cantered him to the start. Once the tapes went up, Tudor Minstrel began to fight a battle with Gordon, pulling hard for his head whilst Gordon did everything in his power to restrain the wilful colt. At the end of the first half-mile the futility of continuing the struggle caused Gordon to allow the impetuous Tudor Minstrel to race into the lead. Although he gave some hope to his supporters at the foot of Tattenham Corner, by the time the final three furlongs were reached he was a spent force. Passed by Merry Quip and Sayajirao, Gordon was still persevering when Pearl Diver and Migoli appeared on the scene full of running. Pearl Diver, owned by Baron de Waldner, a son-in-law of Mr Edward Esmond who had bequeathed him all his bloodstock when he died in 1945, raced into the lead at the distance to win by four lengths. As he approached the winning post his racing silks of 'white, black hoop' looked similar to those worn by Gordon on Tudor Minstrel, and an unfortunate French radio commentator frenziedly informed his listeners that Gordon Richards was winning the Derby at last! Tudor Minstrel's failure in the Derby stunned everyone—but in truth his inability to stay twelve furlongs proved his downfall.

Racing England felt humbled that their champion could only finish fourth behind French challenger Pearl Diver, and gave total sympathy to the crestfallen Gordon. Fatuous reasons were put forward for his defeat, from the belief that a gypsy had once put a curse on Gordon and sworn that he would not win the Derby, to the only slightly more feasible suggestion that Gordon rode too far forward in the saddle coming down Tattenham Corner and thus threw his mount out of his stride.

If nothing else Tudor Minstrel's defeat showed beyond any doubt the stranglehold of affection in which the general public held Gordon. Naturally he was bitterly disappointed by his twenty-second Derby failure, and quietly left Epsom racecourse for his Shoreham house to bathe in the sea, having won the race subsequent to the Derby on a two-year-old owned by the Aga Khan.

The Derby result was a notable landmark in the career of William Hill, who had made up his mind that Tudor Minstrel was a non-stayer and could not possibly win at Epsom. He had taken a similar view with Big Game and would have been a very heavy loser if the colt had won the 1942 Derby. In consequence, he unwisely discarded the elementary principles of bookmaking, and before the Two Thousand Guineas laid the Darling-trained colt at 10–1 for the Derby to a Midland bookmaker to the tune of £30,000. After Tudor Minstrel's brilliant Guineas victory, the colt became an even money chance for the Derby. However, Hill was still not perturbed, for unbeknown to anyone outside his office, one of the most respected professional punters had been persistently backing Blue Train. When quizzed about his bets by Hill, the punter admitted that a considerable part of his wager was on behalf of another—whom Hill assumed to be Fred Darling. When Blue Train was scratched, Hill was left with a hopelessly lop-sided book, with Tudor Minstrel a loser to almost a quarter of a million pounds. He could see little hope of getting out of his liabilities—although he was given a faint hope by Percy Carter, the trainer of Pearl Diver, who told him that the colt was certain to reach a place *if* a little rain took the jar out of the ground.

On the eve of the Derby a gentle drizzle commenced which proved totally advantageous to Pearl Diver. After the race the eldest son of a well-known member of the Jockey Club said to Hill, with undisguised relief, 'Thank God

Tudor Minstrel was beaten. Now I shall be able to sleep tonight.' Hill was dumb-founded and asked, 'What on earth do you mean?' To which came the reply, 'Why if Tudor Minstrel had won the Derby, and after you paid that enormous price for Chanteur II only a few days prior to the Coronation Cup, everyone said that you would be sure to have "knocked" and I would not have received the £50,000 that I won off you at Kempton on Monday!' Hill then recalled that throughout Derby week some of his heaviest gambling clients had fought shy of him.

Earlier in the week William Hill had won the Coronation Cup with his new acquisition Chanteur II. The sale had been agreed with the owner, Monsieur P. Magot, but after winning in Hill's colours at Hurst Park the colt returned to France before attempting to win the Ascot Gold Cup. On arriving back in France the colt was impounded by the Ministry of Agriculture who forbade the sale to go through unless a further £10,000 was paid. Hill paid the money, which he never regretted, due in no small measure to a colt sired by Chanteur II in his second crop. The colt was given the name Pinza.

Days after the Derby Gordon was invited by M. Marcel Boussac to ride Djelal, second in the French Two Thousand Guineas and winner of the Prix Lupin, in an international race at Belmont Park. Gordon was attracted by the idea of riding in the USA and meeting his American contemporary jockeys, but was compelled to refuse the invitation on the grounds that he had too many racing commitments in Britain at the height of the racing season. Tudor Minstrel redeemed his reputa-tion by winning the St James's Palace Stakes at Royal Ascot, but his defeat by Migoli in the Eclipse proved conclusively his lack of stamina.

During mid-summer negotiations were put in hand for Mr J. A. Dewar to purchase Beckhampton 'lock, stock and barrel' from Fred Darling, who had announced that ill-health was causing him to retire at the end of the season. For fifteen years Gordon had been the stable jockey and an immensely strong mutual respect for each other's ability had been forged between Gordon and the great trainer. Darling saw in Gordon the stable jockey par excellence, for not only was he the supreme champion in the saddle, but out of the saddle he showed every characteristic which he required. Gordon was invariably punctual, always im-maculately dressed, meticulous in his business affairs, unfailing in his complete integrity, and impeccable in his manners towards Beckhampton patrons and other owners for whom he rode. Despite the overwhelming demand for his services, he never antagonised owners, as other jockeys did, by arriving on the racecourse having engaged himself to ride two or more horses in the same race. If his genius in the saddle was analysed, one minor criticism was that he lacked the polish which other jockeys, particularly Donoghue or Beary or Beasley could show in the hunting field or in a steeplechase. Steve loved to tell the story of Gordon taking a toss when jumping a huge daunting bank whilst hunting on one of his few visits to Ireland. He got up unhurt and remarked, 'I'm going back to England where the banks keep money!'

He had not the artistry of Donoghue or Carslake, the hair-breadth sense of judgment possessed by Childs, or the terrifying confidence of Smirke, yet in total Gordon's talent in the saddle outweighed the accomplishments of all those with whom he was compared. His build, being light and powerful, was of inestimable advantage, but so too was his determination, his acute sense of balance which enabled his horses to run on an even keel, and his uncanny appreciation of how best to ride each and every horse allowing for his idiosyncrasies. He never rode with too short leathers, as did some Australian and American jockeys, and he usually rode with a long rein, keeping a light contact on his horse's mouth. He never attempted to be too clever and win by the narrowest margin if a three-lengths victory was a possibility and in consequence seldom lost a race by a short head through over-confidence.

Two stories illustrate his complete integrity. Firstly, Steve Donoghue once wrote to a young admirer who had asked his advice about betting, 'If you must back a horse and do not know anything, back Gordon Richards. You will always get a good run for your money.' Secondly, was the occasion at Birmingham when he agreed to ride a very indifferent selling-plater; moments later came a request to ride the red-hot favourite owned by Lord Glanely. He immediately refused the ride, explaining that he was already booked. His word was always his bond.

His virtues were such that no other jockey of the era matched up to Gordon in the estimation of Darling, who in reality was a lonely man who thought it infra-dig to outwardly show emotion. On Darling's retirement it was finally agreed that thirty-seven-year-old Noel Murless was to take over the Beckhampton Stables, with Gordon remaining as stable jockey despite a stupendous offer from HH Aga Khan for him to accept a first retainer.

Murless was Cheshire born and a man who had learned his job the hard way. He had ridden for a short period as an amateur and then as a professional associated with Frank Hartigan at Weyhill, where he first met Gordon. Subsequently he spent five years as assistant to Hubert Hartigan in Ireland before setting up on his own at Hambleton, near Thirsk, set amidst the bleak but beautiful Yorkshire Wolds. Life was harsh, particularly during the freezing cold of the winter months, and with only a few horses in his care Murless would work alongside his head lad putting up fences and hurdles, crushing corn by hand and drawing water from the well. With brains, a sense of humour and a willingness to work hard from dawn to dusk, he was bound to succeed. Gordon often stayed with him for York races and realised his potential great ability.

The question of his successor at Beckhampton had occupied Darling's mind for a considerable time. One night after dinner at his house he asked Gordon for his opinion on the matter. Many names were mentioned, but Gordon was adamant that Noel Murless was the ideal man for the job. Darling knew little about him, and Gordon tentatively suggested that Darling should go to a meeting at Ascot at the end of the week to watch Murless, who had several runners. Darling was impressed, particularly by the fact that Murless carried his own saddle instead of delegating the burdensome task to an underling, and seemed pleased that Murless appeared to have an instinctive gift for understanding his horses. When, at a later date, Murless received Darling's proposition he hesitated to accept until his old boss Hubert Hartigan told him, 'If Gordon stays, you go to Beckhampton.'

Darling ran Beckhampton in a despotic and dictatorial manner, which had resulted in his saddling nineteen Classic winners and training more fashionably-bred horses for immensely rich and influential members of the Jockey Club for three decades than any other trainer. So for Murless, accustomed to the quieter surroundings of Hambleton, this was to prove a very different way of life. It is not unfair to state that he was never totally happy or at ease whilst training at Beckhampton, partly due to his inability to be on the same wavelength as Mr Dewar.

At Goodwood Gordon won the Stewards' Cup on Closeburn, trained by Noel Murless, but the success was lucky to materialise. A coach had crashed at Petersfield, and further traffic congestion was caused by a car smash on the Petworth–Goodwood road. Closeburn had been stabled at Frank Hartigan's Weyhill yard and only arrived in the parade ring with minutes to spare, having been jog-trotted by his enterprising stable lad for the final two miles after his horsebox had become embroiled in a solid traffic jam.

Three months later Darling saddled his final runners at Newmarket before retiring after a career which had made him a veritable 'Colossus'. At the Second October meeting he had the satisfaction of seeing Gordon ride The Cobbler to victory in the Middle Park Stakes. It was a hard-fought contest, but Gordon prevailed by a head over Birthday Greetings, ridden by Charlie Smirke, to give Darling one final major triumph in the last week of his distinguished career as a trainer.

Half-an-hour later Gordon won the Newmarket Oaks on Lord Astor's filly Mitrailleuse trained by R. J. Colling, and highlighted a brilliantly successful meeting by scoring on Migoli in the Champion Stakes, High Stakes in the Lowther Stakes, Weighbridge in the Suffolk Nursery, and Queenpot in the Prendergast Stakes. Having ridden The Cobbler and Queenpot for Darling, it was perhaps appropriate that his final victory of the meeting was on Closeburn, trained by Murless, who openly admitted that without Gordon's wholehearted support he would never have dared to undertake the task of training at Beckhampton.

By mid-November Gordon had equalled his 1933 record of riding 259 winners in a season, and although he had never deliberately attempted to beat his own record, the winners were steadily achieved. At Leicester on 10 November, where Mr Alec Marsh, the former amateur jockey, was officiating as starter for the first time, he won by a short head on Twenty Twenty, owned by Charles Jerdein and trained by George Beeby, to bring his total for the season to 260. It was the final race of the afternoon, and the huge crowd, who had thronged to the Midland track purely to see their hero Gordon, were not to be denied their pleasure of cheering him to the echo. Gordon felt that he could not face so great a number of admirers and arranged for his car to pull up on the 'blind' side of the jockeys' changing room. Moments later he attempted to make his escape through a back window, but was spotted, caught and compelled to sign hundreds of autographs. One of those who cheered him to the echo was a veteran racegoer who had seen him ride his first winner—Jimmy White's Gay Lord—on the Leicester course in 1921. Gordon told the veteran that White had given him a £10 note after the race, that he had started a savings bank account with it, and that it was still there, never having been touched.

Statistically Gordon's 1947 triumph was greater than that of 1933 for during that season he had 975 mounts, whereas in 1947 he had only ridden in 792 races. Before the final day of the season, Gordon had ridden nine more winners, including the last race of the year at Lingfield, to bring his total to 269. To balance and counteract such an achievement, before Christmas he endured the slowest ride of his career when he rode a two-year-old elephant around the ring at Harringay Circus!

Noel Murless commenced his first season at Beckhampton in spectacular style, for on The Cobbler Gordon was only beaten a head by My Babu in the Two Thousand Guineas, and on Queenpot won the One Thousand Guineas forty-eight hours later. From the outset Murless found that Gordon was the perfect stable jockey, and could never over-emphasise the sense of reliability that he received from him. No matter how inclement the weather Gordon would arrive at Beckhampton 'on time', and applied the same concentration and conscientiousness to routine training gallops as he did when riding in a race. Murless always thought that this was one of the secrets of Gordon's success. He rode work at Beckhampton at least twice a week, and knew the peculiarities of each horse that he rode so intimately that Murless thought it superfluous to give him instructions in the paddock before a race.

Surprisingly the Derby meeting at Epsom found Gordon without a winner, and within ten days his bad luck was to increase when he was injured at Brighton, having already ridden twenty-seven consecutive losers before the meeting commenced. Two more losers at Brighton were followed by a crashing fall in the fourth race when he broke two ribs and injured two more. Halfway down the hill to the winning post the filly he was riding crossed her legs and toppled over. Gordon was pitched over the filly's head, but luckily was not touched by any of the other horses as he crashed to the ground. One of the first to reach him was Archie Burns, who started undoing the neckband of his racing silks. 'Leave it,' Gordon told him. 'I might catch cold.' Taken to Sussex County Hospital, where he was later visited by Michael Beary who was substituted for him on the winner of the afternoon's final race, Gordon was driven to the home of ex-trainer Gil Bennet at Polegate, near Eastbourne, in the early evening. The following day, after listening to the Test Match on the radio and disgustedly hearing that two of his Brighton mounts had won, he was taken back to Marlborough.

It was announced that he would be fit enough to ride at Royal Ascot, much to the relief of the household at Clements Meadow, for he was never an easy patient when incapacitated by injury, and the telephone began ringing as trainers attempted to book him for their fancied horses. Rumours then became rife that he would not ride at the meeting after all, and the Marlborough telephone exchange was jammed with as many as one hundred trainers and news reporters attempting to confirm the rumour. Gordon, delighted that one of his pigeons had won an event in the Guernsey Old Bird National Race by flying home to Marlborough at 1,586 yards a minute, was less pleased when he realised that Royal Ascot was not a possibility as far as he was concerned. He rode a hack at Beckhampton on Sunday morning and afterwards felt sore around his ribs. The following morning he gave himself a good test in a gallop and then appreciated that his muscles were too sore to allow him to do himself justice. He cancelled all riding engagements and decided to rest for another week.

Happily his first ride on his return to the saddle was successful, and by mid-July he had ridden eighty-seven winners including the first Beckhampton treble of the season, achieved at Salisbury. At Chepstow in August he rode four consecutive winners and the following afternoon returned to Brighton, scene of his fall earlier in the year, where he rode the first two winners to prove that his brilliance was unimpaired.

At Ascot in September he was sensationally beaten on Royal Forest who started at 25-1 on — much to the financial agony of at least one professional punter — but despite such a setback he headed the winning Jockeys' List for the twenty-first time. He rode 224 winners, and as he came home ahead of his rivals in the final race of the season at Lingfield the huge crowd applauded him. No jockey had ever done more for Racing than Gordon and the crowd were not to be denied the pleasure of showing their approval. Noel Murless, in his first Beckhampton season, headed the winning Trainers' List, due in no small measure to Gordon's prowess in the saddle.

In December, Gordon holidaying in Torquay, was negotiating with a film company who wished to make a film based on his life. The idea was that the film, in Technicolour and lasting ninety minutes, would be made in the spring of 1949 with Gordon taking the star role.

Before the season opened Gordon had been in the curling team skippered by W. Griggs, which won the Cornwell Cup at St Moritz. The cup had been presented by Ronnie Cornwell, father of author John le Carré. On his return from Switzerland at a lunch given by the *Sporting Life* to the Jockey Club and the National Hunt Committee he referred to an occasion when he was being hounded by sporting writers for his life story. Needing advice, he had asked Lord Lonsdale for his opinion and was told not to have anything to do with the Press or television where his biography was concerned. Within six weeks it was announced that Lord Lonsdale had sold his life story to the newspapers.

The star of Beckhampton was Abernant, whose dam, Rustom Mahal, was a daughter of the flying Mumtaz Mahal. Abernant had been placed top of the Free Handicap as a result of victories in the Chesham Stakes at Royal Ascot, the National Breeders Produce Stakes at Sandown, the Champagne Stakes at Doncaster and finally the Middle Park Stakes at Newmarket in the autumn. Gordon had greater affection for Abernant than for any other horse he ever rode. On one occasion the start of a race was delayed, and as Gordon walked the brilliant colt behind the starting gate he espied some children playing marbles. Abernant also noticed, insisted on moving closer, and lowered his head in an effort to join in the fun! Minutes later, he reverted his attention to his appointed task, and as the tapes went up, was into his stride like a bullet from a gun and won with consummate ease.

In the Two Thousand Guineas Abernant was beaten a short head by Nimbus, but despite the fact that his stamina limitations precluded any thought of his contesting the Derby, Gordon seemed to have bright prospects for Epsom, since Beckhampton stabled top-class three-year-olds in Ridge Wood, Krakatoa, Royal Forest, Faux Tirage, and Berrylands owned by King George VI.

Royal Forest gave a sparkling performance at Sandown to win the Sandown Park Trial Stakes and was installed Derby favourite. It was pointed out that if Major Reginald Macdonald-Buchanan's colt was successful, it would be the first time in Turf history that a husband and wife had both enjoyed the good fortune to own a Derby winner, for Mrs Macdonald-Buchanan, daughter of the late Lord Woolavington, had won with Owen Tudor in 1941. The only doubt about Royal Forest seemed to be his temperament, for on more than one occasion he had worked himself into a lather of sweat before a race. At Sandown he lashed out with his heels and squealed in the paddock, but once the race started his bad habits were forgotten, he settled down quickly, and when asked for his effort by Gordon accelerated in the manner of a high-class colt.

As Derby Day approached the public made it clear that they believed that Royal Forest would give Gordon his first Derby triumph. Their belief was heightened when Gordon rode five winners off the reel during the first two days of the Epsom Summer meeting, to prove that he was in top form. On the eve of the race he stayed with friends near Epsom, and refused to take any messages from well-wishers. Meanwhile in London a drama was being enacted as Madame Suzy Volterra, whose husband owned Derby runner Amour Drake, arrived at Victoria station on the Golden Arrow from Paris. Half an hour after reaching the Savoy Hotel with Jack Hylton she received a message that her husband was desperately ill. Hylton organised a charter flight and she flew back to Paris from Croydon at 10.30 p.m.

Derby Day was hot and sultry, and in one of the closest finishes ever witnessed Nimbus, ridden by Charlie Elliott, won by a short head from Amour Drake with Swallow Tail a further short head away third and Royal Forest fourth. A sad but philosophical Gordon told friends after the race that he had another twenty years riding ahead of him, and would one day achieve his ambition. Meanwhile, as he

Gordon on Top Walk with Captain Rupert Laye.

Below (l to r): Tom Reece, Quintin Gilbey, Gordon and Richard Tauber at
Torquay 1947.

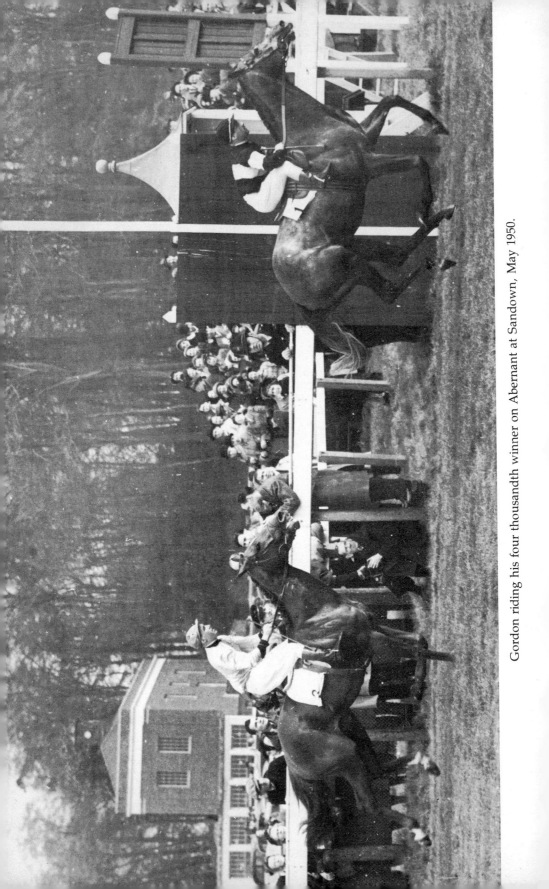

Gordon riding his four thousandth winner on Abernant at Sandown, May 1950.

prepared for rides later in the afternoon, Madame Volterra was telling her dying husband that his horse, Amour Drake, had won — thus giving him the pleasure, in his final hours, of thinking that success at Epsom had been his.

For William Hill, who had bred Nimbus, the Derby was an unforgettable experience. As he stated at a later date, 'You cannot put a cash price upon the thrill of breeding a Derby winner. The following morning I woke up with a victory hangover that few men in a moment of triumph ever have to face. Winning the race brought Mrs Glenister the then record prize of £14,245, but Nimbus' victory cost me £200,000. You see, I had backed Amour Drake to win me that amount, but that did not matter now . . .'

Royal Ascot found Gordon in scintillating form, for he rode three winners, Pambidian, Palestine and Faux Tirage, on the first afternoon, another winner on Gold Cup Day and three on the final day of the meeting to make a grand total of seven victories, in addition to being placed on six other occasions. When he won the final race, the King's Stand Stakes, on Abernant he was deservedly given a rousing reception as he returned to the winners' enclosure. Before the end of the month he had scored another treble at Chepstow to bring his number of winners on the course to 151 since he rode his first winner on the Monmouthshire track in 1927 and once again bookmakers cried out that 'mixed doubles Gordon at Chepstow' would ruin them!

At the Newmarket July meeting he added to Abernant's great reputation by a clear-cut victory in the July Cup, which finished for the first time at the Bunbury Mile winning post instead of at the downhill Exeter course post, in order that the photo-finish camera could be used if necessary. As Abernant slaughtered his two opponents, Star King and Combined Operations, the camera was not required. However, on occasions that it was used, and Gordon was one of those jockeys involved in a close finish, it was very noticeable from studying the photo-finish print that he, much more than many of his contemporaries, sat down in the saddle and drove his horse in front of him, instead of trying to get to the winning post ahead of his mount.

By the beginning of July it seemed that he was on the road to smashing his previous best for a season, for he had already ridden 120 winners, thirty more than at the corresponding period in 1948 and six more than the combined totals of Douglas Smith and Edgar Britt, who were lying second and third in the Jockeys' Table. His supremacy was unchallenged, and his brilliance unimpaired despite the fact that he had reached the age of forty-five. However, he temporarily succumbed to sunstroke. Having ridden the final winner at the Ascot Heath meeting on Friday 8 July, he went home to Marlborough. The following morning he rode out at Beckhampton, and on his return for breakfast complained of a headache. Sunstroke was diagnosed, he retired to bed, cancelled his rides at Ascot that afternoon and stayed out of the saddle for a fortnight.

On his return he thrilled the Goodwood crowds by four consecutive victories on Palestine, Abernant, Krakatao and Diableretta, and was then involved in the verdict given by the Judge, Mr Malcolm Hancock, in awarding the Bentinck Stakes to High Stakes, ridden by Gordon, over Hornet III, ridden by Rae Johnstone, after he had consulted the freak and astonishing photo-finish. It seemed that the Judge had been the victim of an optical illusion for it appeared that the heads of High Stakes and Hornet III had been transposed on the neck of the other. The 'weighed in' was announced, and although under Jockey Club Rules there was no appeal against the result, Joseph Lieux, trainer of Hornet III, asked for an interview with the Stewards. He knew that he and the owner and those who had backed Hornet III had lost their bets, but he hoped that on a technical objection, he might at least receive the winning prize money. When the photo was published, the crowds straining to see it made way for Gordon to scrutinise the print. Diplomatically, he winked and exclaimed, 'It's a near thing', but one disgruntled punter who had invested £3,000 at 6–1 on that Hornet III had won the race was less diplomatic in his observations and his opinion of the unfortunate Mr Hancock. Rae Johnstone commented that when a similar instance had occurred at Le Tremblay the Tote had paid out on both horses to avoid the crowds carrying out their threat of burning down the grandstand. Eventually the High Stakes rumpus came before the Stewards of the Jockey Club who agreed that a mistake had been made, but confirmed that there could be no alteration to the result. High Stakes was the nine hundred and eighty-third winner for Jack Colling, who announced that at the end of the season he intended to leave Newmarket and commence training at Eric Stedall's Ilsley stables.

Gordon rode six more winners at Goodwood which included superb last-moment challenges on heavily-weighted horses to confound the critics who claimed that he could not ride a 'waiting race', and continued on his triumphant way at Chepstow, to bring his total number of successes for the week to fifteen. On the Saturday, news, totally untrue but persistent, was flashed to London newspaper offices that Gordon had been killed in a car crash, and was still pouring into Fleet Street when it was announced that he had just won the first race of the afternoon, at a starting price of 33–1 on! It was also announced that Mr Winston Churchill had purchased the French three-year-old Colonist II, and that Gordon would ride the Walter Nightingall-trained colt whenever possible. Mr Churchill had originally registered his colours as 'chocolate, pink sleeves and cap', but as these were considered to be too similar to those of Jack Jarvis' 'chocolate, pink sleeves', they were altered to 'pink, chocolate sleeves and cap'.

The crowds at Goodwood remained on the Sussex coast to bask in the sunshine, swim in the English Channel and enjoy the racing at Brighton and Lewes the following week. Gordon, on his way to Lewes from Shoreham, got ensnarled in a traffic jam, jumped out of his chauffeur-driven car and began to walk to the races. Recognised by a taxi driver he was hailed with 'Jump in, Gordon. I know a quick way round the back which will be a short cut.' The quick way proved useless and Gordon eventually had to run a further half mile to reach the weighing room in time. 'Not bad for a man of my age' was his subsequent remark, having won the first race on Tommy Carey's filly, Doorlight, trained by Harold Wallington. Later in the afternoon he learned that American Champion Jockey, Johnny Longden, the only contemporary jockey in the world other than Gordon to have ridden more than three thousand winners, was planning to come to England where he hoped to ride against Gordon to size-up the difference between British and American race-riding styles.

Thirty-nine-year-old Longden had left Wakefield in Yorkshire at the age of two when his father, a miner, had decided to emigrate. On his return to England Longden was a millionaire, who flew his own aeroplane from race track to race track in the USA, owned a ranch in Nevada and an estate in California. In his youth he had worked on a Canadian ranch, before becoming Champion Jockey on three occasions. On his arrival in England he made a personal application to the Jockey Club for a jockey's licence, which was granted to him. He spent his first weekend as Gordon's guest at Clements Meadow, and was delighted when his host gave him a conducted tour of Beckhampton.

Days later Gordon was involved in a farcical two horse race at Birmingham, the Midland St Leger Trial, which would have mystified Longden. Noel Murless had given Gordon, on Ridge Wood, instructions not to make the running, and identical orders had been given by Dick Perryman to Tommy Lowrey who had the mount on Courier. In consequence, when the tapes went up, neither horse made a forward move! They stayed put until the starter's assistant cracked his whip in the air behind them. Eventually Ridge Wood and Courier condescended to start, but the race took 5 minutes $13\frac{4}{5}$ seconds, more than double the usual time, and was run amidst louder catcalls and booing than ever heard before on an English racecourse. Not since Gordon had ridden Colorado Kid against Michael Beary on Nitsichin in the 1933 Doncaster Cup had such a ludicrous race been witnessed. Gordon and Tommy Lowrey were both riding to orders, so little blame could be attached to either of them, and with the starter and his assistant not allowed under the Rules of Racing to hit a horse to make it start to race they were powerless to help. Eventually Ridge Wood won by three lengths, and Noel Murless admitted, 'I told Gordon not to make the running. Ridge Wood runs his best race coming from behind. No rule was broken, they can take as long as they like.' If the race had taken place in New South Wales a rule would have been broken, for a schedule of times had recently been laid down for long distance races in Australia, and if the schedule was exceeded the stake money awarded to the winner was halved.

At Bath two days later Gordon rode five consecutive winners, one of which was a two-year-old colt sired by Bois Roussel out of Isle of Capri and owned by Fred Darling. In consequence of these winners, bookmakers refused to accept each way accumulators on his five mounts the subsequent afternoon, for racegoers were beginning to think that he was in the midst of an unbeatable run, reminiscent of his twelve successive victories in 1933. In fact only two of his five fancied mounts obliged, and in the last race he was beaten by his brother Clifford. Gordon's mount started at 9–2 on and Clifford's at 25–1. Nevertheless, the last week in July and the first fortnight in August brought him thirty-six winners from sixty-eight rides and he was so far ahead of his rival jockeys that it was reported as being the equivalent of Henry Cotton winning the Match Play Championship final by ten and eight every year for a quarter of a century.

Inevitably, his every success was analysed and the chance held by his every mount assessed and weighed up. The reasons for his outstanding achievements were discussed and criticised *ad nauseam* — but from such discussion two reasons for his brilliance in the saddle emerged. The first was the fact that at the gate he always had his horse balanced with his legs under him, so that when the starting gate went up, his mount went forward propelled as though a spring had been released, and Gordon, prepared for such jet propulsion, rocketed forward with him. The second factor was that inside the final half furlong Gordon would often give his mount an imperceptible 'easy' to get him on his legs and let him catch his wind. No one knew better than Gordon that it was useless to 'scrub' a horse which was off its balance, but once on an even keel he would hold any horse in a grip of steel with his exceptionally strong legs and drive him relentlessly onwards. Horses ran as straight as a gun-barrel for him and proved time and time again that it is only the perfectly balanced horse who does not swerve under pressure. Years earlier Brownie Carslake had said:

> Gordon has the knack of doing the right thing every time. His perfect balance helps him to stick close to the rails on a round course, and when he throws the reins at a horse in a driving finish his balance keeps the horse straight.
>
> Make no mistake about it. No other jockey could copy Gordon Richards. He is a law unto himself. If any of us tried throwing the reins at a horse the way Gordon does, the horse would swerve all over the place.

From the grandstand it often seemed that Gordon was harsh on his mounts, but in reality he seldom hit them hard with his whip. He had a rhythmic style of swinging his whip at the same pace as the movement of his hand upon the reins, and when he was forced to hit a horse it became necessary to miss a beat, which he was reluctant to do. One interesting criticism, however, that was put forward in some quarters was that he taught the Beckhampton two-year-olds 'to come swinging out of the gate, to sprint and not to stay and thus lost several Derbies'. Such a criticism might be justified if it was levelled at Darling the trainer, but was not justified when held against Richards the jockey.

Confidence and determination were Gordon's stock-in-trade, and although he was superstitious to the extent of believing that if a black cat crossed his path on the way to the races he would ride two winners, his strongest desire was to lead a natural and a normal life. Over the years, he never changed his outlook, never lost his sense of fun, never attempted to lead the life of a hedonistic playboy. During the racing season his invariable routine was to ride work in the morning, race ride in the afternoon, and fly or drive back to Marlborough in the early evening to be with his family, eat a modest supper and go to bed long before midnight. For his veritable army of supporters, many of whom had never been on a racecourse or laid a bet in their lives, it was evident that whatever the secret of his peerless success in the saddle, his sense of sportsmanship and his integrity made him a legend in his lifetime.

10

The Post-war Period

At the Doncaster St Leger meeting Johnny Longden rode for the first time against Gordon – with Gordon finishing first on Beckhampton-trained Wat Tyler and Longden trailing in eighth on the Aga Khan's El Arabi. English jockeys, who watched the race, expressed their opinion that the American style of riding, with its pronounced crouch, did not allow Longden enough control on the wide straight Doncaster course and thought that he would do better on a twisting and turning track.

In the St Leger Gordon rode Krakatao, after Royal Forest was scratched, having strained a tendon. Once again he suffered the frustration of being unplaced on the more fancied Beckhampton colt, seeing another Murless-trained horse romp home to victory. Michael Beary rode Ridge Wood, thus completing five remarkable and unusual Classic results throughout the season, in that each Classic race was won by a horse bought at public auction.

At the end of the season Gordon, who headed the Jockeys' List with 261 winners, whilst Douglas Smith was in second place with 136 and Edgar Britt in third position with 112, gave his opinion that it was not necessary to import overseas jockeys to ride for the largest and most influential English stables. He even suggested that certain members of the Racing Press spent too much time praising certain jockeys, criticising others, and never giving the lesser lights a break, and added the interesting and provocative thought that it might be better to import a few foreign trainers.

In December the Shropshire Sportsmen gave a celebration dinner at the Forest Glen Pavilion, Wellington, with Gordon Richards and Billy Wright the two principal guests. The Forest Glen Pavilion, presided over by genial and beloved John Oswald Pointon, had been built at the end of the nineteenth century after Lord Forester had granted Pointon's father a lease of land upon which to erect the Pavilion which was to become the scene of many festive occasions. At many of these a toast was given, and one which was well known to Gordon: 'Here's to His Majesty the King and all members of the Royal family. England never has and never will lie at the foot of a proud conqueror, and may the Devil rain pebble-stones on the feet of our enemies that we know the b . . . s by their limp.'

Gordon, whose reputation as a first-class after-dinner speaker steadily increased over the years, did not fail his fellow diners, and inspired them when he remarked, 'Whatever we've done, whatever we ain't, it's been worth it.' He told them about an old lady in Sheffield who had supposedly put a curse upon him, demanded a fiver, and warned him that until he paid up he would never win the Derby, and suggested that it was about time he paid up. He then received thunderous applause when he continued, 'I am going to win the Derby. Now look. All of you. Keep your menu cards of tonight, and when I have done it, come and join me here under the old Wrekin.'

The winter of 1949–50 passed happily and uneventfully for Gordon who made his annual pilgrimage to St Moritz. However, the farcical race, Ridge Wood versus Courier, still gave ammunition to those who disliked such events, and the contest had political overtones when a Parliamentary correspondent wrote:

> It may be remembered that towards the end of last year's Flat Racing there was a remarkable incident when the entries had whittled away until only two horses went to the starting post. One was ridden by the Champion Jockey Gordon Richards.
>
> But the race was run so slowly that the crowd began to jeer and after an interminable length of time the race was finally won by Richards whose horse meandered slightly faster than the other.
>
> The Stewards demanded an explanation, and it was revealed that each jockey had been given orders to ride a waiting race behind the other.
>
> There was no suggestion of crookedness, but the jockeys were fined and also warned.
>
> After listening to the King's Speech in the House of Lords and after attending to the opening stages of the debate in the House of Commons I have an uneasy feeling that we are going to see something like the race that I have just described.
>
> His Majesty as the First Servant of the State manfully read the stuff which the Prime Minister had provided for him. The Government had nothing to say and tried to hide the fact by making the speech one of the longest on record.

Two days after the opening of Parliament Gordon was an honoured guest at a luncheon given at the Savoy Hotel by the *Sporting Life* to the Stewards and members of the Jockey Club and the National Hunt Committee. At the lunch where the toast, 'The *Sporting Life* and the Racing Press', was proposed by Lord Mildmay of Flete, the health of Gordon was proposed by Lord Rosebery who, as a nine-year-old boy, had seen Common win the 1891 Derby. Lord Rosebery described Gordon as 'the greatest jockey that I have ever seen' and caused laughter by adding, 'I say this in spite of the fact that he is here listening to me.' Lord Rosebery continued:

> I do not believe in praising jockeys very much, for it is apt to turn their heads, but I repeat Gordon is the greatest jockey that I have ever seen ... People say to me, 'But surely Danny Maher was better?' and after all he rode many winners for my father and sometimes I watched his tactics with terrible apprehension!

The acid test for an owner as regards a jockey is that he should never lose a race which he ought to have won. Of course, every jockey wins races that he ought to have lost, but Gordon Richards, in my opinion, has lost far fewer races that he ought to have won than any other great jockey. He shows the greatest vehemence in all races, whether important ones or selling plates, and never finishes riding until the winning post is well passed . . .

After Lord Rosebery's accolade, the champion was presented with golden spurs by the editor of the *Sporting Life*, A. B. Clements. In his reply Gordon said, 'I never thought that I would get so far along the road, but I suppose that Dick Turpin never thought that he would get to York. The moral is "you never know".'

Gordon began the new season in great style by winning the Lincolnshire Handicap on the George Todd trained Dramatic, who landed one of the most substantial gambles of the post-war years. He missed riding on the first day of the Liverpool meeting later in the week, where Australian jockey Scobie Breasley had his first ride on an English racecourse, and by mid-April was headed in the Jockeys' Table by Doug Smith. Defeated on several odds-on chances, his detractors began to claim that he was ageing, losing his dash and likely to forfeit his crown. In reality many of the horses that he rode were not yet fully fit and his detractors were talking nothing other than balderdash!

He celebrated his forty-sixth birthday in spectacular fashion by riding Abernant to success at Sandown Park. It was his four thousandth victory and the final race of the afternoon. Hundreds of racegoers delayed their departure to greet him on his return to the winners' enclosure. No other jockey in Turf history had ridden so many winners, and as he signed autograph after autograph with the words '4000 not out' the thought that one day he would no longer grace the Racing scene seemed impossible.

Yet for all his brilliance Gordon was criticised as a jockey, as were all other English jockeys, by those whose experience gave them little justification for such criticism. Australian jockey, Jack Thompson, who had begun riding in Ireland, was reputed by a Sydney newspaper to have said, 'English jockeys ride in a fool's paradise. They all ride the same way, reins loose, legs straight. As a result the horses become lazy. The horses are the masters, not the jockeys.' Although Thompson subsequently denied the remarks, they were also refuted by Gordon, by Edgar Britt and by Scobie Breasley, who claimed that in England horses were trained to run lazily and if they were not then they would run themselves into the ground.

As Derby Day approached the question of Gordon's Epsom mount once again became a topic of importance. It was suggested that he might ride Telegram II for M. Francois Dupré, but no one thought that the French colt had more than an outside chance of beating Prince Simon, who was one of the 'talking horses' of the decade and only narrowly beaten in the Two Thousand Guineas by HH Aga

Khan's Palestine, whom Gordon would have ridden had he not been claimed to ride the Beckhampton outsider The Golden Road. Eventually in the Derby he rode a forlorn hope, Napoleon Buonaparte, for thirty-three-year-old Mr Anthony Samuel, a son of the late Lord Bearsted, but they failed behind Galcador and Prince Simon.

In August Gordon had an unhappy day at Bath when he was disqualified for interference after passing the post first in the initial race of the afternoon, and two hours later finished second in the Westgate Stakes to Tai-Yat, ridden by fourteen-year-old Lester Piggott. A week later Gordon clashed again with Piggott at Folkestone, and after winning the third race by a short head from 'the wonder boy' he failed in each of the last three races, in which Piggott was successful on both Blue Sapphire and No Light and second on Corrieuin. Piggott showed that these victories were no flukes by further wins over such champions as Gordon, Carr, Breasley and Britt at Lingfield later in the month. When he won by a head on Lancashire Lassie, beating Oceana (subsequently the dam of Todman and Noholme), he was creating a historic moment for seventy-nine-year-old owner, George Beard, who had seen his 'orange and black' colours carried to victory for the first time when his horse, Leontodar won at Gatwick ridden by Lester's grandfather, Ernest Piggott, in 1899.

Once again Gordon ended the season as Champion Jockey, having ridden 201 winners. The non-staying Fair Trial, eighteen years of age, became leading sire for the first time, to vindicate at long last Gordon's confidence in the Beckhampton-trained horse on whom he had won the Queen Anne Stakes and the Rous Memorial at Royal Ascot, and who had sired Palestine, Petition and Court Martial. A disturbing feature of the sires' list was the absence of young sires amongst the leaders, with Dante's failure to maintain his brilliant promise at stud a disappointing fact.

Gordon returned from St Moritz weighing 9 st 4 lbs and immediately began to go into training to lose 10 lbs before the commencement of the 1951 season. He needed little dieting, and constant road work in the vicinity of Clements Meadow and the occasional game of golf had the desired effect. His legion of followers on the Flat were convinced that he was still the best jockey in the world and were willing to have doubles, trebles and accumulators on his mounts every afternoon. The old cry, 'Follow Lord Lonsdale – you'll get a chance of picking up a half-smoked cigar', had long since changed to 'Follow Gordon – you'll back a winner', and in return Gordon instinctively felt that he owed it to his public to give of his best on every occasion.

He opened his winning account for the season at Kempton and Lincoln, but so too did Lester Piggott who had ridden four winners before breaking his collar-bone in a fall during the first race on Lincoln Day. However, Gordon drew level at Alexandra Park the following Monday where newly-licensed trainer Michael Beary saddled his second winner of the season. Eight Australian jockeys including Breasley, Billy Cook and Neville Sellwood were riding in England during the season and all of them were determined to show the 'jaunty, self-confident Gordon of rolling gait' that they intended to challenge his supremacy. Gordon accepted the challenge and was equally determined to defeat it. To prove his point he won four races including the One Thousand Guineas on Belle of All, trained by Fred Darling's former head lad Norman Bertie, on the eve of his forty-seventh birthday and celebrated his birthday at Newbury by winning on Hard Sauce, Sports Master and Rupert Bear. Greeted on his return to the winners' enclosure by huge crowds singing 'Happy Birthday to You' he was constantly asked if he had decided upon his Derby mount in a year where there seemed no outstanding three-year-old colt. Two Thousand Guineas winner Ki-Ming, trained by Michael Beary, was not considered a great Classic winner and his stamina was suspect, and consequently Turco II, owned by American Mr William Woodward, who had won every major Turf prize except the Derby, was installed the favourite for the Epsom Classic.

It was rumoured that Gordon would ride Stokes, who had been second in the Guineas, for Sir Victor Sassoon, but the horse cut a hind leg as he was being unloaded from a horsebox and became a doubtful runner. Sybil's Nephew, trained by Jack Jarvis, and the winner of the Dee Stakes at Chester, was a possible mount, but even a week before the race when Gordon made a visit to the Stork Club on a charity evening and sang old-time songs to the guests, nothing had been settled. Eventually Stokes satisfied the Newmarket vets that he had recovered from his accident which had required fifteen stitches in his leg, and Gordon took the mount—but to no avail. In a sub-standard year Arctic Prince beat Sybil's Nephew by six lengths, with Stokes toiling in their wake. It was the first time that Gordon had worn the 'peacock blue and old gold hoops' of Sir Victor Sassoon in a Derby, but it would not be the last . . .

Epsom was 'black' for Gordon as he failed to ride a winner, and he rode twenty-nine consecutive losers before breaking his run of bad luck at Lewes. That his long run of misfortune should be banner headlines in newspapers and not merely on the sports pages was proof of the enormous importance attached to his career and to his popularity.

On the opening day of Royal Ascot he was second on Ki Ming in the Queen Anne Stakes, second on Snowdon in the Gold Vase and second on Kameran in the St James's Palace Stakes, in addition to winning the Coventry Stakes on King's Bench. The next day he rode Belle of All to a five length victory in the Coronation Stakes, but despite these triumphs the meeting belonged to Neville Sellwood who won the Hunt Cup, the Bessborough, the Cork and Orrery and the King's Stand Stakes.

Belle of All disappointed Gordon a month later when unplaced behind Supreme Court in the newly instituted King George and Queen Elizabeth Festival of Britain Stakes, but Glorious Goodwood made up for the disappointment, for he succeeded on Bakshishi, Le Sage, Tayeh, Librarian, Agitator, Abadan, Prince d'Ouilly, Sea Parrot and Zante. On two of these winners, Abadan and Prince d'Ouilly, he inadvertently dropped his whip a furlong from home, but still won handsomely. Frivolously, he was asked by Charlie Elliott if he would like to borrow a shooting stick with a loop around the handle or else a whip and some string—but the offer was declined.

On his return home he received a letter from his twenty-year-old son Peter, who was being taught the art of training by Paddy Prendergast, telling him that he was working harder than ever, due to a strike of stable lads, who were demanding an increase of ten shillings a week on their average four pounds a week wages. For Peter the strike meant that he had to get up at 6 a.m. to groom and exercise nine horses instead of his usual two. Prendergast, refusing to give in to the strikers, rounded up his neighbours, friends and farm workers to groom and exercise his thoroughbreds.

By mid-August Gordon was continuing to show brilliant form with twelve winners in a week, including four winners in an afternoon at Folkestone, of which the first three were a treble for Miss Dorothy Paget, which should have been a four-timer but for the refusal of the 11–2 on Snowdon to exert himself. A furlong from the winning post Gordon was sitting as still as the proverbial mouse and looked a certainty. Tommy Gosling on Knuckleduster had other ideas, and began to close upon the leader. As he did so, the holiday crowd yelled a warning to Gordon, but the yell appeared to go unheeded. Snowdon began to go slower and slower as Knuckleduster increased the tempo of his challenge, and at the vital moment was a length clear. A disconcerted Dorothy Paget asked Gordon, 'Were you caught napping?' 'Emphatically no,' was the reply, 'I knew what the crowd were shouting for, but Snowdon is a horse that you simply must not move on or he starts to go backwards. I just had to sit and hope and suffer. Maybe if the crowd had not made such a noise he would have done enough to win.'

At York Gordon won the Gimcrack for American owner Ray Bell, a former cowboy from Wyoming, on Paddy Prendergast-trained Windy City. As the tapes flew up, Gordon lost both his irons, and it was not until halfway that he had regained control of his brilliantly fast colt. Ray Bell liked to both buy and sell horses, and called the yearling Windy City, the nickname of Chicago, in the hope that a wealthy Chicago businessman might wish to purchase him if for no other reason than the horse's name.

Five months later, Ray Bell's speech was read at the historic Gimcrack Dinner. Business commitments prevented his attendance, and Gordon, suffering from a strained groin, was another absentee. Bell declared that America could give Britain lessons in Racing showmanship, and advocated running commentaries on every race. He said:

There were occasions last autumn at Newmarket when I would have been grateful for the harsh tones of an American race announcer, and I believe that even my most conservative neighbours in the grandstand would have forgiven his strident tones for the sake of the forthright information and a suggestion of what was going on out there in the invisible distance . . . Crowds are important to us in America. We go out of our way to attract crowds, and through long experience we have gained wisdom in the way of crowds. Our way of doing things is to allow crowds to dictate their own terms . . .

The 1951 season produced few more highlights for Gordon. At Bath in September he was unhorsed but unhurt when his mount dug in his toes on the way to the start as a fair-haired little girl, who had been picnicking with her family, put her head under the rails to gain a better view of the horses. Such an indignity was remedied when he heard that his nineteen-year-old niece, Betty, daughter of his brother Clifford, and secretary to George Beeby at Compton, had won the Newmarket Town Plate, but was reinflicted when he attended a Royal Variety Show at the Victoria Palace. An attractive woman approached and asked for his autograph. Gordon was about to sign when the woman said, 'You are Wee Georgie Wood, aren't you?' She should have known better, for Gordon, Stanley Matthews, the 1951 winning Cambridge boat race crew and other famous personalities were parading in 'British Champions of Sport'.

The end of the season shock was the news that Noel Murless had decided to leave Beckhampton. Murless announced, 'I have never felt very well at Beckhampton, therefore not entirely happy there, so I have decided to give up my appointment. There has been no trouble, it is just that I wish to go. Of course, I am sorry in many ways. I do not think that I shall go back to Yorkshire, and I have no immediate plans, but I shall continue to train.' In four seasons he had sent out 220 winners of £178,405 and won both the One Thousand Guineas and the St Leger.

As soon as the news broke that Murless would depart at the end of the 1952 season Gordon was asked if he would give up riding and begin training at Beckhampton. To such questions he wisely refused to make any answer and 'no comment' was his constant reply. Many of his admirers thought that it would be pointless for him to give up riding for he seemed to have matured with age, perfected his tactical approach to each and every race and curbed his natural impetuosity. Years of riding over the same race tracks had enabled him to master their intricacies, and on such courses as Bath, Chepstow and Brighton he was almost invincible. He knew the precise moment at which to begin his challenge and time and time again snatched victory on a horse which was not the best in the race.

Gordon returned in February from his annual trip to St Moritz suffering from flu. He was compelled to miss the stable lads boxing at Marlborough for the first time since the end of the War, walked about wearing a cap with ear-flaps to counteract earache, but felt sufficiently well to take a week's holiday in Torquay with Dudley Williams. Whilst in Torquay he learned that Frank Hartigan, who had been training since 1906, planned to retire 'sometime this year'. At the age of seventy he felt that he had been in harness for long enough, and when asked to mention the highlights of his career always put the victory of Gordon upon Golden King at Liverpool in November 1933 as the most memorable moment of his Racing life.

Gordon was expected to retain his Champion Jockey title during the year, despite the claims of Manny Mercer, Eph and Doug Smith, W. Nevett, J. Sime and sixteen-year-old Lester Piggott, who rode for the first time since he had broken his leg at Lingfield in August 1951, when he partnered Princess Pet in the Stonebow Selling Plate at Lincoln on the first day of the season. Unfairly, and without justification, it was rumoured in the Lincoln pubs that he had greeted Gordon at the start with the words, 'Move over, grandpa, make way for the winner', but quite rightly such a remark was denied by both Lester and Gordon. The Press were beginning to compare the two jockeys, treating them as the veteran and the rising young star, and whenever Piggott defeated Gordon the newspapers highlighted the result in unnecessary fashion.

At the Epsom Spring meeting Gordon was thrown on the way to the start of the Great Metropolitan by his mount Approval, a top-class hurdler who shied violently at a path crossing the course and shot Gordon out of the saddle. An ambulance came up the course to collect the injured jockey, but after rubbing an injured knee Gordon decided that he was fit to ride. Approval failed to reach the first four.

The same afternoon, the 1952 edition of *Who's Who* was published. Amongst leading sportsmen Gordon, Jack Hobbs, Walter Hammond and Donald Bradman were included, but no mention was made of Len Hutton, Fred Perry or Stanley Matthews. The publishers, in their preface said 'It cannot be stated too emphatically that inclusion in *Who's Who* has never at any time been a matter for payment or of obligation to purchase the volume,' so Gordon, alongside Hobbs and a very few champion sportsmen, may well have felt pleased to have been included when such men as General Franco and Marshall Tito had never been amongst the *élite* whose biographical details were listed.

It was thought that Gordon would win his fourth Two Thousand Guineas on Mr John Dewar's Agitator, but the colt ran a very disappointing race behind French challenger Thunderhead II, and left Gordon in a quandary for the umpteenth time as to his Derby mount.

Ironically, in 1952 Murless did not have a top-class three-year-old colt at Beckhampton in a season which evidently was not a vintage year for Derby contenders. Eventually Gordon decided to ride Monarch More and in the Derby Dinner Sweepstake at the Savoy Hotel bid £150 for his mount, which had been drawn by the Duke of Norfolk. There was no further bid and Gordon had his mount knocked down to him for the lowest price for any of the runners. At the dinner consensus of opinion was that if a 'dark horse' had made rapid improvement in the past few weeks then he would win the Derby.

Tulyar proved to be such a horse and in the capable hands of Charlie Smirke won the Derby by three-quarters of a length from Gay Time, ridden by Lester

Piggott, to give HH Aga Khan his fifth Derby. Smirke and Gordon had both enjoyed their first Derby ride in 1924, whilst Charlie Elliott, who rode Argur for M. Marcel Boussac in the 1952 race, had first been given a Derby mount thirty years earlier when he rode Satelles in Captain Cuttle's year.

Gordon fared no better in the Oaks, but at Chepstow the following Monday had the pleasure of winning on Her Majesty's Ardent, running in the name and colours of the Duke of Norfolk. It was the third winner since her accession and the first by a horse leased from the National Stud, the other two victories being achieved by Sandringham-bred horses trained by Captain Cecil Boyd-Rochfort.

At the Lingfield June meeting, held on a dreaded Friday 13th, Gordon had a marvellous day, riding four winners including Hoar Frost, trained by his long standing chum Midge Richardson, who had been given his first ride in public as long ago as 1913. Gordon and Midge had acted as perfect foils in the weighing room for many years and some of Midge's famous bowler hats had been demolished by Gordon in friendly jockeys' dressing-room rags. After the day's racing was over, Gordon went to the nearby headquarters of the International League for the Protection of Horses and opened a horsebox named after Golden Miller and endowed by Dorothy Paget.

At Royal Ascot Gordon won his fifth Gold Cup on the Maharaja of Baroda's Aquino II, and his first at Ascot since scoring on Felicitation in 1934, for the other three victories had been at Newmarket during the Second World War.

Throughout the summer he was preoccupied with thoughts as to his future after Noel Murless's departure from Beckhampton. He had lived in the Marlborough area for almost thirty years, and to uproot himself and his family from a part of England that they all adored was unthinkable. Therefore, any offer, however tempting, which would necessitate leaving Marlborough would be rejected out of hand. What were the alternatives if he remained a jockey? To accept a retainer from Mr Dewar who still controlled Beckhampton was one possibility, but Mr Dewar might decide to sell Beckhampton. Miss Dorothy Paget, HH Aga Khan and Sir Victor Sassoon had all made attractive overtures to him, but their horses were not trained in the vicinity. Another possibility was to accept a new career as a trainer, but his life-long ambition of riding the winner of the Derby was still unfulfilled, and when all was said and done he was continuing to ride far more winners than any of his rivals. There had been a thought that he might accept a retainer from Mr James V. Rank, for Druid's Lodge was not far from Marlborough, but Mr Rank had died suddenly in January.

Six months later Mr Rank's bloodstock empire, including stallions Orthodox, Hyperbole and Jock Scot, were sold at Newmarket. Six horses in training were excluded, one of whom was Gay Time, selected by his widow and bequeathed to her in his Will. Bidding was sticky and at one moment Gordon found himself bidding the ridiculously low figure of six hundred and sixty guineas for the two-year-old Fellermelad, who ultimately made three thousand guineas. Druid's Lodge was purchased by Mr Jack Olding who insisted that Noel Cannon remained as his trainer. Cannon also took over the horses of Mr Dewar who had sold Beckhampton during the summer to Mr Herbert Blagrave.

Fifty-three-year-old Herbert Blagrave lived at The Grange, Beckhampton, and had substantial property interests in Reading. In 1941 he had acquired the Harwood Stud near Newbury from the executors of Lady James Douglas and during the 30s and 40s had considerable success with horses acquired from M. Leon Volterra. Couvert, Atout Maître, Master Vote, Vic Day and Royal Drake all carried his colours successfully. When he heard that Mr Dewar was contemplating selling Beckhampton he made an offer which was accepted and Mr Dewar joined forces with Mr Olding.

Herbert Blagrave always thought that Dewar had only acquired Beckhampton to satisfy Fred Darling and never had as great an interest in the training establishment as he did in his Homestall Stud at East Grinstead. In 1938 Colin Richards had become travelling head lad to Blagrave and had returned to Beckhampton at the end of the War. As loyal and dedicated as Gordon, he epitomised the perfect travelling head lad and was of the greatest assistance to his employer.

Years earlier Gordon had 'crossed swords' with Mr Rank as a result of an incident in Ostend. Gordon considered that a hectic and hard-working six-day week was ample toil for any man, and seldom accepted rides on the Continent on Sundays. When, however, a horse from a stable who retained him ran in France or Belgium on the Sabbath he rode it. In 1937 he flew to Ostend to ride His Grace, owned by Mr Rank in the Grand International d'Ostende. On his arrival on Saturday evening Charlie Elliott told him that M. Boussac's Corrida was a certainty. Gordon, together with Tom Reece, Quintin Gilbey, Donald Snow and Archie Burns dined in style and then went to the casino, where Mr Rank saw them in the early hours of the morning. His Grace was unplaced behind Corrida, and days later Gordon was astonished to receive a letter from Mr Rank upbraiding him and complaining that he did not pay a retainer to a jockey to spend his nights in the casino. Gordon was justifiably furious, and at the Doncaster St Leger meeting told Jack Clayton, who was Mr Rank's racing manager, that he intended taking Mr Rank before the Stewards. Happily the storm blew over, for both Gordon and Mr Rank were too 'big' to allow such an incident to mar their relationship.

In mid-July Gay Time was acquired from Mrs J. V. Rank by the National Stud for £40,000 and leased to the Queen for the remainder of his racing career. Gordon rode him in the Gordon Stakes at Goodwood and won comfortably, much to the delight of members of the Royal family. Historically, the occasion was memorable as the Queen's attendance at Glorious Goodwood was the first by a reigning Sovereign since 1929. After the race the Queen congratulated trainer Walter Nightingall, in whose care Gay Time had been during the summer, and who was now to lose the colt. Gay Time was put into a horsebox and taken to his new abode at Beckhampton later in the afternoon.

Gordon rode Gay Time in the St Leger, but to the disappointment of the Queen, who had travelled overnight from Balmoral, he was unplaced behind Tulyar who won with contemptuous ease, to prove that he was the best three-year-old in training. However, Gay Time's future was not without interest, for an invitation had been received at Buckingham Palace requesting his inclusion amongst the runners for the Washington DC International at Laurel Park. If the invitation was accepted Gordon would have the mount and fulfil Eddie Arcaro and Johnny Longden's long-anticipated dream of persuading him to ride on American race tracks. Eventually the invitation was declined on the grounds that Gay Time had already had a hard and strenuous season, and in consequence did not cross the Atlantic. Longden had always insisted that Gordon might take three or four months to acclimatise to conditions in America, giving as his reasons the facts that their track surfaces were hard instead of soft, and that American breeders bred for speed and not stamina, so that the majority of races were run 'flat out' from start to finish.

Despite Gay Time's failure in the St Leger, the Doncaster meeting was not without significance in Gordon's career. He rode seven winners, including Aquino II who won the Doncaster Cup and Whistler the Rous Stakes in the colours of the Maharanee of Baroda, and in the Tattersall Sale Stakes won by six lengths on the favourite, Sir Victor Sassoon's Pinza. It was only the big colt's second race, and Gordon felt that the power and strength of his mount was exceptional and that his future was full of promise.

By the beginning of October Gordon had ridden 200 winners for the seventh consecutive year, had attended the opening night of the Horse of the Year Show at Harringay where he presented his own trophy for a Show Jumping Competition, and had learned that his fame had spread to Communist Rumania when two Englishmen on a courtesy visit to Bucharest University had announced to cheering crowds that they brought greetings from their great democratic England where the heroes included Gordon Richards. 'Richards, Richards, Richards' chanted the throng of spectators, who clapped with delight when it was explained that Gordon Richards had a huge following of supporters.

A week before the end of the season Gordon was riding at Liverpool on the same afternoon as his son Peter rode for the first time in England when he contested the Final Amateur Riders Stakes at Windsor. Gordon rode a winner but Peter, although having ridden nine winners in Ireland, was unplaced behind Hutchin, ridden by 'ace' Mr John Hislop. Amongst the Windsor spectators was Margery Richards who had come to watch and report to Richards senior concerning the ability of Richards junior.

More important for the family as the season ended was the belief that at long last Gordon might have an outstanding chance of winning the Derby. Norman Bertie, former head lad to Fred Darling, trained a useful two-year-old named Fountain for Mr R. F. Watson. One morning on the Newmarket gallops Gordon was riding Fountain and seemed to be winning the trial gallop with ease when a huge backward colt came alongside him and strode away to make Fountain and his rivals look second-rate. The colt was Pinza. Gordon's opinion was that this

Discussing the prospects in the paddock with Her Majesty the Queen and the Duke of Edinburgh, Derby Day, 1953.

Gordon on Pinza in the winners' enclosure, Epsom 1953.

Sir Gordon Richards and his wife relax at Clements Meadow on the day after Pinza's Derby victory.

A week before the 1954 Flat season opens, Gordon and his trainer George Garrard set the pace ahead of Soda.

ungainly young horse must be 'something out of the ordinary' even though Darling described him on first sight as 'nothing but a great big Suffolk Punch'. The opinion of Gordon was endorsed when Pinza won at the Doncaster St Leger meeting. Although subsequently Pinza was beaten in the Royal Lodge Stakes at Ascot, the five length victory which he had gained in the Dewhurst Stakes made Gordon believe that at long last his Epsom dreams might come true. Years of disappointment, when he had been compelled to ride non-stayers had blunted his exuberance, but deep in his heart he was beginning to wonder whether 1953 might not be his greatest and most memorable year.

II

The Glorious Year

Gordon's plans for the winter remained unvaried, and whilst Charlie Smirke flew to Jamaica, Bill Rickaby to India and Lester Piggott to Athens where he intended to ride throughout January and February, Gordon took a short holiday in Torquay, spent happy days shooting in the vicinity of Marlborough, and then travelled to his beloved St Moritz. In the spring of 1953 he was unable to attend a lunch at the Savoy to celebrate the bicentenary of the Jockey Club, at which he was to have been one of the principal speakers, due to a mild attack of influenza, but proved that he had lost none of his brilliance by riding six winners in the first week of the season.

Much to his annoyance a black eye caused by a horse rearing up and striking him in the face during a Newmarket gallop precluded his riding at Kempton on Easter Monday, for he loved all Bank Holiday meetings, but he was back in action within two days. Frustratingly, he was soon to be in the wars again, and a strained leg muscle prevented his riding at the Epsom Spring meeting. The injury proved more serious than expected, and he was also compelled to miss the Two Thousand Guineas meeting at Newmarket.

He did not ride for three weeks and the constant refrain in newspapers from John o'Groats to Land's End was 'Is the champion about to retire?' It was mentioned that at the age of forty-nine he was bound to feel the stress and strain of his professional life far more than a younger man, and the hoary chestnut of 'What will Gordon ride in the Derby?' once more became front page news. Every conceivable statistic concerning his Derby record was dragged into prominence, but the most crucial factor seldom highlighted. This was that he had always been restricted to riding horses from stables for which he had retainers, unlike Donoghue who rode six Derby winners, having treated owners with total disdain and lack of loyalty in his determination to win 'The Blue Riband of the Turf'.

However, although rumour-mongers persisted in decrying Gordon on the grounds of his age, and wiseacres claimed that he would never ride again, Gordon was to confound them in no uncertain manner. At the Newmarket Second Spring meeting Pinza made his debut in the ten furlong Newmarket Stakes against five opponents, two of whom had already won at Sandown since the start of the season. Pinza toyed with them to win by four lengths, with Gordon looking over his shoulder for non-existent danger. Trainer Norman Bertie was thrilled at the ease of Pinza's success, especially since his training had been carried out under difficulties. In December Pinza had skidded and fallen when crossing the Bury Road and several gravel stones became embedded under his skin. The wound was washed out and appeared to be healing, but two months later it again became inflamed. A tiny stone, more deeply embedded than the others, had not been noticed and now had to be cut out. This setback prevented his running in the Two Thousand Guineas as planned, and in which he would have been ridden by another jockey as Gordon was 'on the sidelines'.

Admittedly, paddock critics at Newmarket were disparaging about Pinza's 'common' look, but none could claim that on his breeding he would not stay the Derby trip, and after his decisive victory he was immediately made second favourite for the Epsom Classic, with Two Thousand Guineas winner Nearula favourite and Aureole third favourite. A recurrence of Nearula's lameness, after a foot injury which stubbornly refused to answer to treatment, caused Captain Charles Elsey's hope to drift in the Derby betting, and Aureole was installed as favourite after his convincing victory in the Derby Trial at Lingfield.

Yet Pinza continued to please everyone at Newmarket, and Stanley Matthews having at long last won a Cup Final medal was considered a very favourable omen for Gordon, who was inundated with letters and cards from well-wishers in the days before the Derby. Lady Munnings sent him a good luck charm from her Pekinese Black Knight, with a message that he would employ all the vocal cords at the command of a Pekinese to 'bark you home, Gordon', but such a message was as nothing compared with those which poured into Clements Meadow when it was announced in the Queen's Coronation Honours List that Gordon Richards was to receive the accolade of knighthood for services to horse-racing in Great Britain. No honour was ever more richly deserved, and as cricket acclaimed the knighthood awarded to Jack Hobbs and the theatre that given to John Gielgud, Racing extravagantly wallowed in the pleasure and excitement of Gordon's honour, knowing that no one would wear the dignity more fittingly or more modestly than he.

The knighthood aroused considerable interest in America, and a leading sports writer commented that 'It may break down snobbery towards professionals who are forced to use the tradesman's entrance.' It also caused amusement at Kingswood School near Epsom where two general knowledge questions were 'What is the longest day of the year?' and 'What is the shortest night?' The answer to the first was invariably correctly put as 'June 21–2'. To the second so many scholars answered 'Sir Gordon Richards' that the examiners accepted it!

Gordon had originally been told of the great honour in a letter from the Prime Minister. The night that he heard the news he went to bed early, but on his own admission never slept a wink! Days later Sir Winston Churchill personally congratulated him at Lingfield where the Prime Minister's colt, Prince Arthur, was unplaced to Aureole, and explained that the Queen was very pleased, but added 'keep it all under your hat until the Honours List is announced'.

When the news was made public Gordon said:

I find it difficult to express in words what I feel about this great honour. Naturally I am very proud, but my greatest delight is that the Queen has honoured the jockey profession. Among my treasures at my Marlborough home is a gold cigarette case given me by the Queen's grandfather, and a Munnings painting of the best horse that I ever rode, the 1942 winner of three Classics, Sun Chariot, which was presented to me by the Queen's father. I said to my wife only a short while ago that I hoped before long to add a present from the Queen to my possessions, but I never dreamed that I should receive such a high honour.

He added

I have now been riding for thirty-three years and cannot continue indefinitely. I shall have to consult the owners who retain me before making a final decision, but I suppose that I shall retire at the end of this season or perhaps next year.

In private his pleasure was intense, with the heart-felt wish that his parents could have been alive to share his joy. Appropriately he rode his first winner since becoming a 'Knight of the Turf' at Leicester, where he had ridden his first winner as an apprentice, and was almost mobbed by the crowd. When the announcer, giving the runners for the first race said 'Number eight—ridden by Sir Gordon Richards' a huge cheer rent the air. Perhaps it was significant that the next race on the programme was won by Lester Piggott.

Once the Leicester meeting was over, Gordon was driven to Newmarket to gallop Pinza before returning to the house at Worthing which he had rented for Derby week. At the London Press Club lunch Lord Derby quipped that 'Gordon was the first man to have been made a knight for his equestrian performances since the Middle Ages. I only hope he is not so much moved that he turns out to ride Pinza in a suit of armour and a lance.' Sir Victor Sassoon summed up the sentiments of everyone present when, having extolled the virtues of Sir Gordon Richards and the confidence that he had in Pinza's ability to triumph, he added, 'There is one fly in the ointment. We should all like to see the Queen win the Derby in her Coronation Year, but she has already won something much more precious—the hearts of all her people.'

Two days before the Derby Gordon was second in the Oaks riding Kerkeb for HH Aga Khan. As he returned to the unsaddling enclosure, a wit shouted at him 'Don't do that in the Derby', and leading racing journalist Clive Graham wrote, 'Never, never, never have I seen a leading jockey ride a worse judged race than Gordon did on Kerkeb. He pushed her from a position away back, fourteenth or fifteenth, went round the outside of five, checked her from running over to the stand-side rails, straightened her out to take the lead rounding Tattenham Corner, and was then overhauled by Ambiguity. If Pinza gets a ride like that, he'll need twenty-one pounds in hand.' However, even Homer occasionally nodded, and Gordon was only human. No one could ride as many races as he did, without an occasional lapse.

During the next twenty-four hours he rode two Epsom winners to show that his skill and judgment were as good as ever despite the criticism of Clive Graham, and in an early morning gallop down Tattenham Corner on Derby Day Pinza proved to him that he was fit to run for his life. After dismounting Gordon told well-wishers, 'Pinza was all right, absolutely grand.' He was enormously impressed with the improvement made by Pinza in his ability to negotiate Tattenham Corner. At his first attempt he had, according to Gordon, seemed 'like a camel', whilst at his second attempt he had rounded the notorious turn 'like a bird'.

The news that Mount Everest had been successfully conquered added zest and jubilation to the morning as 750,000 people made their way to Epsom Downs. Hours later Pinza seemed nervous and excited in the paddock, whilst his chief rival Aureole, owned by the Queen, was calm and sedate. Few had eyes for any of the other twenty-five contestants for the one hundred and seventy-fourth renewal of the Derby Stakes, and only those intimately connected with them gave them more than a cursory glance. For the Queen to win the Derby in Coronation Year would be like a fairy tale having the happiest of endings, whilst for the newly knighted Sir Gordon Richards to achieve success would be equally exhilarating. A dead-heat might be the perfect solution, but if either Aureole or Pinza was victorious, then jubilation would be boundless.

In the pre-race parade in front of the packed grandstands the roles of Pinza and Aureole were reversed, with Aureole beginning to buck, kick and lash out whilst Pinza became more placid with every moment. The start was not long delayed, and since the early pace was not strong, Charlie Smirke elected to send Shikampur into the lead at the mile post. He maintained his lead until the straight was reached, with Pinza moving through into second place, some three lengths ahead of Aureole, Premonition, Mountain King and Good Brandy. As the race approached its dramatic climax it could be seen that Pinza was full of running, and that bar an accident the race was within his grasp. But 'bar an accident' can be ominous words and few spectators realised that Gordon's reins had become unbuckled.

Luckily the buckle held, Gordon never noticed that anything was wrong, and Pinza stormed clear to win by four lengths from Aureole to bring himself immortality and Gordon the complete fulfilment of a life's ambition. What thoughts go through the brain of a man at such a moment of glory? Exultation, a sense of relief, a feeling of humility, a realisation that one has reached the peak of one's endeavour. These and many other thoughts, all of them instant and instinctive, are immediately overtaken by the appreciation that reality is the keyword to the occasion.

As Gordon rode back in triumph to the incessant roars of the crowd his face was impassive — outwardly hiding his innermost knowledge that his heart was pounding with excitement. It would have been understandable if he had flung himself from the saddle, grabbed the nearest spectator and cried out, 'I've done it, I've done it.' But such an exhibition was not in his character, and as he was led into the hallowed winners' enclosure, congratulated by owners, trainers, Jockey Club members and friends, his credulity was stretched to the utmost limits. Had he really won the Derby? Had he succeeded at long last—and within days of becoming a knight? Or was it all a dream from which he would wake up to the cold dawn of reality? That it was reality was proved to him within minutes, for having weighed-in, he was taken to the royal box where the Queen, hiding her own disappointment at Aureole's defeat, congratulated him, Sir Victor Sassoon and Norman Bertie on their moment of triumph.

In retrospect Gordon told reporters that:

Pinza is a grand horse. Don't say I won. Say he won. I could not have done it without him. I know. I've tried to win the Derby before on goodness knows how many other animals. He took it all in his stride, the parade, the starting gate, everything. Even the race itself. He's a fighter. We were lucky enough to get a place on the rails right at the start. And there we were, lying seventh or eighth at the top of the hill. We had a clear run down to Tattenham Corner on the inside, no interference at all. I somehow knew, even then, that this was going to be it. This was my year. And at the Corner I knew that I had the race won. Pinza's a fighter, he'd fight all the way home. Shikampur was still in front . . . Three furlongs out I began to put in my challenge. I never touched Pinza with the whip. I did not have to. Everything that I asked him to do, he did in the way that only a good colt will. The moment that I asked him to go he responded, and we were in front. Nothing came near us . . . At first I could hardly realise that I had won—but now I am as happy as can be.

As a token of his happiness he generously asked his valet George Smyth to make a list of every gateman on duty at Epsom and gave each of them a fiver, and every jockey's valet a tenner in addition to the two hundred and fifty pounds which he gave to George Smyth, thus keeping a promise made thirty years previously that he would give that specified sum to his valet when he won the Derby for the first time. Amongst the Epsom spectators were several of his St Moritz friends who came to England every year to watch the Derby from a grandstand box.

Throughout the weekend messages of congratulations poured into Clements Meadow from every corner of the world. From Jockey Clubs as far apart as Egypt and Hong Kong, from well-wishers who had never seen a racecourse, from overseas friends and local councillors. Johnny Longden phoned Gordon from California, and his beloved ninety-year-old Newmarket landlady Mrs Seamans sent him a telegram—one of more than a thousand received at the Marlborough post office within twenty-four hours. It had always been Mrs Seamans dearest wish that Gordon would win the Derby—but misguidedly she was worried that his knighthood might affect his concentration in the saddle and wished it had not been announced until after the race. She died a few days after Pinza's victory.

Gordon went to bed early on Saturday night knowing that his most important self-appointed task on Sunday would be to go to Beckhampton to give the dying Fred Darling a stride for stride account of the race. During Sunday morning before he set out for Beckhampton an aeroplane gave a victory roll over his house, and his motor-salesman son Jack, who had listened to the commentary on a car radio at Lord's cricket ground, arrived to congratulate him and also, as Gordon explained, 'in the hope that he can sell me a new car!'

Fred Darling had always been convinced that Pinza was potentially a champion. He had asked Mr Dewar to buy his dam Pasqua for him at the 1949 Newmarket December Sales when she was submitted by Mrs Morriss from the Banstead Manor Stud, explaining to Mr Dewar that he would not have returned from South Africa at the time of the sales. Mr Dewar agreed to Darling's request and bought Pasqua for two thousand guineas. Twelve months later Darling re-submitted Pasqua at the Newmarket Sales and also sold her yearling colt by Chanteur at the 1951 Tattersalls Sales. The purchaser was Sir Victor Sassoon who gave the absurdly low price, by his standards, of one thousand five hundred guineas for the colt whom he named Pinza.

When Gordon visited Darling at Beckhampton to give him a first-hand account of the Derby, the great trainer was only being kept alive by his own indomitable courage. Weighing little more than six stone he fought death in order to be alive at the time of the Derby, the commentary of which he listened to on the wireless. Pinza's victory, and a gracious letter he had received from the Queen, wishing him a return to health and explaining that if Aureole did not win the Derby she hoped that Pinza, whom he had bred, would achieve success, made his final days memorable and brought him contentment. He died on 9 June, three days after the Derby. Gordon learned of his death at Lewes races. He had realised two days earlier that 'the Guvnor's' death was imminent, but nevertheless the shock was great and his sorrow immense.

In his Will Darling made many bequests to his relations and those who had worked for him at Beckhampton. He specifically bequeathed some of his best Racing pictures, the gold cuff links that Gordon had given to him and other valuable souvenirs of great triumphs, but did not name Gordon as a beneficiary.

A fortnight after the Derby Gordon found to his disgust that during the night Clements Meadow had been burgled. He discovered the robbery when he went downstairs at 7 a.m. and saw that several rooms had been ransacked. The golden spurs presented to him at a *Sporting Life* lunch, the gold cigarette case given to him by King George V after he had broken Archer's record in 1933, and about fifteen pounds in cash had been stolen. Gordon appealed for the return of the stolen items, which were of great sentimental value. Happily his appeal did not fall upon deaf ears, and within days the stolen items were returned.

Two days after the burglary Gordon went to Buckingham Palace to receive his accolade. Later in the day he flew to Newmarket where he rode three horses into second place during the afternoon and suffered the indignity of being accosted by a woman who took an ice-cream out of her mouth and kissed him as he walked to the paddock. At his request, and by permission of the Stewards of the Jockey Club, he continued to be referred to as 'G. Richards' over the public address system and on the number-boards.

Pinza duly won the King George VI and Queen Elizabeth Stakes with Gordon in the saddle, and Aureole again the runner-up. A month later Gordon scotched all rumours that he would retire when he announced that he had arranged his retainers for 1954 — Noel Murless at Newmarket would have first claim, Norman Bertie second and thirdly the Maharanee of Baroda, whose horses were now trained at Lambourn by Peter Nelson.

Before the end of the season Gordon had won three races on the Queen's Landau, sired by Dante out of Sun Chariot, and racecourse gossip was that he might complete a notable Derby double by winning the 1954 Epsom Classic in her colours riding this superbly bred colt. He had also won the Cambridgeshire upon Lord Lambton's Jupiter to land a considerable coup for Rufus Beasley's Malton stable. Rufus had been very confident that Jupiter would win the Britannia Stakes at Royal Ascot but he ran badly, and on dismounting, Willie Snaith stated that the horse required blinkers. Three days later, wearing the 'rogues badge', he won the Wokingham by three lengths. When the Cambridgeshire weights were published Jupiter had been allocated 8 st 2 lbs and Beasley immediately contacted Gordon and asked him to ride. Gordon agreed to do so, and the stable commission was commenced at 33–1.

A week later the colt was ante-post favourite when disaster struck, for Jupiter began to cough. Beasley had the Devil's own task to keep Jupiter fit, and at one time, after he had run badly at York, Gordon suggested that he might be released to accept the offer to ride the top-class colt King of the Tudors. Beasley persisted that Jupiter had a great chance; Gordon agreed to abide by his original decision, and the stable became even more confident after Lord Lambton's colt put up a brilliant trial gallop at Malton, giving Brunetto a stone and beating him three lengths. In the Cambridgeshire Gordon rode a perfect race and won comfortably, not only to land the very substantial gambles for the patrons of Wold House, but to achieve his own first Cambridgeshire victory. For Beasley it added to his great record in the race, for he had saddled Sterope to win in 1948 and 1949, whilst Brunetto had been third in 1951.

Throughout the autumn the Urban District Council at Oakengates were considering the manner in which they could permanently honour Gordon. Many local inhabitants wished to erect a statue to their hero, but Gordon would not contemplate such a suggestion. He proposed that a permanent dispensary for sick animals be established — and at his request this was done, with veterinary surgeons giving their services free.

At the end of the year Gordon and his wife returned to Oakengates for several days of celebrations. At the outset he attended a service in Wrockwardine Wood Church and heard the rector say, 'many of us remember you as a small boy who used to ride bare-back on a pony here, and ride remarkably well. That small boy has now grown into a great national figure of whom every one of us is extremely proud.' Later Gordon was presented with an illuminated address at the local cinema. The address, the work of a Shrewsbury artist, included illustrations of Buckingham Palace; his birthplace; Donnington Wood C of E school; Clements Meadow; the church at Gerrards Cross where he was married, and Pinza. He gave away prizes at the local school and visited his old home in Ivy Row. There he met a very old lady whom he had known when he was a boy. As they were introduced, the old lady said, 'Well, if it is not old Gordon', and added, 'You know I have been practising to call you Sir Gordon and there, I've forgotten all about it!'

In the evening he was guest of honour at a public dinner organised by the Chamber of Commerce and the Oakengates UDC. At the dinner and dance, he was presented with an illuminated address which ended, 'May you long be associated with Racing where your illustrious name and motives are regarded as an influence for the good.' Geoffrey Gilbey proposed the toast to 'British Racing' to which Noel Murless replied. Gordon's health was proposed by Lord Forester and at the end of his speech and before Gordon's reply, the radio commentary by Raymond Glendenning of Pinza's Derby victory was played. As Gordon stood up on a chair, in response to the clamorous demands of his audience who wished to get a better view of him, the guests spontaneously began singing 'For he's a jolly good fellow'. In his speech he told his audience how he came home one night after racing in the spring:

I was greeted by my wife with 'Good evening, sir.' This 'sir' business went on, 'Will you have some soup, sir?' 'Will you have this and that, sir?' my wife kept saying. It took me some time to discover what the 'sir' business was all about.

Then I was given my mail and among it was a letter from No 10 Downing Street. The letter said that Sir Winston had put my name forward to the Queen for a knighthood and if I had no objection the matter would be proceeded with.

Well, I never had a wink of sleep that night. I could imagine fellow jockeys like Charlie Smirke saying as I went into the weighing room 'Morning, Sir Gordon.' They would pull my leg properly.

A few days later I saw Sir Winston. He said to me, 'I have put your name before the Queen and she was delighted. But whatever you do keep it under your hat.'

With those words Sir Gordon looked with a smile towards his wife – obviously inferring that she had kept the news under her hat anyhow.

He ended his speech:

When a fellow leaves his home town or village they often say that they are glad to get rid of him. But you know you sent for me to come back, and what a come back it is. To be surrounded by a host of old friends makes everything that I have done seem so worthwhile.

Such words delighted his audience.

Behind the scenes Gordon worked hard on his speeches and would rehearse his words over and over again at Clements Meadow. He would ask Margery and his children for their opinion on certain points and took endless trouble to get his words 'just right'.

Throughout the three days of the Oakengates festivities, which helped to collect money for the Sick Animal Dispensary, Gordon and Margery stayed with his unmarried sister, Vera, who had built a house immediately across the road from Bonita where Gordon's father had lived for the last twenty years of his life.

To commemorate the occasion of Gordon's visit a local poet, M. Parkinson, whose family had known the Richards' children in Ivy Row, wrote:

Sir Gordon Richards

In Shropshire village years gone by,
A group of colts would past you fly;
On leading colt—perched up on high,
    Wee Richards lad was riding.

The folk would scatter in dismay,
As thud of hoofs would come their way;
No saddle or bridle in display,
    Madly that boy was riding.

What dangerous tactics! What the heck!
That lad will surely break his neck!
His folk should act! Such madness check!
    He deserves a darned good hiding!

The wizard lad came to his own—
In famous stables world renowned;
And Shropshire folk with pride were blown,
    Watching his wizard riding.

As stage by stage, success his aim,
Proud villagers were glad to claim;

This youth out-classing Archer fame,
Great winners he was riding.

By grit and purpose do we see,
A famous jockey now is he;
A nation's pride—by Queen's decree—
Sir Gordon Richards is riding.

A month later Gordon kept the promise made to almost four hundred Salopians four years previously at the Forest Glen Pavilion that he would be their host at a dinner if he ever won the Derby. At the dinner he disclosed for the first time part of the conversation that he had with the Queen after winning the Derby on Pinza. The Duke of Edinburgh had said, 'Well, Gordon, I suppose that you are going to retire now,' when the Queen stepped forward and exclaimed, 'Oh, no, he is not. He is going to win the Derby for me on Landau next year.'

Before the evening ended, Gordon and his fellow guests were unexpectedly 'kidnapped' by members of the Wrekin Round Table, the Junior Rotary Club. The kidnapping was done in the most gentle but totally determined manner— with the price of ransom being a donation from everyone towards the Table's funds for a Christmas party for blind children to be given to a local Home adopted by the Round Table. The ransom was willingly paid and with alacrity.

The day after the dinner Gordon drove to Torquay for a short holiday. On the Saturday afternoon Shrewsbury were playing Torquay—and Gordon spent several minutes at half-time telling his local team how to play football. His efforts were in vain, but nevertheless he was the first to go into their dressing-room to commiserate with them at the end of the match.

1954 started in its usual manner for Gordon, when he, his wife and daughter, together with his great friends Chris Jarvis and Bill Griggs left for St Moritz. Whilst they were there it was announced that his son Peter, who had just completed three years with Paddy Prendergast, was to become assistant trainer to Noel Murless at Newmarket. With Gordon retained as first jockey to the powerful stable which housed more than eighty horses, it seemed a logical step for Peter Richards to join the establishment, particularly as so many people believed that eventually Gordon and his son would set up their own training establishment. When the offer was first made, Peter was reluctant to accept it at a time when there was a ban on Paddy Prendergast-trained horses running in England and felt that he should delay a move, however golden the opportunity, until the ban was lifted. Paddy was insistent, however, that Peter should return to England and this he did.

Gordon was now approaching his fiftieth birthday and finding it difficult to alter his life style. He still ate sparingly, although he did not believe in going hungry, and continued to drink a considerable quantity of milk. Although virtually a non-smoker, he enjoyed a glass of port, of which he was a connoisseur, and during the War had acquired large quantities of various vintages, which rumour had it he had stored in air-raid shelters! One of his maxims was 'the harder you work the more rest you need', and he seldom slept less than eight hours a night.

He still practised the same procedure for keeping fit, by skipping, physical exercises and seven or eight mile jog trots in the lanes around Marlborough, aided and encouraged by ex-boxer George Garrard, who worked for most of each year as a plasterer in his family's building firm, but insisted on being released for the month of March to help Gordon with his training. He still rode out at Newmarket and Lambourn almost every morning, but found time to devote to the hundred and one calls upon the time of a famous man from unexpected sources. He allowed sculptor Vasco Lazzolo to do a bust which was included in the series 'The Ten Most Eminent Men in England' and patiently answered a host of questions from Roland Orton, the scriptwriter of the BBC tribute to him on his fiftieth birthday.

Orton was told, 'Do not go writing a lot of flowery stuff that will make me into a hero', and the suggestion was made that a meeting at Clements Meadow might be advisable so that 'we can have a little chat'. The time proposed was 8.30 a.m., and Orton, as punctual as his host, found that the first hour of the 'little chat' was devoted to a discussion on racing pigeons with Gordon, in Orton's opinion deliberately steering the conversation away from his career as a jockey. When the broadcast was heard, it included tributes from Noel Murless, the Duke of Norfolk, Harry Wragg, Geoffrey Gilbey and Norah Laye.

On his fiftieth birthday Gordon, who was beginning to find it necessary to wear glasses for reading, rode a winner at Sandown. Days later he told the Press that he would ride Landau in the Derby and that he was confident of victory. However, a fortnight before the race, his hopes were shattered when he was injured in a fall at Salisbury. His mount and that of the apprentice, R. Manders, fell after a mile had been covered in the Devizes Handicap. When the ambulance arrived, Gordon was suffering badly from concussion but appeared unhurt, whilst Manders was still unconscious and had broken his leg. Gordon told his brother Clifford, 'I do not remember a thing about it,' before both jockeys were taken to Salisbury Infirmary. There a house surgeon said, 'Sir Gordon Richards might—I emphasise might—have to rest and not ride for a fortnight. No bones are broken but he has some bad bruising. He has had a really bad knock and was unconscious for nearly half-an-hour. Complete rest and quiet are essential.' The doctor's diagnosis was to some extent countermanded by Gordon's announcement that he was determined to be fit enough for his Derby ride on Landau, who had failed to be placed behind Darius in the Two Thousand Guineas. His announcement was understandable, for what achievement could compare with riding the Derby winner for the Queen of England? Noel Murless made it clear that should Gordon not be able to ride at Epsom, then Landau would still run in the Derby, although no substitute jockey had been engaged.

The Queen sent Gordon a message of sympathy as did Sir Winston Churchill, and he left hospital to return home three days later. As he departed from the hospital, he faced a battery of cameramen and jokingly remarked, 'I hope that there are not thirteen of you.' Diplomatically, but sincerely, he added a tribute to the sister in charge of the private wards and exclaimed, 'I am sorry that I cannot take her with me.'

Four days before the Derby Gordon was advised by his doctors not to ride — unless his headaches disappeared very quickly. Eventually the decision was reached that he could not do justice to Landau, and it was announced that he would not ride at Epsom. Bitterly disappointed, he told reporters that he would be listening to the radio commentary on the race from Clements Meadow, that it was only the second Derby that he had missed in thirty years, and added that he firmly believed that 'if you are in doubt, cut it out'. Willie Snaith was engaged in Gordon's place.

On the eve of the Derby a historic moment came at Epsom when 'ace' American jockey, Johnny Longden, who had flown to Marlborough with his wife earlier in the day to see Gordon, rode Lord Cadogan's Bird Song to win the Durdans Stakes. Using his acey-deucy, one leg shorter than the other style, and inspired by the tips he had received from Gordon, Longden won by a neck, and acquired considerable experience of the Epsom track before riding in the Derby, which gave Lester Piggott his first victory on Never Say Die.

Gordon rode for the first time since his accident when he partnered Sun Festival at Sandown on 11 June, three weeks after he had crashed to the ground at Salisbury. When Royal Ascot opened the following week he seemed fully recovered and won the Cork and Orrery Stakes and the New Stakes on Gold Cup Day. Unplaced on Souepi in the Gold Cup he next proceeded to win the King Edward VII Stakes on Rashleigh, and quickly found himself at the centre of a storm of controversy.

One of the most sensational and dramatic contests ever witnessed by Gold Cup Day spectators and a race in which the Derby victor, Never Say Die, and the runner-up Arabian Night, renewed their rivalry. It resulted in the Stewards lodging an objection to the winner on the grounds of crossing, and after hearing evidence, withdrawing their objection. Gordon, Rickaby, Poincelet, Gosling and Piggott were interviewed, and Piggott was informed by the Stewards that they considered he had ridden in a dangerous manner. They suspended him for the remainder of the meeting and reported him to the Stewards of the Jockey Club. At the subsequent hearing in London, Piggott was told by the Stewards that they had taken notice of his dangerous and erratic riding, both in 1954 and in the previous season, and that in their opinion, in spite of numerous warnings, he continued to show complete disregard for the Rules of Racing and for the safety of other jockeys. The Stewards of the Jockey Club withdrew his licence to ride. Many racegoers, including Lester's father and Lester himself, thought that the verdict was far too harsh — and that it might have been less severe had a camera patrol been in operation.

Unquestionably, it was a race in which an immense amount of scrimmaging took place and with Piggott on Never Say Die attempting to go through a gap which closed in his face. Perhaps Gordon's judicious comment that evening summed it all up: 'Some race! That's all I can say!'

The following afternoon he won the Rous Memorial on Landau for the Queen and proved that he was back to his best form by riding three winners on the first afternoon of the Newbury Summer meeting. He improved his total for the year at Newmarket First July meeting when he won on Tamerlane, Nullabor, Landau and Gloria Nicky, and was also placed second in eight races during the three day meeting.

Early in July it became apparent that Gordon for the first time in his career was seriously considering retirement. However, this train of thought was in no way brought about by a notice which appeared in the *Racing Calendar*: 'Newbury Summer Meeting—Stroud Green Handicap. The Stewards asked G. Richards, rider of Kriss Kringle, why he eased his horse out of a place. They drew his attention to the notice in the Sheet Calendar of 6 May and cautioned him.' What may have influenced Gordon was the knowledge that Colonel Dick Warden, a tenant of one of the Beckhampton yards, was intending to quit the yard in the immediate future. If a new tenant was required, then it was an opportunity for Gordon which might never be repeated.

On the first day of the Eclipse meeting at Sandown Gordon won the final race on Sir Victor Sassoon's Princely Gift. Unbeknown to anyone it was the last winner that he was to ride, the final time that he would thrill racegoers with his inimitable artistry and magic, and provide one of his patrons with yet another triumph.

On Eclipse Day he was unplaced on Miss Dorothy Paget's Apple Tree, who started favourite for the first race, did not have a ride in the second contest, was third on Rhinehart in the Sandown Anniversary Handicap, and third on Landau in the Eclipse. Half-an-hour later he was due to ride the Queen's grey filly, Abergeldie, sired by his favourite horse, Abernant, in the Star Stakes. As he was taking the filly out of the parade ring, she suddenly reared up and toppled over backwards. As she did so, Gordon tried to jump clear, but the stirrup leather held him and he crashed to the ground with Abergeldie. The disaster happened so quickly that horrified spectators were mesmerised, and for an instant seemed as though turned to stone as Gordon lay prostrate and obviously seriously hurt.

Noel Murless, Captain Charles Moore and Gordon's chauffeur, who happened to be on the scene, rushed to his aid. A stretcher was brought and he was quickly taken to the ambulance room clutching a handkerchief and in excruciating agony. Within minutes he was on his way to the Rowley Bristow Orthopaedic Hospital at Pyrford—a distance of twelve miles—whilst frantic telephone calls were made to his surgeon, Mr E. G. Slesinger of Guy's Hospital, and to Lady Richards at Marlborough. Later that evening Mr Slesinger issued a bulletin: 'Sir Gordon Richards' condition is serious, but he is not in any danger. He has dislocated a bone of his pelvis and will not be able to ride again for at least two months.'

The filly which had caused the accident, Abergeldie, had been named after a famous Scottish Castle in Aberdeenshire, where the Duke of Windsor, as a young boy, had climbed the clock tower and put the hands of the clock an hour fast. Locals 'corrected' their watches, but the culprit was found and duly punished by his father.

One of the consequences of Gordon's tragic accident was that it precluded his intention to purchase yearlings at the Newmarket July Auctions, and necessitated his waiting until the Dublin, Doncaster and Newmarket Sales in the autumn. Although few knew how far negotiations with Herbert Blagrave and Jeremy Tree had progressed, it was common knowledge that Gordon had already engaged a skeleton staff and hoped to be installed at Beckhampton before winter approached.

The day after the accident, which *inter alia* brought critical abuse at the dilatory manner in which the Red Cross staff coped with Gordon's condition and bitter complaint from one racing journalist that at least ten minutes elapsed before Gordon was taken to the racecourse hospital, his wife and sister, Rhoda Miller, drove from Marlborough to see him at the Rowley Bristow Hospital. The Queen, staying at Windsor Castle for the weekend, was kept informed of his condition, and sent a get-well message to him.

Eventually his doctors accepted that he was fit to travel, and he flew from nearby Brooklands Aerodrome to Shoreham and was driven to Grand Avenue, West Worthing where he had rented a house. On the eve of his departure television viewers saw him on *Sportsview* when he was interviewed by Peter Dimmock, and in answer to the inevitable question, 'Do you intend to retire?' he answered that he would make up his mind within the forthcoming fortnight.

Few, if any, doubted what his final answer would be, and when the news broke, with poignant finality, that he had decided to retire no one was surprised. Equally there was no one who was not saddened by his decision, for it meant the end of an era. For thirty-four years he had enjoyed every minute of his great career, and realised that he would miss the excitement and thrill of riding winners. What he failed to realise was the immense void which would be left and the sense of loss which the sporting public would suffer on the retirement of their idol. He had ridden in 21,834 races and had won 4,870 of them. Far more important than the honour and glory that these victories brought him was the fact that for more than three decades his integrity and his determination always to do his best had been an example to all jockeys in particular and to all sportsmen in general.

In every era there have been jockeys who have lingered in the saddle for too long, becoming failures as they battled unsuccessfully with age and increasing weight. Others have allowed their financial resources to dwindle until the prospect of retirement has become an appalling nightmare. Gordon's affluence was constantly mentioned in the Press, with ridiculous and exaggerated claims as to his income and his accumulated capital. In truth his capital was not vast—due in some measure to unwise advice to invest heavily in War Loan. Such a course of action, though patriotic, precluded any appreciation to keep pace with inflation.

Tributes to Gordon as a gentleman, as a husband, a father and a jockey flooded national newspapers and it was no exaggeration to claim that every lover of Racing wished him success as a trainer.

Boxer Tommy Farr claimed that Gordon allowed no softness in himself and none in those around him and that he hated vanity, conceit and affectation. John Hislop, doyen of racing journalists, pointed out that to be as successful a jockey as Gordon had been was as severe a test of character as any walk of life could offer, and Gordon had passed the test with flying colours. The good wishes were typified by Charlie Smirke's letter to the *Daily Mail*:

Sir Gordon Richards' decision to leave the saddle and become a trainer will be a great loss to many of us in Racing. We jockeys will miss him especially, for to us he was not only the leading jockey, but also a friend and adviser. Many young jockeys have to thank him for a friendly word of advice, and we older ones always admired his fairness in a race and his calm in a crisis. He was one of the most energetic jockeys I have known . . .

Days later Smirke elaborated his views upon Gordon in an article in the *News of the World*:

You wouldn't believe how different it is in the weighing rooms, now that we know the smiling, helpful, competent Sir Gordon won't ever again come bustling in through the door to join in our joking and fun. You wouldn't understand—unless you, too, lived in this little world that belongs to us jockeys alone—just how much difference the sudden, premature departure of one character makes. Yet it isn't surprising, really.

For, leaving aside all the nice things that are usually said whenever a sporting personality packs up, I am sure there isn't a jockey in the country who wouldn't agree that Gordon Richards is as good as they come—and then some.

Certainly he was one of the finest jockeys and one of the best *men* I've ever ridden against. Certainly he was as good a friend and adviser as a youngster in Racing could ever hope for. Certainly he was the hardest working, fairest, cleverest of us all.

Gordon would fly from his home at Marlborough, perhaps to Newmarket, ride work on five of six horses there, fly to Lambourn to ride five or six more, fly to a racecourse to ride, maybe, in every race on the card, and then get home late at night—ready for another day, just like that.

I couldn't do it—not that and sweat too. I don't think many of us still riding today could face up to such hustling.

I'm a couple of years younger than Gordon but, believe me, I know what a strain this sort of a life can be for a man of forty-eight as I am.

Remember those fighting finishes of his? Gordon never gave up on any horse in a finish. That's a very fine thing to say of a jockey. And it can be said of very few of us. But it was typical of the man.

Sir Gordon Richards with jockey Jock Wilson and Miss Dorothy Paget (second from right) in the paddock at Windsor before The Saint gave him his first success as a trainer.

...f Peace ridden by A. Breasley ...he Middle Park Stakes at New-market, 1956.

These are my instructions. Gordon at
Ogbourne.

Gordon with ace American jockey
Johnny Longden at the 1954 Doncaster
St Leger Sales.

I'll never forget the finish of the 1936 Derby, with Gordon on my tail. You'll remember that both of us were riding for the Aga Khan. I won on Mahmoud and Gordon was second on Taj Akbar.

I was a little lucky, I think, because I was on a horse that was very easy to ride, whereas Taj Akbar certainly wasn't. Besides, Gordon's mount had to be waited with until the last half furlong — which is very hard to do in a great race like the Derby.

Yes, I think I was lucky all right. And that's just one reason why I was so pleased — why all of us were — that he won at last on Pinza after waiting all those years.

And now for Gordon the trainer. My tip is that he'll do just as well at that job, too.

He has ridden for one of the best trainers there ever was, Fred Darling. He has ridden nearly all the best racehorses and, obviously, he is a fine judge of racehorses or he wouldn't have gone as far as he has.

So he has all the makings of success.

Whilst messages of goodwill were being received from many quarters, Gordon began to map out his new career. The weather at Worthing was poor, and the lack of sunshine at the seaside depressed him. In consequence his family packed up and returned from Worthing to Clements Meadow a week earlier than planned. There was little doubt that many owners wished to send him horses, and HH Aga Khan who had only two fillies in training in Britain as compared with the huge number of horses that raced in his colours during the 1930s, was one of those expected to send him yearlings when he moved into the Top Yard at Beckhampton.

12

A new career

The entire Beckhampton property belonged to Mr Herbert Blagrave and comprised the magnificent gallops, the large red-brick house and main yard built by Fred Darling's father, and the Top Yard, which stabled the yearlings and was reputedly built with money won from Captain Cuttle's Derby victory. This yard, which Gordon sub-let from Jeremy Tree, consisted of twenty-six red-brick boxes, with the woodwork painted dark brown. In comparison with the majority of boxes in trainers' yards they were sumptuous and could be described as being as warm and comfortable as a five-star hotel. From them Gordon's horses could walk to the cantering grounds maintained by Herbert Blagrave, and on to the famous trial grounds and Derby gallops on the top of the Downs. He had already engaged Morgan Scannell as his head lad, a travelling head lad and three apprentices, one of whom was Bobby Elliott, to whom he said, 'I entered my first stable on New Year's Day, and you can do the same. It may be lucky.' Jack Blake, who had been at Beckhampton for forty years and had broken Manna, Coronach, Captain Cuttle and Cameronian, was another to join Gordon's team.

Scannell had commenced his racing career with Atty Persse at Chattis Hill and joined Darling's staff in 1925. At Chattis Hill, when he weighed less than five stone he 'did' the flying Tetratema and the Cambridgeshire winner Verdict. He remained with Darling for nearly twenty years before being called up and at the end of the War he took out a licence to train at Sandy Brow, near Tarporley, which had once been the training headquarters of Colonel Hall Walker.

Gordon could have chosen no one better for his head lad, for Scannell was steeped in the Beckhampton tradition. He had walked horses into Marlborough on Sunday evenings, stabled them overnight at the Ailesbury Arms and seen them boxed on the race trains to go to Newmarket, York and Chester. He had ridden all the Beckhampton champions; had looked after Myrobella who at times could be wicked; had been convinced a week before the race that Bois Roussel would beat Pasch in the Derby; and was so indoctrinated with Darling's creed concerning stable management that efficiency was second nature to him. Darling had insisted that his stable staff were immaculate at all times, with boots so highly polished that they shone as brightly as the coats of his horses. The horses would be fed at 6.30 a.m., and although only seriously worked on Wednesdays and Saturdays Scannell and the other stable lads would be lucky if they sat down to their own dinner by 3 p.m. on any day of the week. Hard work never harmed the character or the health of anyone and Scannell was happy to be back at Beckhampton with his new 'Guvnor'.

Gordon had the gift of knowing exactly the correct attitude to take with others and could, as implied by the line in Rudyard Kipling's poem *If*, 'walk with Kings nor lose the common touch'. He always called Fred Darling 'Sir', but throughout his career as a jockey, no matter how great his success, never 'put on side' or was 'swanky' with the stable employees to whom he was invariably kind and considerate.

Scannell was sent by Gordon to an auction sale of stable equipment at Upper Lambourn at the end of August, and bought breaking-in tackle, saddles and horse clothes. The following month Gordon was at the Doncaster Sales and took a half share in a bay colt by Vilmorin out of Hi-Yalla submitted by the National Stud, and bought by Mr Chris Jarvis for one thousand two hundred guineas. The colt was named Caspar Badrutt, after the famous St Moritz hotelier whose ancestor, Johannes Badrutt, had been responsible for founding the modern St Moritz. A more expensive colt, by Alycidon out of Eastern Empress, and therefore a half-brother to Tamerlane, was bought by Greek shipping magnate Mr Basil Mavroleon, Chairman of London & Overseas Freighters, for eight thousand six hundred guineas and sent to Gordon, for the promise had been made that when the Champion Jockey retired, the ship owner would send him yearlings.

Due to Gordon's fame and the fact that Racing England idolised him, he received hundreds of letters from teenagers asking for jobs as stable lads. Believing that one could assess much concerning a person's character from their handwriting, he went through each letter carefully in his efforts to build up an impression of the writers. Aided by Walter Lawrence he sifted through the applications and eventually selected six fifteen-year-olds whom he arranged would live in a hostel, and whom, on his own admission, he hoped would include a future Champion Jockey.

In mid-September he received an invitation from John Schapiro, President of Laurel Park, to act as an honorary Steward when the third Washington DC International was run in November. Schapiro had also invited Mr Robert Sterling Clark to send Derby winner Never Say Die to America for the race, and had expressed his hopes that Lester Piggott would have the ride. Both invitations were declined, although Gordon admitted that he would not have hesitated if he had been one hundred per cent fit.

One invitation that Gordon did accept was to be guest of honour at a dinner organised by Sir Percy Loraine, Roderic and Frank More O'Ferral and Paddy Prendergast to coincide with the Dublin Yearling Sales. Gordon flew to Ireland where he purchased two more yearlings for his Beckhampton yard, a colt by Ballyogan and a filly by Preciptic. At Newmarket a week later he added to his purchases when he paid top price of £9,450 for an Arctic Prince colt from the Loughton Stud in Co Kildare.

Inevitably the question of whether or not Gordon would retain a stable jockey was discussed, and the names of Eph Smith, Tommy Carter, Joe Mercer, Geoff Lewis and Wally Swinburne were suggested. Gordon took some time to make up his mind, and then gave the job to twenty-one-year-old 'Jock' Wilson, who had served his apprenticeship with Jack Readon and during the year had been riding with considerable success for Staff Ingham. Equally important was the question of a successor to Gordon as stable jockey at Warren Place.

Noel Murless deliberated long and hard before offering the plum job to Lester Piggott within a week of the Stewards of the Jockey Club announcing the lifting of the one hundred and three day ban upon the young jockey. There had been speculation that Piggott would ride for Gordon, but the offer of riding for the powerful Warren Place Stable was far too good an opportunity to turn down. Once accepted it commenced one of the greatest and most successful trainer-jockey partnerships in Turf history and one which for all time will rank alongside that of Darling and Richards.

At the end of the Flat season Gordon was entertained to dinner by the Stewards of the Jockey Club in Newmarket, thus becoming the first jockey ever to be honoured in this manner. At the dinner Gordon sat between Sir Randle Feilden and Mr James Rothschild. On the walls of the dining-room were paintings of famous champions including Coronach, Captain Cuttle and Hurry On, and the long mahogany table glowed in the light cast by the silver candelabra. As the guest of so many distinguished members of the Jockey Club Gordon thought the evening one of the most memorable in his life. Since the foundation of the Club in the mid 1750s they had been considered socially to be aloof and although the Chifneys, Archer and Danny Maher had been shown hospitality by Jockey Club members who were their patrons, there had been no previous occasion comparable to that honouring Gordon in the long and significant history of the Club. At the dinner deserved praise was showered upon Gordon, who received little praise and much criticism the next day from Cassandra of the *Daily Mirror*:

> I wonder what bright advertising genius hit on the idea of showing Gordon Richards, complete with jockey cap, urging us to join National Savings with his injunction 'Take a tip from your old friend, Gordon Richards, I'm right behind this grand New Savers Campaign. Make it a cert!' Now no doubt Sir Gordon is a thrifty man and an excellent example to us, but if ever there was an occupation which is the reverse of saving for a rainy day it is horseracing. You might as well get the brewers to urge temperance, and the Church to plead for the Devil.

Despite Cassandra's reference to the brewers advocating temperance, a London public house in a street north of Oxford Street, whose name was The Champion, changed its original sign to one of Sir Gordon Richards, riding Pinza in the colours of Sir Victor Sassoon. Few contemporaries were so honoured, although in various parts of England were an Earl Haig, an Admiral Beatty and outside The Abyssinian at Hornsey a portrait on the inn sign of Prince Monolulu!

At the annual Jockeys' Dinner held at the Savoy Gordon was presented with a silver tray bearing the signatures of forty contemporary jockeys. In his speech proposing Gordon's health Sir Randle Feilden, Senior Steward of the Jockey Club, said that owners, trainers, Press, jockeys and valets had one desire in common — the prosperity of Racing run on the cleanest lines. No one in the history of the Turf had done more for the furtherance of this ideal than Sir Gordon Richards.

On a lighter note Sir Randle referred to the occasion when Stewards had decided to reprimand Gordon for his riding of Kriss Kringle at Newbury — and added that he had heard that Gordon was furious at the incident and had asked a trainer, 'What sort of a ride do you think that the Senior Steward would have given Kriss Kringle?' As Sir Randle pointed out Kriss Kringle had gone on to win his next two races, so he felt confident he would have given the horse a very good ride.

In his reply Gordon was in more emotional mood than usual, and told his audience, 'Ninety-nine per cent of us start from very humble surroundings. In my opinion one thing is of paramount importance — set an example wherever you go — everything is up to you . . .'

The number of celebration lunches and dinners that Gordon attended did nothing to help his waistline, and he complained that he had put on more than seven pounds in a fortnight. At the *Sporting Life* luncheon at the Savoy, where once again he was guest of honour he was presented with a silver statuette of Sun Chariot. His health was proposed by the Chairman of Odhams Press, by the Editor of the *Sporting Life*, by the Duke of Norfolk and by Major Macdonald-Buchanan. The Duke, praising the champion, remarked, 'There is one person who always ran true to form. I wish that I could find horses that would do the same!' At the lunch it was announced that Gordon had registered his racing colours — 'rose and black stripes'. These colours had originally belonged to Fred Darling, and there was hardly a dry eye amongst hardened and usually unsentimental racegoers when they learned that Gordon had chosen to take them as his own.

When he replied to the toasts which had bestowed so much praise upon him, Gordon looked ahead to the future, 'I can imagine nothing better than a string of racehorses, up early in the morning, out on the Downs. There is something which smells good to me about it.' He then admitted that the Kriss Kringle affair still rankled, and said, 'Sometimes I have been told off by owners for not riding a horse into a place, but you have to think about the next time. Once I rode a horse of Major Macdonald-Buchanan's under instructions to go all-out, and I rode him right out. We finished second but he never won again. If a horse is ridden all-out and finishes second to a good horse he makes an enemy of the handicapper for the rest of the season.'

By Christmas Gordon needed a holiday and he decided to spend early January in St Moritz. For England it had been a memorable year with an end to rationing and years of austerity, with ration cards finally discarded; and for Gordon the year had brought the end of one career and the beginning of another.

Three reasons brought Gordon, Margery and their daughter home after only a comparatively short holiday in Switzerland. The first was his anxiety to commence preparing his two-year-olds, some of whom had been broken-in by Norah Wilmot, for the forthcoming season. His team had increased shortly before he left for St Moritz when Miss Dorothy Paget had sent him six of her Irish-bred two-year-olds, including a Dante colt and a Nearco filly and he now trained nearly thirty horses for her, Mr Stavros Niarchos, Mr Basil Mavroleon and Mr J. R. Mullion. Obviously he could hardly contain his concern as to their well-being. The second reason for his return was to be able to attend the wedding of his son Peter to Miss Rosario Driscoll, daughter of a Kildare doctor. The third reason was to assist with the preparation of his life story, which was to be published by Hodder and Stoughton in the summer and was to be serialised in the *Evening News*.

In writing his autobiography he had been assisted by Gerard Fairlie in whose colours he had won at Salisbury three years earlier on a filly trained by Noel Cannon. Fairlie, modest, talented and the author of many exciting thrillers, had been a great friend of 'Sapper' and was the man upon whom the famous character Bulldog Drummond was based.

Prior to the publication of *My Story* an application was heard in the Chancery Division when Associated Newspapers Limited were refused an interim injunction restraining Kemsley Newspapers Limited, Aberdeen Journals Limited and the Western Mail and Echo Limited from 'passing off' articles as the life story of Sir Gordon Richards by using the words 'Gordon Richards' story'.

The plaintiffs stated that Sir Gordon Richards had given them exclusive rights in his life story, on which they had spent £14,000 in advertising. The defendants, they claimed, took advantage of this by publishing articles by another famous jockey, Charlie Elliott, referring to Sir Gordon Richards. A similar application was heard in the Court of Session Edinburgh, against the Scottish Daily Record and Evening News Limited, and Aberdeen Journals Limited.

On 9 May 1955, five days after his fifty-first birthday, Gordon had his first runner when he saddled Miss Dorothy Paget's The Saint for the Frogmore Plate at Windsor. Dorothy Paget was determined that Gordon should start with a winner, and The Saint who had been with Charlie 'Romeo' Rogers in Ireland was very forward in condition when he arrived at Beckhampton, only a few weeks before his Windsor race. Smartly into his stride, The Saint was never headed, and won by two lengths. His victory was fully expected and he started favourite at evens. Whilst The Saint was writing his name in the record books as Gordon's first winner, Quick as Light, owned by Gordon, was running at Birmingham, but failed to be placed. Quick as Light was trained for him by David Sherbrooke, whose mother was Norah Laye's sister. The Saint won again at Leicester a fortnight later, but his two victories heralded a lean time for Gordon. Many of his admirers made excuses on his behalf and suggested that he was following the Darling principle of being patient with his two-year-olds and not hurrying their preparation. He had no runners at Royal Ascot and tongues unfairly began to wag that he was treating his horses too gently and not giving them the chance to show their ability on the racecourse. Such criticism, coming so soon after he had commenced his new career, was both harsh and unjust.

For most part the training programme for his horses—and a programme broadly based upon that employed by Fred Darling—was ordinary exercise on Mondays, Wednesdays and Saturdays; Thursdays a more relaxed day and 'work' on Tuesdays and Fridays—particularly for horses with engagements in the near future. Gordon hated running horses, especially young horses, out of their class believing that if the colt had a hard race it might overstrain him, physically and mentally, to his future detriment. With his yearlings he had adopted the policy of having them 'broken in' and cantering by Christmas and would then stop the cantering until he returned from his winter holiday. Only by the end of February would he begin the gradual process of building up their condition to bring them to their peak.

In July Gordon attended the Foyles Literary lunch at the Dorchester, which celebrated the publication of *My Story*. Tributes to him were paid by Sir Alfred Munnings and Lord Brabazon of Tara, who humorously mentioned that he knew Gordon as a first-class and very serious-minded curler in St Moritz and was surprised to learn that his friend was a jockey during his spare time in the summer months. Boxer Freddie Mills caused laughter when he told his audience that as a corporal during the war, he was at Salisbury races and had backed the winner of the first race to win £10 for himself. 'Sir Gordon sidled up to me and marked my card. He told me to have a little bit on each of those. At that moment my CO arrived and, thinking I might wangle a wonderful weekend pass, I marked his card with Sir Gordon's tips. Needless to say not one of them finished in the first three, I had a wonderful weekend—in the barracks!'

By mid-summer Gordon had trained eight winners. The grandeur of the establishment did not over-awe him, nor did the memory of Fred Darling weigh heavily on him, but for some reason he did not appear happy at Beckhampton. His landlord and tenant relationship with Herbert Blagrave and Jeremy Tree, a nephew of Bois Roussel's owner, seemed excellent, and yet he did not appear to be enjoying his new career—probably because he was not the boss at Beckhampton.

Fate decided to take a hand, for fifty-nine-year-old Wing Commander Rupert Laye, third husband of Norah Edwardes, had died at Ogbourne in March. Gordon had often ridden for him since the end of the War, had won on his horses, including The Bite and Leica, and was never happier than riding in trial gallops on the Downs above his beloved Ogbourne, where he considered the best fourteen furlong peat gallop in England was to be found. Norah Laye appreciated that she must find a new tenant/trainer, and the thought crossed her mind that Gordon would be the ideal person to take over the establishment where her nephew David Sherbrooke had held the licence since Rupert Laye's death. A proposal was made to Gordon and accepted.

From a sentimental and nostalgic viewpoint his return to Ogbourne as a trainer after having worked there as a young apprentice thirty years previously was almost like a fairy tale come true. No romantic novel could have had a more enchanting plot, no film scenario a more happy ending. Gordon knew that by accepting the offer to go to Ogbourne he would be losing money on his Beck-hampton venture for he had spent a large sum on renovating the premises and building new boxes, but nevertheless he decided to move to Ogbourne in the late autumn. He also decided that for the 1956 season Scobie Breasley would ride for his stable with a retainer estimated at more than five thousand pounds.

Breasley had originally come to England from Australia in 1950 to ride for Mr James V. Rank, and had consolidated his reputation as one of the most brilliant jockeys of the era, and the undisputed master as a judge of pace. Noel Cannon had hoped th at he would continue to ride for the Druid's Lodge Stable, but the offer made to him by Gordon was too good to be refused.

Like all other Australians interested in Racing, Breasley knew of Gordon's achievements in the saddle long before he came to England for the first time, and consequently was an ardent admirer of the famous English jockey. The admiration turned to a close personal friendship as the two men became acquainted. Living either at Druid's Lodge or Kingston-upon-Thames, Breasley often shared Gordon's chauffeur-driven car or his aeroplane to and from racemeetings. As Gordon watched Breasley's artistry in the saddle he knew that he was the jockey above all others to whom he wished to give a retainer.

In fact Gordon had high hopes for the 1956 season, for he had several fashion-ably-bred horses in his stable which he had patiently allowed to mature despite criticism that he ought to have allowed them to make their racing debut earlier. Critics pointed out that he had only collected £3,553 in prize money for his patrons and that he was finding the life of a trainer considerably less attractive than that of a jockey. As a jockey each job was over in less than three minutes, whilst for the trainer it was often necessary 'to sit tight for long periods, batten down the hatches and wait for tempestuous times to abate'. Above all else this was the lesson learnt by Gordon in his first season, when he was plagued by water-logged gallops in the spring, hard ground in the summer and an epidemic of coughing among the horses in the autumn.

When Gordon moved his horses to Ogbourne he had a string of almost fifty, including expensive colts bought at the sales in the autumn of 1955. David Sherbrooke remained in a new capacity as secretary and Peter Richards joined his father as his assistant trainer. Miss Dorothy Paget owned more than half of the horses in Gordon's yard, and he had high hopes for her colt Patty; for Mongol Warrior, the half-brother to Tamerlane, owned by Mr Basil Mavroleon; and for Mr Stavros Niarchos' Ardent Knight and Testament, a filly bought at the dispersal sale of the horses of Mr Dewar who had died at Montecatini in Italy in August 1955.

In the spring of 1956 Gordon was involved in an accident which eventually led to a long drawn out and complicated legal action. The three-year-old Hamama, trained at Chantilly by Jack Cunnington, was bought by former Labour MP Mr John Lewis for a sum rumoured to be £7,000, the horse arriving at Gordon's stables a week before the Two Thousand Guineas. At Newmarket he finished a distant last and pulled up in obvious distress. Sent to the Equine Research Station at Newmarket for an examination for a possible heart complaint, Hamama had a week of extensive electro-cardiac tests, and was taken out of training for the remainder of the season.

To add to Gordon's troubles the five horses that he trained for Mr Basil Mavroleon departed from Ogbourne in mid-summer and were sent to Matt Feakes at Lambourn. The reason given was that Mavroleon wished to concentrate all his horses with Feakes, with whom he had had some horses in training since 1953, because he preferred to be the patron of a small stable. Earlier in the year Daemon, owned by Mavroleon, had won the Burwell Stakes at Newmarket, beating Hugh Lupus, and had started second favourite for the Coronation Cup at Epsom, but finished last behind Tropique. Subsequently it was announced in the *Racing Calendar*, 'The Stewards enquired into the riding of Daemon. After hearing the evidence of the trainer, Sir Gordon Richards, and Breasley they decided to accept the latter's explanation, but considered he had ridden an injudicious race.'

In August Gordon was invited by Johnny Longden to visit America for a special occasion, his imminent achievement of riding his four thousand eight hundred and seventy-first winner, thus beating Gordon's total. Due to the pressure of his commitments as a trainer, Gordon was not able to accept, and thus missed seeing forty-six-year-old Longden surpass his record at the Del Mar course in California. Gordon was philosophical about his record being broken, sent Longden a telegram of congratulations, and commented, 'I know what hard work it is to ride nearly five thousand winners. It must be even harder in America where the tracks are sharper and they are at it all the time from the moment that the gates go up. Jockeys reckon to be finished at the age of thirty—yet Johnny is forty-six.' However, just to prove that he too could go fast, Gordon was fined two pounds by Brighton magistrates for speeding!

Before the end of the season Gordon had sent out Mr Stavros Niarchos's Pipe of Peace to win at Salisbury, Goodwood and Newmarket where he won the Middle Park Stakes by a neck from French challenger Wayne II, with Military Law a length away third, and a strong attractive-looking colt of Sir Victor Sassoon's named Crepello fourth.

Pipe of Peace who had been bought by the BBA for seven thousand guineas, headed the colts with 9 st 5 lbs in the Free Handicap, and Gordon was entitled to think that the horse might bring him a Classic success in 1957. Never a big colt, and built somewhat on greyhound lines, yet full of quality, Pipe of Peace wintered well and delighted Gordon in the spring when he won the valuable Greenham Stakes at Newbury on his debut. In the Two Thousand Guineas he was third, beaten only half a length and a head by Crepello and Quorum; and in the Derby he was a gallant third to champions Crepello and Ballymoss, being defeated less than three lengths by the winner. He was again third, in the St James's Palace Stakes at Royal Ascot, and ended a commendable three-year-old career by winning the Gordon Stakes at Goodwood. Many of the huge holiday crowd at the Sussex track were under the impression that the Gordon Stakes was named in honour of Pipe of Peace's trainer, and were disappointed when they were told the true reason for the name of the race, which was that it commemorated the family name of the Dukes of Richmond who own the racecourse.

The performances of Pipe of Peace proved that Gordon had the ability to train potential champions. So too did the victories of Court Harwell at Salisbury where he won the Bibury Cup, at Goodwood when he scored an easy success in the Warren Stakes, and at Newbury where he trounced a high-class field in the Oxfordshire Stakes, and which stamped the colt as in the top flight.

But the training of top-class thoroughbreds left little time for relaxation, and Gordon and his wife made the sad but wise decision to sell Clements Meadow where they had lived so happily for twenty-one years, for the house was too large for them now that their children were no longer at home. Their eldest son Jack, now thirty years old, was a motor salesman in London, Peter was assisting him at Ogbourne and twenty-three-year-old Marjorie was studying domestic science in Cheltenham after being educated at Battle Abbey.

In consequence, they agreed to build a bungalow at Ogbourne from where Gordon could supervise his horses twenty-four hours a day, seven days a week and fifty-two weeks a year—except when he was holidaying in St Moritz. However in September, when Clements Meadow was expected to be offered for sale by auction, the property was withdrawn. The auctioneer announced that Sir Gordon Richards would continue to live at the house, but that the grounds would be reduced by selling part of the land and the gardener's cottage. Eventually Clements Meadow was sold in February 1959.

In August Gordon and Scobie Breasley, also a keen golfer, were compelled to make a forced landing on Bloxwich golf course, six miles from Wolverhampton, when a freak cloud of fog enveloped their aircraft, which was *en route* for the races. 'We had a bump or two over the bunkers and in the rough,' quipped Gordon, but, thankfully, neither trainer nor jockey nor pilot was hurt.

However, although Gordon was in the best of health, Pipe of Peace was 'in the wars', and sustained a badly bruised joint which interrupted his training programme. Eventually it was decided he would not be able to do himself justice in the St Leger, for which he was greatly fancied, and he was taken out of the race. Court Harwell proved a worthy substitute, finishing second to Ballymoss, and then proceeded to win the Jockey Club Stakes to end a successful season on a high note. Pipe of Peace recovered rapidly from his injury in early September and Gordon ambitiously set his sights upon the Prix de l'Arc de Triomphe, the race in which he had ridden Felicitation into third place behind the French champion

Brantome twenty-three years previously. He believed that Pipe of Peace must have a great chance at Longchamp, but the colt could only finish twelfth to shock winner Oroso.

Before the end of the year, when Gordon finished twelfth in the trainers' list, he had become a proud grandfather for the first time, but announced after seeing his son Peter's baby, 'I doubt whether there is much chance of him becoming a famous jockey. He is so fat that I should think he will become an all-in wrestler!'

Gordon had his first training success of the 1958 season at Bath in May, but later in the month seven horses that he trained for Mr John Lewis, the owner of the ex-French colt Hamama, left for Epsom, to be trained by Tommy Carey. Forty-six-year-old John Lewis was a remarkable man, whose wealth was based upon the fact that he was joint inventor of the high temperature thermal reclaiming process adopted and sponsored by the Ministry of Supply in 1941. He was also the joint inventor of rubber substitute for cable and general rubber production. From 1945–50 he had been Labour MP for Bolton West and was acknowledged as an outspoken critic of many aspects of Parliamentary life who found that Racing offered a solace to his busy existence. Amongst Mr Lewis' seven horses who left Gordon's care were Technion and Firestreak, whom Gordon had sent out to win the Warminster Stakes at Salisbury upon his debut the previous week. Firestreak won by five lengths and in the opinion of many was the best two-year-old seen in action since the commencement of the season.

A fortnight later Gordon unveiled a pair of gates at Epsom in memory of Steve Donoghue. The ceremony took place on the opening day of the Derby meeting, but through mismanagement was held so early in the day that few people attended. Only Atty Persse of the veteran trainers, for whom Steve had ridden, saw Gordon unveiling the gates which had been sponsored by the Crazy Gang, who were represented by Chesney Allen.

Firestreak was to start second favourite for the Gimcrack Stakes at York, but was unplaced to Be Careful owned by William Hill. When, in December 1958, William Hill rose to his feet to address the Gimcrack Club it was the 188th historic dinner held by the club. Not all of his words were acceptable to many of his highly influential listeners.

He began by saying that he was the first member of his profession ever to win the Gimcrack. 'Betting is the life-blood of the Racing industry', he remarked, 'and I believe the future of horseracing and British bloodstock depends entirely on the patronage of the punters, the paying customers at the turnstiles. Whether it is a good thing or not, the majority of people go racing, not because of their love of horseflesh, not because it is the Sport of Kings, but because they want to bet.'

Warning his audience that there were rival betting industries such as football and dog racing (casinos and bingo had not then been legalised) and that there were other serious competitors to horseracing in television, motor-racing and show jumping, he said, 'The blame for the parlous state of the Racing industry cannot be laid at the door of the bookmaker; neither can the remedy be to tax the book-makers who were taking all the money out of the game, but nothing could be further from the truth. Whatever you gentlemen may think, the few hundred bookmakers who operate on the racecourse make only a very precarious liveli-hood, and competition, diminishing crowds, and heavy overheads are gradually reducing their numbers.'

During the summer an event occurred which was to have an outstanding effect upon Gordon's future when he was introduced to sixty-year-old industrialist Mr Michael Sobell, one of whose daughters was married to Stanley Rubin, joint Master of the South Oxfordshire, the other to the joint Managing Director of Sobell TV, Arnold Weinstock. Mr Sobell had been far too busy in the post-war years to allow time to find relaxation as the owner of bloodstock, for he had been working intensely hard to build up a vast and highly successful television and radio manufacturing empire. Yet the love of horses instilled into him as a boy by his father, who had been a cavalry officer in Austria, had never been far below the surface.

Mr John Lewis had suggested to Mr Michael Sobell that he should purchase a horse, and recommended Gordon as the most suitable trainer. Shortly after the Derby Mr Sobell met Gordon at lunch in John Lewis' London flat and explained that he would like to enter the ranks of ownership and asked Gordon to buy him a horse. He made it clear that his Racing horizons were modest, and that although he was happy to dream of owning a Classic colt, in reality he would be delighted to win a small race at a minor meeting. He added, however, that should he and his wife find hoped-for fun in Racing, then the sky might one day become the limit.

Understandably Gordon was delighted at the prospect of a new owner with such ideas on the ownership of thoroughbreds, and gladly accepted the commission. Good fortune elected to smile upon him and Mr Sobell, for the horse acquired was London Cry, who was purchased for three thousand five hundred guineas from Mr R. F. Watson. London Cry proved a 'gold mine', winning the Craven Stakes at Epsom, other races at Brighton, Salisbury and Newmarket, the Chester-field Cup at Goodwood and ended the season in a blaze of glory with a fluent victory in the Cambridgeshire under the huge burden of 9 st 5 lbs, to set a new weight carrying record for the race. The victories of London Cry stimulated Mr Sobell's interest in Racing, with the happiest of results from Gordon's point of view, and were to lead to one of the most significant and successful periods of his career.

At the end of the season he was instructed to buy five more horses for Mr Sobell and this he did before leaving for his annual holiday in St Moritz, where he captained his team of Chris Jarvis, Henry Berli and young jockey Edward Hide to win the coveted Kurverein Cup, one of the most important international curling trophies.

On his return he was called as a key witness in the High Court action being brought by Prince Said Toussoun, a cousin of King Farouk, and Madame Marguerite Cunnington, against the St Simon Bloodstock Agency (International) Limited and Mr John Lewis. The defendants denied liability and Mr Lewis counter-claimed for damages. In a second action the Agency sued Mr Lewis in respect of a cheque for £7,420, payable to them in connection with the purchase of Hamama and their commission. The Prince alleged breach of contract and claimed recovery of the £7,000 from the Agency, run by former trainer John de Moraville.

The action, heard in the Queen's Bench Division, took a melodramatic turn on the fifth day when Mr Gilbert Beyfus QC for Prince Toussoun and Madame Cunnington asked Gordon, who was under cross-examination in the witness box, 'You train at Ogbourne Maisey. Do you know anyone living there at the time in question who in any way at all had been mixed up in any sort of doping scandal?' Gordon hesitated before replying, 'I think that my head lad had been.' Gordon wrote the name of the head lad on a paper which was handed to the judge before continuing to explain that the head lad was at one time a trainer and had lost his licence because a horse trained by him had been found to be doped at the end of a race. Mr Beyfus interrupted to ask, 'Does the Jockey Club withdraw a trainer's licence under these circumstances irrespective of the guilt or negligence of the trainer?' Gordon replied in the affirmative before the judge commented, 'It is fair that it should be realised that it does not mean the man was personally concerned with the doping.'

It was immediately pointed out by Mr F. H. Lawton, the QC representing Mr Lewis, that in fairness to Sir Gordon Richards' head lad a few facts should be given. Therefore he asked Gordon the question, 'How long ago did your head lad lose his licence as a trainer?' Gordon replied 'I have no idea. It must be something like ten or twelve years.' To a supplementary question, 'You investigated the position before you employed him?' Gordon answered 'Yes, he had been employed by another trainer.' The judge interrupted the cross-examination by posing this question to Gordon, 'Had you any reason to suppose that the head lad personally had taken any part in it, or was cognisant with doping?' Gordon replied without hesitation, 'No, he was given back his licence by the Stewards of the Jockey Club and is perfectly entitled to apply for it and get it.'

After Gordon had completed his evidence, W. Rickaby, who rode Hamama, Frederick Day, the Newmarket veterinary surgeon who had examined Hamama after the Two Thousand Guineas, Professor W. C. Miller from the Equine Research Station at Newmarket, and Mr John Lewis were also put into the witness box.

At the end of almost two weeks of the hearing, the costs of which were estimated at £14,000, and in which seven counsel were engaged, Mr Justice Paull announced that he would consider his judgment, and added, 'Quite frankly it is a case which causes me a good deal of trouble.' Subsequently he entered judgment in the first action for Prince Toussoun and Madame Cunnington for £405 against

Mr Lewis, and judgment for Mr Lewis for £630 on his counter-claim, leaving £225 to be paid by the plaintiffs to Mr Lewis. Plaintiffs were ordered to pay three-quarters of Mr Lewis' costs.

In the second action judgment was entered for the St Simon Bloodstock Agency (International) Limited, of Clarges Street, London, against Mr Lewis for £420 commission with no order as to costs.

Leave to appeal was granted in both actions.

The prolonged action caused Gordon worry and anxiety and made him realise more than any other incident the responsibilities and hazards attached to the life of a trainer.

In June, after Clements Meadow had been bought by a former Treasurer of the Bank of England, Gordon sadly watched the sale of some of his household effects and his cellar. His love of port caused him to keep back some Jubilee '97, a little 1912 and a few cases of 1927 – but the fact that his new bungalow would not have a cellar necessitated the sale of the majority of his stock of wine. Jeremy Tree bought fourteen dozen bottles of Taylor '48 at 300 shillings a dozen, Lord George Scott acquired a dozen bottles of Pol Roger '43 for 324 shillings and magnums of Krug Private Cuvée '47 went for 70 shillings.

Another death which was to stun Gordon was that of Miss Dorothy Paget in February 1960. Gordon had thirty-six of her horses in his charge, and she had telephoned him less than twelve hours before her death to ask for a progress report upon some of them. He had told her that she had much to look forward to in the coming season, and she was thrilled.

She virtually never visited her horses in their trainer's stables, relying on her secretaries for information about their progress. Her real love was to have a horse upon which to go 'banco', or even better two horses for two bancos at the same meeting. Invariably her first question to Gordon on arrival at the course was 'How is the wretched Breasley? Has he got a cold today?' And to her jockey for whom she had enormous admiration, 'Now, Breasley, do not cut it too fine this time.' In the winter months when Gordon was in St Moritz endless telegrams would be sent from her Chalfont St Giles home about plans for the forthcoming season. Some of these telegrams ran to pages.

When she was buried under a group of cypress trees in the fifteenth-century churchyard of St Mary's at Hertingfordbury near Hertford, Gordon was one of the many trainers, jockeys and other members of the Racing fraternity who attended the funeral. Also amongst the mourners was her cousin, John Hay Whitney, and the tall bearded Russian Orthodox Bishop of Sergievo who assisted at the service and represented the White Russian exiles in France, and whom she had helped with great financial generosity after the First World War. The day after the funeral Gordon stated that he would not race any of her horses until their future was decided upon by the executors. Later it was announced that the horses would stay with Gordon throughout the season, after letters of administration had been granted to Lady Baillie, Dorothy Paget's sister.

Only days prior to Dorothy Paget's death Gordon had returned from a brief visit to California where he had provided the surprise 'star turn' in a Hollywood *This is your Life* television programme on Johnny Longden. The following day he had presented the main trophy to Longden after the great American jockey had won the principal race at Santa Anita.

A month after his return from America Gordon was caused additional worry when he was involved in a confused 'Nat Gould' type of incident, highlighted by the suicide of sixty-six-year-old Bertie (Bandy) Rogers, who shot himself at his home in the Berkshire village of Compton. Rogers was thought to be a pedlar of horse dope used by crooks throughout the country, and detectives had found letters, supposedly orders for dope, in his bedroom at the thatched cottage where he had lodged for almost thirty years. Members of the Flying Squad had taken Rogers to various stables including those of Gordon at Ogbourne only days before his suicide. After his death his landlady said that the night before he killed himself Rogers had admitted, 'I've been giving powders to Sir Gordon Richards' horses' which appeared an admission of his guilt. When this information became public Gordon refused to confirm that it was he who had started the Flying Squad probe by calling at Scotland Yard with a complaint that some of his horses appeared to be doped, and added, 'I can say nothing at all until the enquiry is complete—not even to the friends of long-standing who have asked.' In fact he had contacted Scotland Yard after Colonel Neville Blair, head of Jockey Club security, had warned him privately that if it was proved that his horses were doped, then, under the Rules of Racing, he would lose his licence.

Whilst the unpleasant drama resulting from Roger's suicide was slowly unfolding, a brighter item of news appeared on the horizon when it was announced that Mr Michael Sobell had taken over the entire bloodstock empire of Miss Dorothy Paget, retaining Gordon as trainer and Charlie Rogers as manager of the three hundred acre Ballymacoll Stud at Dunboyne, Co Meath. Sobell had told Gordon some months earlier that he was prepared to buy a stud farm if and when a suitable one appeared on the market. He had no particular stud in mind, but provided its history was sound he would be advised by Gordon's knowledge and expertise. It was fortuitous for Gordon that he knew so much about the Ballymacoll Stud and its bloodstock, and its purchase was the logical sequel to Sobell's desire to increase his Racing interests. The initial negotiations were carried out at the Royal Hotel at Ascot before being finalised in London.

Gordon advised Sobell on the benefits which would accrue from the deal, the price of which was reputedly £250,000, and which proved to be one of the wisest investments that he ever made, for amongst the brood mares acquired was Pin Prick, grand-dam of 1979 Derby winner Troy.

Gordon had always thought that any owner wanting to make a total success of his Racing should have his own stud and breed his own horses, provided that he could afford the colossal financial outlay. He had made this clear to Sobell, explaining that in his opinion an owner-breeder received far more pleasure from victories achieved on the racecourse by horses foaled at his own stud than that gained by the owner of horses bought at yearling sales.

Gordon had been intrigued by the breeding aspect of Racing whilst a jockey and had owned two brood mares. On buying Ballymacoll for Sobell he was convinced that in the long term it was necessary to be ruthless, expressing his view that 'like breeds like—only perhaps a little worse', and that in consequence the bloodstock which seemed temperamental and unreliable should be sold forthwith. He added that he did not think that sentimentality should ever be allowed to influence such a decision. Eventually twenty-two mares were sold at the opening session of the Houghton Sales. Offered without reserve they realised thirty thousand one hundred and forty guineas.

Whilst the future of Ballymacoll was being considered a sensational development in the Rogers doping scandal occurred at Salisbury races on 5 July. A jockey was arrested after riding in the second race; earlier in the day a stable lad was arrested at Bob Turnell's Ogbourne yard, another was arrested at R. J. Colling's stable, and an unemployed Newmarket stable lad and a chemist's dispenser from Hednesford in Staffordshire were also requested 'to help police enquiries'. The five men, all given bail, were accused of conspiring to administer drugs to horses between 1 January 1958 and 31 August 1959 in order to 'cheat and defraud owners and bookmakers'.

At the end of the trial in which one of the accused was freed during the third day, the four others—the jockey, two stable lads and a chemist's dispenser—were found guilty.

In imposing sentences the judge said that all four men were of excellent character. He continued:

It is indeed a disaster that you have allowed yourselves to become involved in what, I am afraid, was obviously a quite widespread fraudulent scheme to tamper with racehorses. It was a scheme and practice which, if it were allowed to go unchecked, would undermine, as you all know quite well, the whole integrity and cleanliness of the sport which such a vast number of people in this country are interested in.

Nevertheless, some considerable general good came from the trial, for as a result of it a committee headed by the Duke of Norfolk was appointed to enquire into the use of drugs on racehorses and into the efficiency of the existing methods of detecting their presence. The Duke's Committee also examined the operation and the efficiency of the Rules of Racing relating to the subject. When their report was published they recommended that in future it should be at the discretion of the Stewards of the Jockey Club whether or not to withdraw the licence of a trainer whose horse had been doped. From that moment far greater co-operation was given to the authorities by trainers who had previously been reluctant to give details of attempts made to dope horses in their care or their suspicions regarding doping.

A serious discussion with Doug Smith, St Moritz, 1959.

Goodbye to training, November 1970.

To add gloom and depression to the year from Gordon's viewpoint, his horses started coughing in mid-September and many of his intended runners were withdrawn from their engagements. Lester Piggott seemed assured of the jockey's crown, but caused worry to the banqueting manager at the Savoy Hotel, by not making any provisional arrangements for the traditional end-of-season dinner given by the top jockey. From his parents' Berkshire home Lester stated that he had done nothing about the dinner because he had not yet won the championship, and added that he was uncertain whether or not he would hold a party even if he was successful.

It seemed that 1961 might be a great year for Gordon, even though before Christmas Peter Richards had left Ogbourne and started training on his own account on The Curragh, for his sixty horses included Spaki, Persian Lancer, Nicodemus, Primus, Mural and The White Girl. Primus began the season promisingly by winning the Greenham Stakes at Newbury, but during the race was struck into and received a cut on his near hind tendon, which prevented his running in the Two Thousand Guineas. Gordon was very disappointed for he thought that Primus was a top-class colt with a chance second to none.

As Derby Day 1961 approached, Gordon, speaking at the Press Club lunch in London, pointed out the folly of valuable horses having to run on ground as hard as that at Epsom. 'It is a tragedy that we have one million pounds worth of horse-flesh racing at Epsom on this hard ground and yet can do nothing about it. The Derby is the greatest race in the world, yet it is followed in a fortnight's time by the greatest racemeeting in the world—Royal Ascot. Twenty-five or twenty-six horses would have to go on from Epsom to Ascot. Can anyone produce them properly fit at Ascot after running at Epsom? Something ought to be done about it.'

'Something ought to be done about it' were words fresh in Gordon's mind for at the Derby Dinner at the Savoy the previous evening he had asked Henry Cotton to explain how he played such brilliant golf shots, and in return tried to explain how he held the reins when riding more than four thousand eight hundred winners. Later Henry Cotton commented, 'Gordon apparently never thought about it. He just did what came naturally and won. It would not do in golf.' Gordon had been one of the speakers at the dinner. A few days later Margery Richards received a letter from Lord Brabazon of Tara which gave her great pleasure. 'Brab' wrote:

. . . tell you how proud you would have been of your husband at the Derby Dinner. I know, of course, that Gordon is the world's greatest jockey, a very great trainer and a fine curler—as you are yourself, but I was a little anxious when I found that he was to address an enormous gathering at the Derby Dinner at the Savoy. He got up on a chair and made one of the best after-dinner speeches that I have ever heard in my life—and, mark you, I am a good judge of speeches, having had to listen to them in Parliament and elsewhere for most of my life. It was informative, amusing, subtle, entertaining and arresting, and got an ovation at the end which he well deserved. It was a wonderful feat of great confidence and without a note. I cannot tell you how proud I was to be a friend of his.

Twelve months later there were rumours that Gordon would be compelled to leave Ogbourne when his lease expired at the end of the season. For six years he as tenant, and Norah Laye as landlord, had enjoyed a peaceful relationship. Admittedly there had been minor altercations, involving such small disputes as the removal of a gate-post or a few railings, but for the most part there had been no serious differences between them. It seemed, however, that Norah Laye now required a change of tenant and wished to regain possession. Sobell instructed Gordon to buy the entire establishment, virtually regardless of price, but the stubborn, elderly, and by now eccentric, Norah Laye would not contemplate such a proposal. Consequently Gordon, backed financially by Sobell and his son-in-law Arnold Weinstock, attempted to negotiate elsewhere. There was a chance that George Todd might sell Manton, and rumours spread that Whatcombe could be a feasible proposition, but stumbling blocks of one kind or another forestalled any progress towards a sale being made.

Gordon looked at several other establishments, including Fergus Sutherland's Carlburgh Stables at Newmarket, and it seemed that he might be forced to make Newmarket his final choice. It was a worrying time for him although his three apprentices, Kimberley, Proctor and German, were meeting with considerable success. He was not the only trainer with problems, however, for Major Dick Hern, private trainer to Major Lionel Holliday, was also on the move, and planned to depart from Lagrange Stables, Newmarket to Ilsley to train for the Astors on the retirement of Jack Colling. Finally Norah Laye and Gordon agreed that he should stay at Ogbourne for another twelve months, so that he faced the 1963 season with confidence, and hoped to surpass his 1962 total of sixty-four winners when one of his victories included the *News of the World* Stakes with Tamerlo, owned by Mr Michael Sobell.

The season brought him no significant success, and at the end of the year he finally vacated Ogbourne. Mrs Laye commented, 'I fear that the break is irrevoc- able, but we are parting on friendly terms. I intend to use the stables as a home for a few brood mares.' However negotiations with William Hill for him to lease Whitsbury appeared to be bearing fruit.

When these negotiations were completed he moved to Whitsbury, before holidaying in Nassau with Mr and Mrs Sobell—his first break with St Moritz— but Sobell insisted that the warmth of the West Indies was a better climate for 'old bones'.

The history of Whitsbury had commenced in 1923 when Sir Charles Hyde, proprietor of the *Birmingham Mail* and the *Birmingham Weekly Post*, began to take an interest in Racing, and three years later bought the Whitsbury estate, near

Fordingbridge, where he installed Norman Scobie as his trainer. Scobie had trained in Australia as a young man before being persuaded to try his luck in England by Frank Bullock. He found his first year in Britain exceedingly difficult and remarked, 'England is the hardest place I know to get a start as a trainer. No matter what a man has done previously, he has got to prove himself here before he is believed in, and I would not like again to go through what I did before I met Sir Charles Hyde.' Hyde dropped dead in his office in 1942 and the following year William Hill bought Whitsbury.

When Sir Charles Hyde's bloodstock was sold at auction Mr Phil Bull, on William Hill's behalf, bought the ten-year-old mare Kong, who had won the 1937 Wokingham Stakes at Royal Ascot, for seven hundred and ten guineas and her filly foal by Umidwar for nine hundred and seventy guineas.

Gordon's arrival at Whitsbury was quickly crowned with success when he won the Free Handicap at Newmarket with his first runner since moving to Fordingbridge. Port Merion, owned by Major Macdonald-Buchanan, won by a comfortable two lengths and was immediately made third favourite for the Two Thousand Guineas. However the colt was well beaten in the Newmarket Classic, finishing out of the frame to Baldric II.

On his sixtieth birthday whilst opening shoals of congratulatory telegrams, Gordon remarked that training was far harder than riding and added, 'I no longer ride racehorses. I just go out on my hack. But to be working with horses is the next best thing to riding. The most enjoyable thing is to be by the winning post and see one of your horses come first.'

He had been saddened to learn on the eve of his birthday that Rae Johnstone had collapsed with heart failure at Le Tremblay, within minutes of saddling a runner. He had ridden thirty Classic winners—sixteen more than Gordon—and had been known to Parisian racegoers as 'The Crocodile' because of his habit of waiting to gobble up the opposition.

During the next two years Reform proved the best of Gordon's horses. This horse was trained for Michael Sobell, who also owned the useful colt Dart Board, who won the Dewhurst Stakes, and was third to Royal Palace in the 1967 Derby. Reform, who had been bred at the Ballymacoll Stud, suffered from slightly malformed forelegs, and was so unprepossessing as a foal that it was decided that it would be unwise to submit him at the yearling sales. As a two-year-old he won six races, including the Clarence House Stakes at Ascot, and was allotted 9 st in the Free Handicap, 7 lbs below Bold Lad. In 1967 he proved one of the best colts in the country, and after defeating Bold Lad in the St James's Palace Stakes at Royal Ascot, won the Sussex Stakes at Goodwood, the Queen Elizabeth II Stakes at Ascot, and the Champion Stakes at Newmarket, where he beat Taj Dewan, Royal Palace and Pia.

The previous autumn Gordon had proposed the health of the bride and groom when Julie Murless had married Henry Cecil, with five-year-old Maureen Piggott one of the bridesmaids. Six months later his daughter Marjorie married Richard

Read, an Andover farmer, at Fordingbridge Parish Church. As Gordon smilingly commented, 'When a daughter gets married, mother does the shopping and father signs the cheques.' One of the bridesmaids was Zonda Swift, granddaughter of Scobie Breasley.

Gordon was happy at Whitsbury, and believed that in addition to the brilliant jockeyship of Scobie Breasley who rode his horses, much of his success stemmed from the fact that the turf on the gallops had never been cultivated. It was the same in 1967 as it had been in the Stone Age, and always provided soft, lush grass. The going was never hard, and never heavy. Gordon was often asked why he had become a trainer when he gave up riding. His invariable answer was that once a man had been with horses he could not give them up, for they got into the bloodstream. When he announced his retirement, the Aga Khan had quizzed him as to his future. He had replied that, although he could buy a farm or a cottage by the sea, he believed that the choice lay between training and standing for Parliament. And his former patron had exclaimed, 'Good God, Gordon, you'll have to do something or you will go mental. Both your choices are rackets—but training seems the lesser of two evils.'

In his heart Gordon knew that it was not strictly true to claim that he could not give up horses. The real truth was that horses would not allow him to give them up, for they had become a way of life with the two impostors, success and failure, for ever at his side. He realised the implications of training more than half a million pounds worth of thoroughbreds, did not relish the thought that the financial profit at the end of the year might be minimal, and only reluctantly accepted the volume of paper work involved with entries and correspondence with owners. However, despite everything he would not exchange his life for any other even though the pressure was never relieved. In comparison with his days as a Champion Jockey, when he could relax on each and every Sunday, he now found the Sabbath to be the busiest day of the week. Yet the satisfaction of bringing a horse to concert pitch and then seeing him win on the racecourse made it all worth while.

In 1968 he was asked to train some horses for Lady Beaverbrook, widow of the world famous newspaper proprietor whose filly Micmac had been third to Rose of England in the Oaks, to give Gordon his first Classic winner. Lady Beaverbrook had taken up Racing after her husband's death in 1964, at the suggestion of Lord Rosebery, choosing Walter Nightingall as her trainer. It was an obvious choice for he trained for Sir Winston Churchill, who had been one of Lord Beaverbrook's greatest friends, and his Epsom stables were only a few miles from her home at Cherkley near Leatherhead.

Within the next four years Lady Beaverbrook's appetite for Racing had been whetted due to the victories of Rosebid and Hametus, who won the 1967 Dewhurst Stakes at Newmarket. Seventy-three-year-old Nightingall died in 1968 and Lady Beaverbrook, whose horses were invariably given names containing seven letters, which was thought to be her lucky number, decided to divide her horses between Gordon and Scobie Breasley, who was commencing his career as a trainer, having acquired Nightingall's South Hatch yard.

Four times Champion Jockey fifty-four-year-old Breasley had announced his decision to retire at Goodwood early in August. He said that, 'In fairness to Sir Gordon Richards, to whom I owe so much, I should make a statement so that he and all those that support me have good time to make their plans for 1969.' Breasley had been Gordon's staunch ally since he began riding for him, and praised him as 'the best and nicest man I have ever met' in addition to acclaiming him as a trainer.

Throughout the years that he was retained by Gordon, Breasley was never given riding instructions for the reason, admitted by Gordon, 'that he would not take any notice of them in any event.' Often he would elect to win races by the shortest possible margin, giving Gordon and his owner heart-failure. After one race Gordon told him that he had frightened the life out of everyone by delaying his challenge until the last moment, and was aghast when Scobie commented, 'I frightened the life out of myself!' Induna, Greengage and Wrekin Rambler were three top-class horses, in addition to Reform, Dart Board and Pipe of Peace, trained by Gordon on whom Breasley won notable victories. Breasley always thought that Pipe of Peace was a champion three-year-old, who would have won both the Two Thousand Guineas and the Derby in any average year. On Derby Day as he cantered the colt to the start, Breasley felt that he had never been on the back of a more perfectly trained racehorse. On Breasley's retirement Edward Hide took over as Gordon's stable jockey.

Gordon continued to train at Whitsbury until the end of 1970, sending out, amongst other winners, Jacobus, Miracle, Biskrah and Richboy in the colours of Lady Beaverbrook. Unlike Dorothy Paget, Lady Beaverbrook never bet; invariably made her own telephone calls to Gordon to find out how her horses were progressing; visited the stables several times every season; and proved the perfect owner even though she had the knack of 'keeping everyone on their toes'.

Although outwardly everything appeared to be harmonious in Gordon's relationship with William Hill, inwardly much was on a discordant note. Hill would arrive at Whitsbury on a Friday evening to spend the weekend wandering around the estate, and openly criticised everything and everyone when he felt in the mood to do so. Eventually the relationship became unbearable and when Gordon's lease expired, William Hill would not renew it, although to help him and to please Michael Sobell he extended it for one more season.

Gordon attempted to find an alternative training establishment to lease, and when his efforts were unavailing, decided to retire. His decision was to some extent made for him, in the light of a munificent offer from Mr Michael Sobell. The radio and television millionaire had recently bought the West Ilsley stables from Mr J. J. Astor and proposed that Gordon managed his horses which would be trained by Dick Hern. Gordon accepted the offer. Sobell recognised the fact that Gordon was beloved by Racing England, and knew that Gordon was far too important a man with far too great a knowledge and experience of Racing to be inactive. Wisely, he decided to make use of Gordon's expertise before his services were snapped up by anyone else. Lady Beaverbrook also requested that Gordon manage her horses.

In November 1970 the auctioneer's hammer fell on more than five hundred lots as Gordon sold up his training establishment. Saddles, bridles, blinkers and training tack were sold. So too were outside effects including a three-stall starting gate and a Ferguson plough. At the end of the afternoon a forlorn and wistful Gordon explained that what he would miss the most was the sound of horses munching at night when all was quiet in the yard. The sale fetched almost eight thousand pounds, and was attended by far more potential buyers than were expected, many of them hoping to acquire a memento of their hero, whose best year had been 1967 when he finished second on the Trainers' List.

In December Gordon was elected an Honorary member of the Jockey Club. The significance of the word honorary was that the beneficiary did not have to pay any annual subscriptions. He could attend all Jockey Club meetings and speak at their debates, but would not be entitled to vote. Commenting on the election, Sir Randle Feilden remarked, 'It was the wish of members of the Jockey Club that Sir Gordon Richards services to Racing should be recognised. Since he held a trainer's licence until recently, and before that a jockey's, this was our first opportunity.' Other Honorary members were the Dukes of Edinburgh, Gloucester and Windsor. Gordon was delighted at his election and felt that he had received one of the greatest honours that Racing could bestow. He had often wondered if he would have to pay to attend racemeetings after he had finished training but being a member of the Jockey Club presented the solution.

The following month Gordon and Margery departed with Mr and Mrs Sobell for a holiday at the Coral Reef Club in Barbados. He found himself succumbing to the sunshine, to the warmth of his welcome in the West Indies, and the lazy days spent at the side of a swimming pool. He became enchanted by the colour and gaiety of the island and in future was to return every year, forsaking his original love of St Moritz and the Engadine.

At the Newmarket Craven meeting in the spring of 1971 he officiated as a Steward for the first time. His new responsibilities as racing manager for Sir Michael Sobell and Lady Beaverbrook stimulated his interest in Racing in the 70s but were not over-arduous. He enjoyed his early morning visits to Dick Hern's West Ilsley stables, where he would ride out on a hack watching the horses at exercise, before reporting their progress to their owners, and found equal pleasure in his visits to racemeetings to see them in action.

During the summer he moved from Whitsbury to his new home in the Berkshire village of Kintbury, half way between Newbury and Hungerford, and less than ten miles from West Ilsley. Curiously his next-door neighbour at Kintbury was Keith Piggott. Golf, gardening and grandchildren began to take an ever-increasing importance in his life, which never became dull or dreary, although inevitably its tempo slowed down.

During the past eight years Gordon has been associated with the triumphs of many horses owned by Lady Beaverbrook and Sir Michael Sobell, who was knighted in 1972. Biskrah, Zab, Riboson, Relkino and Royalty all achieved notable victories for Lady Beaverbrook who was rewarded still further by the 1974 St Leger and 1975 Coronation Cup triumphs of Bustino and the brilliance of Boldboy who earned more prize money than any other gelding in Turf history. In 1978 Lady Beaverbrook named one of her yearlings Sir Gordon and there is the hope that the colt will achieve great success and live up to the reputation of his illustrious namesake. Throughout these years the horses of Sir Michael Sobell were equally successful with important victories gained by Sun Prince, Homeric and Sallust. But, even in total, all these victories did not provide the glory earned in 1979 by Troy, whose grand-dam had been amongst the mares acquired by Sir Michael Sobell and his son-in-law when the Ballymacoll Stud was purchased on Gordon's recommendation.

Troy was acclaimed as one of the greatest champion thoroughbreds of post-war Europe, and it was disappointing that Gordon was prevented from witnessing his success at either Epsom or The Curragh. by a trapped nerve in his spine which caused paralysis in his leg. However, there were many spectators at Epsom on Derby Day 200 who were saddened by Gordon's absence on the unique occasion. Certainly one of them was Sir Michael Sobell whose overriding thought, as he was driven home after the Derby celebrations, was to speak to Gordon as soon as possible. On arrival he walked quickly into the hall, grabbed the telephone and with his binoculars still slung over his arm, dialled Gordon's number. When Gordon answered, the first words of Troy's jubilant owner were, '*We* have won the Derby.' It was a deserved tribute to all that Gordon had achieved since he had relinquished his licence to train, and added further renown to the great career of a man who will be honoured for ever on the British Turf.

Highlights of career

1904	5 May	Born at Oakengates, Shropshire.
1920		Apprenticed to Mr Martin Hartigan at Foxhill.
1920	16 October	Rode in public for the first time—October Nursery Handicap at Lingfield Park. Unplaced on Mr J. White's Clock-work.
1921	31 March	Rode his first winner—Apprentice Plate at Leicester on Mr J. White's Gay Lord.
1925		Champion Jockey for the first time, with 118 winning mounts.
1933	4 & 5 October	Rode eleven consecutive winners at Chepstow.
1933	8 November	Beat Fred Archer's record of 246 winners in a season set up in 1885 when he won the Wavertree Selling Plate at Liverpool on Mr F. Hartigan's Golden King.
1953	1 June	Awarded a knighthood in the Queen's Coronation Honours List.
1953	6 June	Won the Epsom Derby on Sir Victor Sassoon's Pinza—his twenty-eighth and final Derby mount.
1954	10 July	Rode HM The Queen's Landau into third place in the Eclipse Stakes at Sandown Park. In subsequent race thrown heavily when leaving the paddock on Abergeldie. His final ride.

TOTAL NUMBER OF MOUNTS 1920–1954—21,834.

TOTAL NUMBER OF WINNERS 1920–1954— 4,870.

CHAMPION JOCKEY Twenty-six times.

CLASSIC WINNERS:

Two Thousand Guineas	Pasch	1938
	Big Game	1942
	Tudor Minstrel	1947
One Thousand Guineas	Sun Chariot	1942
	Queenpot	1948
	Belle of All	1951
Derby	Pinza	1953
Oaks	Rose of England	1930
	Sun Chariot	1942
St Leger	Singapore	1930
	Chulmleigh	1937
	Turkhan	1940
	Sun Chariot	1942
	Tehran	1944

Index

INDEX

189